PHYSICAL EDUCATION
A
CONTEMPORARY
INTRODUCTION

Physical Education

A CONTEMPORARY INTRODUCTION

Angela Lumpkin, Ph.D.

Professor of Physical Education
University of North Carolina
Chapel Hill, North Carolina

TIMES MIRROR/MOSBY
COLLEGE PUBLISHING

ST. LOUIS • TORONTO • SANTA CLARA   1986

Editor: Nancy K. Roberson
Developmental Editor: Michelle Turenne
Designer: Susan E. Lane
Production and Editing: Editing, Design & Production, Inc.

Copyright © 1986 by Times Mirror/Mosby College Publishing

A division of The C. V. Mosby Company
11830 Westline Industrial Drive
St. Louis, Missouri 63146

Printed in the United States of America

Library of Congress Cataloging-in-Publication Data

Lumpkin, Angela.
  Physical education.

  Bibliography: p.
  Includes index.
  1. Physical education and training.   I. Title.
GV211.L86   1986   613.7   85-21742
ISBN 0-8016-2998-5

MCC/VH/VH 9 8 7 6 5 4 3 2 1   01/B/041

PREFACE

Physical Education: A Contemporary Introduction provides students with a unique opportunity to discover the exciting diversity of physical education and the wealth of careers available in the field. Students will be introduced to the heritage, the current programs, and the future potential of the field that they are considering entering. The purpose of this book is to guide students by describing this multifaceted field and also by involving them in assessing what physical education offers in terms of career potential.

The intent of this book is to broaden students' understanding of how the philosophies and programs of physical education evolved as well as their current status. Inherent within the changing nature of physical education is a need to examine how Title IX, the mainstreaming of disabled individuals, the fitness mania, increased numbers of senior citizens, past programs in this country and in Europe, and traditional philosophies have affected this process.

No longer is physical education just for grade schools or colleges, although teaching in these settings is certainly a vital work of its professionals. By learning about careers in leisure services, athletic training, corporate fitness, athletic administration, sports communication, recreation for all ages and abilities, coaching, and a variety of other non-traditional pursuits, students will gain a clearer perspective of the future role physical education should play in American society. Individuals who accept the challenges of these careers will help women, minorities, senior citizens, individuals in lower socioeconomic classes, students, and many others benefit from an active, fit life-style. Practical suggestions are provided to students as they choose and prepare for their careers.

To enhance this process, throughout the book the importance of physical education as an expanding and diverse field of service, enjoyment, and employment is emphasized.

FEATURES

1. Written in a conversational and personal style, *Physical Education: A Contemporary Introduction* is designed for freshmen and sophomores who are enrolled in their first physical education course.

2. An overview of the field is stressed rather than an in-depth examination of the disciplinary areas. Some of these relevant topics for students include practical suggestions for selecting and obtaining a job in the chosen career; current issues affecting job security; girls and women in sports; minorities and physical education; teacher, coach, trainer, and exercise specialist certifications; educational outcomes of sports; and the future of fitness for Americans.

3. A career emphasis is integrated throughout, and given special attention in Chapters 5, 6, and 7. Chapter 5 describes over 50 careers in education, recreation, fitness, sports, business, and athletics. Students can learn about job responsibilities, prerequisite education and preparation, salary ranges, and potential availability of these careers. Chapter 6 provides practical ideas for preparing for careers, such as the importance of volunteer experiences, internships, obtaining certifications, compiling and preparing resumes, and hints for interviewing. Since teaching is an essential component of many of the nontraditional as well as traditional careers, Chapter 7 describes the qualities of, contributions to, and planning for successful teaching and emphasizes the attributes of the good teacher—enthusiasm, leadership abilities, and communication skills.

4. Organizationally, the book's three units are self-contained and may be read in any order, although each is important to a full understanding of the field. Unit I provides foundational information in the first four chapters before focusing on careers. As defined in Chapter 1, *physical education is a process through which an individual obtains optimal physical, mental, and social skills and fitness through physical activity.* Its cognitive, affective, and psychomotor objectives expand on how physical education can contribute to improvements in quality of life for all. The philosophies presented in Chapter 2 provide reference points for the essential development of a personal philosophy. Chapter 3 examines the applied sciences which comprise the academic discipline of physical education, while health, recreation, and dance are discussed as allied sciences. The organization of this profession along with professional preparation programs constitute Chapter 4.

In order to assist students in the career selection process, Chapter 5 describes a variety of available career options, Chapter 6 provides practical suggestions for career preparation, and Chapter 7 examines teaching in physical education.

The second unit covers the history and development of physical education and sports from early cultures through today. Athletics in Athens and Sparta, European gymnastics programs, and English sports and games are emphasized in Chapter 8 in terms of their influence on today's programs in the United States. In Chapter 9, early American physical education is traced from early sporting diversions through the formalized gymnastics programs of the late 1800s. Chapter 10 completes the chronology of evolving programs that are diverse in philosophy, clientele, and activity.

Unit III describes issues and trends in physical education. Chapter 11, examining the changing nature of this field, discusses content and control of programs. Issues, such as merit pay, career burnout, and activity adherence, that currently affect individuals in physical education careers are the focus of Chapter 12. The beneficial outcomes and the problem areas of sports for girls and women, minorities, youth, school and college students, and Olympic athletes are addressed in Chapter 13. The final chapter looks at the image and role of physical education in all settings as the twenty-first century approaches.

The pedagogical features of this book are specifically designed to benefit students. Included are the following:

Key Concepts

Each chapter begins with statements that highlight the major topics to be discussed. These provide students with both a focus and direction as they read.

Introductions

The first paragraphs in the chapters briefly set the stage for and preview the text. These further help students gain a perspective on the relevance of the content.

Illustrations

Over 50 photographs help students see the diversity of physical education and its career potential. These photographs also reemphasize the popularity of sports and activities for all, and help teach these concepts.

Boxed Materials

Throughout the text, specially highlighted information is designed to enhance students' understanding, and provide additional insights into the profession.

Summaries

A summary paragraph at the conclusion of each chapter emphasizes the primary areas of importance, which complement the initial key concepts. These summaries help students focus on the major items discussed.

Review Questions

To assist in students' retention of each chapter's content, they are encouraged to answer review questions. Rather than seeking rote memorization of facts, these questions stress understanding of the concepts.

Student Activities

Like the review questions, student activities encourage students to think about and use the chapter content in greater depth, and to extract practical ideas which they may apply to their careers. These also encourage an active participation in the learning process.

References

References provide students with the most current documentation of important issues and developments.

Recommended Readings

Recommended readings furnish students with additional information and potential resources for further study. The *annotations* are especially beneficial to expanding students' knowledge.

Glossary

A comprehensive glossary of important terms reinforces students' understanding of the terminology used in the book and in physical education.

Career Perspectives

An especially unique feature of this book is the integration of biographical sketches of physical educators in several diverse careers. The featured individuals describe their job responsibilities, hours, salary ranges, course work, degrees, experiences needed for their careers, satisfying aspects of their careers, and job potential, and provide advice to students.

It is the desire of the author that this book will awaken and kindle the interest of those who read it to select physical education careers. This challenge emphasizes both the significance and the enjoyment in a physical education career.

SUPPLEMENTS

An instructor's manual accompanies the text, and is available to those who adopt it. The manual includes practical teaching suggestions; chapter overviews; instructional objectives; additional annotated readings; over 450 multiple choice, true or false, matching, and essay test items with separate answer keys; suggested audiovisual materials; an appendix of selected Canadian physical education and sport associations; and 14 transparency masters of important drawings, tables, and charts. These were chosen to help explain difficult concepts within the text. The manual is perforated for convenience of use.

ACKNOWLEDGMENTS

Without the help of numerous individuals, this book would not exist. First, and foremost, my parents, Janice and Carol Lumpkin, instilled in me a love for learning, provided me with many educational opportunities through personal sacrifice, and constantly encouraged and supported all my endeavors. I dedicate this book to them with my love. My sister, Vernell Berry, and my brother, Phillip Lumpkin, and their families have always provided me with love and encouragement.

I am indebted to Linda Prather for her photographs, to Delaine Marbry, Cindy Atkins, and Mattie Hawkins for their typing, to Carol Pinkston for her editorial assistance, and to John Billing for his provision of departmental support and materials. I am greatly appreciative of the time and energy spent by the reviewers, who helped me immeasurably in improving the quality of each draft of the manuscript. Their suggestions were invaluable.

Carl P. Bahneman
West Virginia University

Patsy Caldwell
North Texas State University

Leslie Wayne Carter
University of South Carolina

Judith A. Christensen
Southern Connecticut State University

Mark W. Clark
University of Montana

Carolyn Cody
University of Northern Colorado

Virginia Fereira
Orange Coast College

Sonja S. Glassmeyer
California Polytechnic State University
San Luis Obispo

Elizabeth R. Hall
Texas Tech University

Roy F. Hill
Louisiana State University

Bonnie J. Hulstrand
University of Idaho

O. N. Hunter
University of Utah

Billie J. Jones
Florida State University

Dennie R. Kelley
University of Tennessee

Cynthia L. Meyer
Kent State University

Charles A. Spencer
University of South Dakota

Marianna Trekel
University of Illinois
Urbana-Champaign

Deborah A. Wuest
Ithaca College

Lastly, but significantly, I want to thank the outstanding professionals at Times Mirror/Mosby College Publishing. It has been a pleasure to be associated with each of them because of their commitment to publishing only quality books. Among this superior group, two individuals, Nancy Roberson and Michelle Turenne, have been especially helpful to me in this endeavor. Nancy initially and throughout the development of this textbook has expressed confidence in me and in the potential of a book with a career perspective. Michelle continually focused my attention on the many details of this writing project plus always encouraged me to persevere. They, because of their competent and professional attitudes toward the production of this textbook, deserve the credit for the best qualities of this work. Hopefully, our joint efforts have resulted in a book that will prepare you for an exciting career in physical education.

Angela Lumpkin

CONTENTS

UNIT   II
HISTORY AND DEVELOPMENT OF PHYSICAL EDUCATION AND SPORT PROGRAMS

UNIT III
ISSUES, TRENDS, AND THE FUTURE OF PHYSICAL EDUCATION

PHYSICAL EDUCATION
A
CONTEMPORARY
INTRODUCTION

Unit I

PRINCIPLES AND SCOPE OF PHYSICAL EDUCATION

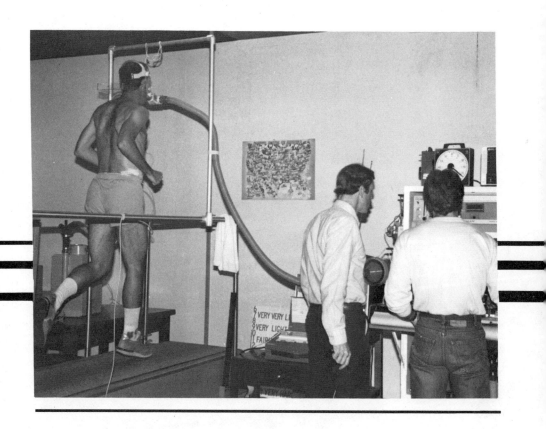

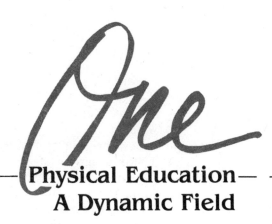

Physical Education— A Dynamic Field

KEY CONCEPTS

- Today's physical education programs have the potential to improve the quality of life for everyone.
- Physical education today has emerged from a rich heritage of varied activities and programs.
- Fitness and optimal physical, mental, and social skills are benefits of physical education.
- The aim of physical education is to improve everyone's life-style. The growing interest in health and fitness helps make this possible.
- Cognitive, affective, and psychomotor objectives are achieved through today's physical education programs.

Physical education today faces the unique opportunity of potentially contributing to the improvement of everyone's quality of life. No other field enjoys such a dynamic future. Millions of people who eagerly enroll in aerobic dance classes, join Nautilus clubs, swim or jog regularly, bowl in leagues, and participate in a multitude of other activities have already determined that these activities are fun and that they contribute to their mental, physical, and social development. These people have already joined the "wellness revolution," but others have not yet been convinced of the values of physical education. Reaching this latter group is the challenge awaiting you when you join the field of physical education.

Physical education programs in the past have been described by various terms that still influence this field today. This rich heritage provides a foundation for the programs that currently exist in the United States. Understanding the definition, aim, and purpose of physical education will help you conceptualize this field, while understanding affective, cognitive, and psychomotor objectives will ensure that you know what physical education

In classes in diverse settings, aerobic dance is a favorite conditioning activity of individuals of both sexes and all ages and body sizes.

Moderate activity often meets both the social and the recreational needs of senior citizens.

programs seek to accomplish. These objectives are related to the purposes of education. Awaiting you is a challenge to become an enthusiastic physical educator who can contribute to the wellness of others.

QUALITY OF LIFE—PHYSICAL EDUCATION'S CONTRIBUTION

What does "quality of life" mean? Is it happiness, wellness, health, fitness, or fun? Maybe it refers to the absence of disease, leisure time, freedom from oppression, or safety from harm. Quality of life, although defined individually, in today's world increasingly means a long and healthy life. Inherent therein is the concept that a feeling of well-being or some level of fitness enhances life. Maybe it is an outgrowth of Americans' search for the fountain of youth, but seemingly "fit is in," or at least the appearance of fitness.

Not a fad, this mania has become an integral part of life for many. Executives may choose their companies based on the availability of exercise programs, or employers may hire employees only if they are healthy and fit (*U.S. News and World Report*). Families often focus vacations and leisure time around various recreational and sport activities. Thousands of people sign up for marathons, 10-kilometer road races, and fun runs. Walking has become popular for people of all ages. Sporting goods and sports clothing sales continue to gross millions of dollars. Sports facilities such as health clubs, aerobics centers, tennis courts, swimming pools, and golf courses increasingly attract people who take their health and/or a sport seriously.

The threat of cardiovascular disease has contributed to a realization of the need to exercise the heart muscle (Watterson, 1984, pp. 144–145). Poor nutritional habits have adversely affected the health of thousands. Longer life expectancies have raised the consciousness levels of many who not only want to live longer but also want to enjoy their later years. Technological advances in modern society have reduced the amount of exercise inherent in our daily lives while simultaneously providing greater amounts of leisure time and discretionary income. Stress proliferates as a frequent by-product of technology and a highly competitive business world. In each case exercise, along with a knowledge of how the body functions in response to activity, has positively affected those participating. These factors reemphasize the importance of activity that can enhance fitness and the overall quality of life.

Millions of people in the United States do not participate in any physical activity due to lack of motivation, time, money, skills, or knowledge (Neal, 1984, pp. 33–37). To encourage participation is the role of physical educators. Are you willing to accept responsibility for changing attitudes and developing programs to get the inactive involved? Teachers, can you sell your students on the value of activity? How do you activate the lethargic? The future is unlimited for physical educators because less than 50% of our population exercises regularly. The inactive frequently are poorly skilled, economically disadvantaged, older adults, and children.

Typically, school athletic teams and city or business recreational leagues attract skilled participants or those at least moderately comfortable with their skills. Those lacking skills are relegated to the spectator role or to their easy chairs in front of their televisions. More instructional programs and introductory skill leagues and teams are needed for these beginners of all ages. Frequently, there is overlap between the lower skilled and the economically disadvantaged. Due to the cost of tennis, golf, and swimming, for example, these have often been categorized as upper-class sports. So, tax-supported recreation departments need to provide opportunities for these and other activities for all individuals. Senior citizens, an increasingly large percentage (more than 11%) of the population in the United States, have recreational needs (Godbey and Blazey, 1983, pp. 229–244). For example, exercise has been found to reduce osteoporosis, a breakdown of the calcium in the bones, especially for women in their postmenopausal years. This group needs activities tailored to its capabilities. On the other end of the spectrum, children have many needs for physical activity that remain unanswered. Daily physical education in kindergarten through the twelfth grade would greatly enhance children's movement skills and fitness capacities. Nonschool sport programs also can provide opportunities for fun. For each of these groups, increased positive opportunities for physical activities will contribute to the development of a healthy life-style and to a commitment to continue it as a quality way of life (McPherson, 1984, pp. 213-230). You, as a physical educator, hold the key to unlock this door of opportunity for them. Before exploring this dynamic field's principles, it is important to gain a historical perspective.

A RICH HERITAGE

This brief overview of the program foci in physical education's heritage provides a framework for the subsequent discussion. The Greeks began the first programs that resemble today's physical education, calling those who contended for a prize "athletes." At wrestling schools, sons of upper-class Greeks learned to run, jump, throw, swim, and wrestle. Upon reaching adulthood these citizen-soldiers trained in military/athletic events at a gymnasium.

Following more than 1000 years of apathy toward physical development, with the exception of the knights during the Middle Ages, European gymnastics emerged in the 1700s and 1800s. Based initially upon naturalistic principles concerning each child's interests, needs, and capabilities, many programs expanded due to nationalistic goals. Participants in school, military, and community programs exercised on apparatus, such as parallel bars, vaulting horses, climbing ladders, and balance beams, and executed command–response movements with little freedom permitted. Some running, jumping, throwing, sports, and games were included, but in most cases these remained secondary to the gymnastic exercises. European physical education today remains gymnastics-oriented.

The English, through worldwide colonization, spread their love of sports and games in the 1700s and 1800s; this contrasted dramatically the continental emphasis on more formalized exercises. English schoolboys and the lower-class factory workers in the industrialized urban areas separately participated in their own sports. Immigrants to the United States, especially from England, brought with them sports and games and ensured their permanence here. The freedom and competition of sports appealed to the nature and aspirations of this new citizenry much more than did the formalized gymnastic systems.

Hygiene, the science of preserving one's health, was the focus of many early school programs in the United States. These programs were often called "physical culture" or "physical training" because of the beneficial effects of exercise. This latter term reflected an emphasis on strength, popular in the late 1800s. Gymnastics, especially from Germany and Sweden, found some adherents around the turn of the century, but few programs fully adopted these systems. "Physical education" at that time became the accepted term for the emerging, eclectic programs that combined gymnastics, strength development, sports, and hygiene.

During the next half-century, physical education, although the accepted descriptive label of the field, faced various identity clashes. Athletics, internationally synonymous with track and field events, in the United States described organized sports competitions between highly skilled individuals. Since athletics in colleges preceded physical education programs and later merged with them, confusion resulted because many people thought that the two were the same. Although in the schools and in small colleges this situation continues, many people have recently separated the two in program and in objectives.

In the 1960s, individuals who led in the emphasis on the subdisciplines wanted to rename "physical education" "human movement," defined as the theoretical structure and scholarly approach of how the body moves most efficiently. Titles such as "human kinetics" and "kinesiology" were also proposed to provide credibility to this attempt to break out of the "play games in a gym" stereotype and to emerge as an academically recognized field of study.

While "physical education" remains the most common title for instruction in various human movements, by the year 2000 "leisure studies" or "sports sciences" may have surpassed it both in popularity and in specificity. Throughout this book the more recognizable term "physical education" is used in a broad sense to encompass programs as diverse as Greek athletics, European gymnastics, English sports, and American programs from *a* (athletics) to *w* (wellness) and from traditional school programs to nontraditional programs in many settings. With this brief perspective of physical education's background, in mind, it is now important to establish the scope, aim, purpose, and objectives of this field.

WHAT IS PHYSICAL EDUCATION?

Just as physical education has been variously labeled and has faced seeming identity crises, it also has been described in a multitude of ways. What does physical education mean to you? Is it synonymous with exercise, play, games, leisure, recreation, sports, or athletics? Before defining physical education, each of these terms needs to be understood. *Exercise*, in the physical dimension, means using or exerting the body. *Play* refers to the resultant action, or what the participants do during physical exertion. *Games* range from amusements or diversions to competitions with significant outcomes governed by rules. Freedom from work or duties describes *leisure*, which may or may not be used for physical activity. Similarly, *recreation* refreshes or renews one's strength and spirits after toil, again with or without activity. *Sport* encompasses all those diversions and physical activities that one does for pleasure or success. *Athletics* are organized, competitive activities in which trained individuals participate. Skill levels vary in each.

DEFINITION

Physical education may include any of these in its diverse programs, because depending on the setting, it may be organized or spontaneous, competitive or noncompetitive, required or optional, job-related or job-excluded, and a diversion or a compulsion. As you can readily determine, defining physical education, at least to the satisfaction of a diverse audience, is not an easy task. The following definition seeks to encompass the varied outcomes experienced by all people in its varied programs: *Physical education is a process through which an individual obtains optimal physical, mental, and social skills and fitness through physical activity.*

AIM AND GOAL OF PHYSICAL EDUCATION

With this definition in mind, what exactly do physical education programs seek to accomplish? *Aims, goals, objectives,* and *purposes* are interchangeable in their usage, although somewhat different in their meaning. An aim and a goal both describe a distant and encompassing end. Establishing a short-term goal of making the dean's list this term or aiming to make Phi Beta Kappa as a senior are examples. A purpose includes a resolution or intention to pursue a goal or aim, although in some cases they may overlap, as may objectives that specify the outcomes. If a hierarchy is required, an aim or a goal then becomes the ultimate aspiration, and the attainment of a purpose and lasting objectives contributes on a lower level.

Traditionally, physical education has accepted as its goal the one offered by Jesse Williams (1964, p. 325), whose ideas dominated this field between 1930 and 1960. He stated:

> Physical education should aim to provide skilled leadership and adequate facilities which will afford an opportunity for the individual or group to act in situations which are physically wholesome, mentally stimulating and satisfying, and socially sound.

Williams' goal challenged physical educators to develop the abilities to impact significantly the lives of those they taught or led. He suggested that physical education could benefit the whole individual, who, in turn, could contribute to the well-being of society. Traditionally, this goal has been associated with physical education's role in the aims of education. Today's goal for physical education involves similar aspirations for its diverse programs in this technological society. *The aim of physical education is to increase every individual's physical, mental, and social benefits from physical activities and to develop healthy life-style skills and attitudes.*

PURPOSE OF PHYSICAL EDUCATION

The purpose of physical education is closely linked with its aim but includes the stated intention to act (i.e., a process). Thus a purpose may encompass a behavior change, a commitment, a determination, and a willingness to alter one's life-style. *Optimizing one's quality of life through a long-term commitment to an enjoyable, personal exercise program that will meet varied needs in a changing world is the purpose of physical education.*

OBJECTIVES OF PHYSICAL EDUCATION

The objectives of physical education are often more specific than the goal, or aim, and purpose and are comprised of particular outcomes. Usually plural, in combination they result in the achievement of a purpose and an aim. Professional colleagues and the general public often learn about physical education's worth through an examination of its objectives and their fulfillment.

Dudley Sargent, a recognized leader in physical education for college students in the late 1800s and early 1900s, was an authority in teacher training and in anthropometric measurements of the positive effects of exercise on the body. He suggested that physical education achieved hygienic, educative, recreative, and remedial objectives. Outcomes that he noted in his programs included improved health, fun, remediation of illness and injury, and enhanced knowledge about how the body moved and learned. Clark Hetherington, one of the "new physical educators," helped lead in the transition from exercising methodically to developing the entire person. In 1910, he recommended that physical education programs seek organic, psychomotor, character, and intellectual objectives.

In 1934, the American Physical Education Association's Committee on Objectives listed physical fitness, mental health and efficiency, social-moral character, emotional expression and control, and appreciations as the desired objectives. In 1950, these were restated by the profession: to develop and to maintain maximum physical efficiency, to develop useful skills, to conduct oneself in socially useful ways, and to enjoy wholesome recreation. In 1965, the American Association for Health, Physical Education and Recreation stated five major objectives (AAHPER, 1965):

1. To help children move in a skillful and effective manner in all the selected activities in which they engage, in the physical education program, and also in those situations that they will experience during their lifetime.
2. To develop an understanding and appreciation of movement in children and youth so that their lives will become more meaningful, purposive, and productive.
3. To develop an understanding and appreciation of certain scientific principles concerned with movement that relate to such factors as time, space, force, and mass-energy relationships.
4. To develop through the medium of games and sports better interpersonal relationships.
5. To develop the various organic systems of the body so they will respond in a healthful way to the increased demands placed on them.

Before examining physical education's objectives in greater detail, it is essential to understand how they relate to those of education.

In 1918, the Educational Policies Commission stated seven objectives of education: health, command of fundamental processes, worthy home membership, vocation, citizenship, worthy use of leisure time, and ethical character. In 1938, these were consolidated to self-realization, human relationship, economic efficiency, and civic responsibility. Through both statements, educational leaders showed a desire to develop the child as a whole. Justification for any educational program was based on what contribution it could make. Led by Jesse Williams and others, since the 1930s, physical education has demonstrated that its alignment with Benjamin Bloom's taxonomy of cognitive, affective, and psychomotor objectives has verified its value as a school subject. These same objectives are achievable in physical education programs outside the schools.

Cognitive objectives focus on the acquisition, comprehension, analysis, synthesis, application, and evaluation of knowledge. Minimal preparation in physical education course work includes the body's structure and function, health, first aid, history and principles, growth and development, organization and administration, motor learning, and exercise physiology. Regardless of the setting, information from these courses is essential for instructors to understand and disseminate and for program participants to comprehend and apply.

Increased cognitive involvement usually leads to better execution of skills and always leads to a better understanding of the activity. Physical educators need to explain not only how, but especially why, so individuals may par-

Jogging to develop and maintain cardiovascular endurance has become an important part of the life-style adopted by many Americans.

ticipate on their own. They also must emphasize learning sport rules, strategies and skills, safety principles, and proper etiquette.

One additional point is that often physical activity enhances one's cognitive development. Reading, math, language, and other subjects may be enhanced through participation in certain physical activities. Mental fatigue from studying or working can be reduced through exercise, so that a subsequent session of either is more productive. Stress can impede cognitive processes, but activity can reduce stress and enhance productivity.

The emphasis of the affective domain is on the development of attitudes, appreciations, and values and contains both social and emotional dimensions. In the social realm, both individual and group needs are met while positive characteristics are developed. Learning self-confidence, courtesy, fair play, sportsmanship, and how to make value judgments benefits the individual directly. From a group perspective, decision-making abilities, communication skills, and affiliation needs are enhanced. Individuals' values and attitudes toward involvement in physical activity are solidified, as are appreciations for participation and performance. On the emotional side, discipline, fun, how to win and how to lose, how to release tension, self-control, and self-expression are learned.

Developing and improving fundamental movement skills and game skills are the foci of the psychomotor objective, as sport, aquatic, and dance skills begin with learning basic and efficient movement patterns. Children need to explore their bodies' capabilities, including learning to walk, run, or jump independently or in conjunction with others or using apparatus. Similar principles can apply as individuals experiment with solving movement challenges. Manipulative skills are developed by exploring the potential of and practice with hoops, ropes, balls, rackets, bats, and other implements. Perceptual-motor skills, such as the eye-hand coordination needed to strike a ball with a racket or the reaction time needed to judge how quickly a partner's thrown ball will reach one, are also important skills. Once these abilities are mastered independently and in combination at each person's developmental level, then game skills, such as catching, throwing, and batting, can be incorporated into lead-up games and mini-sport situations. Although they are not listed specifically, dance, aquatic, and other specific sport skills are outcomes of the psychomotor objective.

Physical fitness, a second outcome of the psychomotor domain, comprises cardiovascular endurance, muscular strength and endurance, and flexibility. Physicians increasingly state that a healthy heart and respiratory system may reduce the risk of disease and certainly may improve the quality of life; they

Physical education helps children develop fitness and psychomotor skills as they learn to enjoy activity. (Courtesy of Gid Alston)

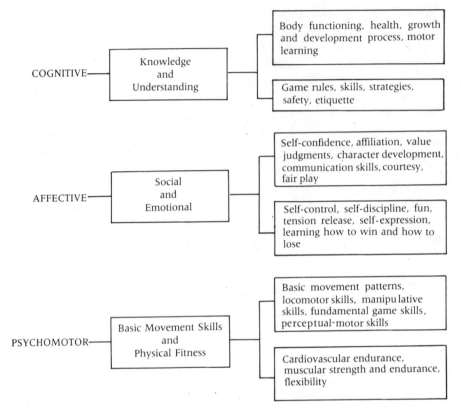

FIGURE 1–1. Objectives of physical education.

encourage cardiovascular exercises. The ability to exert maximal force and to sustain this effort describes muscular strength and endurance, a second component of fitness. Flexibility gained by statically stretching the muscles improves the range of motion in the joints. Other motoric factors that result from physical fitness include agility, balance, coordination, speed, and power.

Figure 1–1 summarizes the cognitive, affective, and psychomotor objectives of physical education. It is essential that these three objectives interrelate rather than exist singularly. For example, while learning to hit tennis balls, people not only enhance their eye-hand coordination, but also learn proper body position for a level swing and cooperation with those with whom they take turns tossing the ball. Box 1–1 provides examples of specific objectives related to each domain. Three additional examples follow; note that each objective is worded so that results can be measured.

BOX 1–1
EXAMPLES OF PHYSICAL EDUCATION OBJECTIVES

Cognitive

1. The participant will explain the principles for playing zone defenses in basketball.
2. The participant will analyze the technique for executing a flat tennis serve.
3. The participant, using the whole teaching method, will synthesize the principles of learning the crawl stroke in swimming.
4. The participant will apply knowledge of cardiovascular functioning in establishing a personal exercise program.
5. The participant will evaluate another person's weight-lifting technique and provide corrective feedback.

Affective

1. The participant will express appreciation of the excellence of an opponent's high-level performance.
2. The participant will enjoy playing hard and doing his or her best, regardless of the outcome of a contest.
3. The participant will cooperate and take turns with others.
4. The participant will demonstrate fair play and good sportsmanship in unsupervised activities.
5. The participant will value the rights of others and the regulations governing the situation.

Psychomotor

1. The participant will improve eye-hand coordination by weekly practicing racquetball forehand and backhand shots.
2. The participant will explore ways to manipulate a ball without using the hands.
3. The participant will design and perform a one-minute dance that includes use of two locomotor movements and use of two objects.
4. The participant will demonstrate the proper technique for executing a volleyball spike.
5. The participant will execute four exercises designed to improve flexibility of the shoulders.

Cognitive—the participant will demonstrate knowledge of the rules of racquetball by answering at least 15 of 20 questions correctly;

Affective—the participant will show communication skills by accurately describing and leading five different warm-up exercises for a group of at least 10 people;

Psychomotor—the participant will use proper technique in successfully executing 7 of 10 dominant-hand basketball lay-ups.

SUMMARY

You might ask yourself, what is the relationship of these objectives to me? Regardless of our future, everyone needs to be educated physically. We should want to benefit from the outcomes of physical education programs. Whether our desire is to have fun, to play games, to learn sport skills, to improve sportsmanship values, to develop a healthy life-style, or to reduce tension, we can affect the quality of our lives directly and positively. Physical education can be a very personal experience.

More broadly, how do these objectives relate to others and possibly to your work with others? That is the challenge that awaits those who choose to pursue physical education as a career. It truly is a unique and dynamic field because its activities can touch and improve everyone's quality of life, but only if the programs are positive and meaningful. Historically, this has not always been the case. Therefore, if you are planning a career in physical education you must consider whether you can achieve the aim, purpose, and objectives that have been presented here. In the chapters that follow you will learn more about physical education and how it presents you with exciting opportunities while challenging you to impact positively on the lives of others.

SUSAN B. JOHNSON

Associate Director and Senior Consultant of the Division of Continuing Education
Institute for Aerobics Research
Dallas, Texas

EDUCATION

B.S., Physical Education, Memphis State University (1969)
M.Ed., Physical Education, Memphis State University (1973)
Ed.D., Teacher Behavior in Physical Education, University of North Carolina at Greensboro (1982)

JOB RESPONSIBILITIES, HOURS, AND SALARY RANGE

Susan develops and conducts certification workshops for exercise instructors and aerobic dance teachers, initiates research, develops new materials, and consults with agencies, businesses, and organizations relative to physical fitness programs. Susan works from 6:30 A.M. to 5:30 P.M. Monday through Friday and 1:00 P.M. to 4:00 P.M. on Saturday and Sunday, typical hours for this career. The salary range for corporate fitness programming and training is between $30,000 and $55,000.

SPECIALIZED COURSE WORK, DEGREES, AND WORK EXPERIENCES NEEDED FOR THIS CAREER

Teaching is a major function of this job, so educational courses are important. It is highly recommended that individuals wishing to pursue this career possess specialized knowledge in health promotion, exercise physiology, psychology, kinesiology, and sociology. Susan states that her doctorate has provided a vital background for her specific responsibilities, although other corporate fitness careers may require only master's degrees. In addition, a medical background as well as a knowledge of statistics, computer applications, and research methodology complement this work. Other abilities needed include competence in speaking before groups, writing skills, leadership abilities, and administrative skills. Jobs that involve teaching and research would best prepare students. Also, administrative jobs would help students acquire necessary organizational and management skills.

SATISFYING ASPECTS OF THIS CAREER

One reason for the need for exercise leaders is the growth in corporate fitness programs. Leaders in business and industry are realizing that taking care of their number one asset, their employees, is cost-efficient as well as an excellent fringe benefit for the participants. Many physical educators are attracted to working with adults in the fitness field, where the major challenges are developing motivational and adherence strategies. Susan especially enjoys training exercise leaders to offer safe and effective programs. She also takes pleasure in her role of seeing individuals make life-style changes that lead to healthier and happier lives.

JOB POTENTIAL

Susan predicts that the fitness boom will continue to expand and will impact on all phases of life—work, home, school, business, and church. Looking to the twenty-first century, the availability of jobs in training exercise leaders and in becoming an exercise leader will expand dramatically. Businesses and industries will continue to provide for executive fitness, and they will offer more programs for blue-collar workers, too. Urban areas where larger companies are located will have more jobs, although businesses in small cities may jointly offer programs for their employees.

ADVICE TO STUDENTS

Susan suggests that students study the field and all its related subdisciplines and acquire as much knowledge as possible from current leaders in the field and from their writings. On an emotional level, she recommends that students find a special area of interest or study that appeals to their sense of commitment. In the field of physical fitness, Susan stresses the importance of functioning as a role model. Credibility is lost if fitness leaders smoke, are overweight, use drugs, or practice unhealthy habits. Susan believes that working as a team player and being willing to do a variety of tasks to reach an ultimate goal are important. She also recommends that physical educators learn to think futuristically and to act progressively and productively to make valid plans come to life.

REVIEW QUESTIONS

1. How can physical education contribute to the improvement in one's quality of life?
2. What general groups in society have not yet joined the fitness boom?
3. How does physical education relate to athletics, sports, play, and recreation?
4. How do physical education's objectives relate to education's objectives?
5. What types of knowledge are important within the cognitive domain of physical education? Give examples of each.
6. What type of objectives focus on the development of attitudes, appreciations, and values?
7. Name several ways that the social aspect of physical education programs can impact on participants positively.
8. What three components are essential for the development of physical fitness?
9. In what setting(s) can physical education's three objectives be achieved?
10. How do you define physical education?

STUDENT ACTIVITIES

1. Interview relatives or friends who are older than 50 years to find out what types of physical education program(s) they experienced. Ask them their perspective of what physical education is today.

2. Ask at least two friends who are not physical education majors what they think physical education is.

3. Read and report on one article that uses a different name or descriptive term for physical education. How is it defined? What is the rationale for it?

4. Write a one- or two-page description of how you would incorporate three affective outcomes into a community swimming program.

5. Write a one-page summary of how the three physical education objectives have impacted on your life and your career choice.

REFERENCES

As companies jump on the fitness bandwagon. *U.S. News & World Report, 88* (3), 36–39, 28 January 1980.

Godbey, G., and Blazey, M. Old people in urban parks: An exploratory investigation. *Journal of Leisure Research, 15* (3), 229–244, 1983.

McPherson, B. D. Sport participation across the life cycle: A review of the literature and suggestions for future research. *Sociology of Sport Journal, 1* (3), 213–230, 1984.

Neal, L. L. Family recreation trends, tenets and model building. *Journal of Physical Education, Recreation and Dance, 55* (8), 33–37, October 1984.

This is physical education. Washington, D.C.: American Association for Health, Physical Education and Recreation, 1965.

Watterson, V. V. The effects of aerobics on cardiovascular fitness. *The Physician and Sportsmedicine, 12* (10), 138–141, 144–145, October 1984.

Williams, J. F. *The principles of physical education* (8th Ed.). Philadelphia: W.B. Saunders Company, p. 325, 1964.

SUGGESTED READINGS

Arnold, P. J. Three approaches toward an understanding of sportsmanship. *Journal of the Philosophy of Sport, 10,* 61–70, 1983. The author proposes three different although related, views about sportsmanship relative to the actions and conduct of individuals engaged in sports—as a form of social union, as a means in the promotion of pleasure, and as a form of altruism.

Bain, L. L. Socialization into the role of participant: physical education's ultimate goal. *Journal of Physical Education and Recreation, 51,* 48–50, September 1980. Physical educators should state participant enjoyment as their central purpose, should base curricular decisions on this focus, and should evaluate to determine whether this enjoyment increases voluntary participation.

Bonaguro, J. A. PRECEDE for wellness. *The Journal of School Health, 51,* 501–506, September 1981. PRECEDE is a model for examining those factors that predispose, enable, or reinforce health behaviors, or have the opposite effect, and for evaluating attitudes, beliefs, and values that impact on one's life-style.

Goldberger, M., and Moyer, S. A schema for classifying educational objectives in the psychomotor domain. *Quest (2), 32,* 134–142, 1982. After reviewing Mosston's three-dimensional model of developmental movement, the authors introduce their taxonomy of psychomotor forms as a mechanism for ordering information about human movement and physical ability hierarchically and as a strategy that is connected to a larger structure of human movement.

Hage, P. Prescribing exercise: more than just a running program. *The Physician and Sportsmedicine, 11,* 123–127, 131, May 1983. Physicians today are more likely to prescribe group exercise and fitness programs, to elicit the assistance of those who apply motivational techniques to encourage adherence, and to involve patients in the selection of their programs.

Holloszy, J. O. Exercise, health, and aging: a need for more information. *Medicine and Science in Sports and Exercise, 15 (1),* 1–5, 1983. Needed are large-scale, well-controlled studies by exercise physiologists who are funded to study the effects of exercise on chronic disease processes and aging.

Kummant, I. Joy of movement: high priority for physical educator. *The Physician and Sportsmedicine, 9,* 147–150, September 1981. Rudy Benton, an elementary physical educator in California, is illustrative of a "new breed" of teachers who stress that children should spend as much time as possible experiencing the joy of movement.

Murphy, J. F. *Concepts of leisure* (2nd Ed.). Englewood Cliffs, New Jersey: Prentice-Hall, Inc., 1981. After providing a background for viewing the impact of leisure in contemporary society, this book examines work-leisure relationships, leisure and time, leisure relative to life-style and socioeconomic status, psychological and environmental perspectives of leisure, and holistic and futuristic views of leisure.

Woodford, R. C. The importance of the affective domain in the education of physical educators. *Quest, 31,* 285–293, 1979. The importance of achieving affective objectives in teacher education programs is stressed through a taxonomy and a listing and description of desirable curricular goals.

C H A P T E R

Two

—Philosophy—
and Physical Education

KEY
CONCEPTS

- ■ Philosophy is the pursuit of truth and the resultant knowledge and values.
- ■ Idealism, realism, pragmatism, naturalism, and existentialism have influenced the growth of physical education.
- ■ Several branches of philosophy, such as aesthetics and logic, have contributed to the development of physical education programs.
- ■ Ethics is a branch of philosophy that deals with moral values.
- ■ The practical application of philosophical theories will help you develop a personal philosophy of physical education.

Philosophy, often misunderstood and neglected, provides focus, a communication bond, a clarity of vision and direction, and an opportunity to analyze the present to expand one's horizons for the future.

The pursuit of knowledge through logical reasoning and analysis is as pervasive today as it was during the development of several diverse philosophies. This chapter examines the importance of philosophy, focuses on five of the traditional philosophies, with emphasis on how they have influenced physical education. Other philosophies are included because of their similar impact. Based on the knowledge gained from this study, each of you is encouraged to develop a personal philosophy of physical education.

WHY STUDY PHILOSOPHY?

Philosophy can be defined as a love of wisdom or more broadly as the pursuit of truth. Philosophy is both the developmental process and the resultant facts, theories, and values. Philosophy is an attempt to understand the meaning of life by analyzing and synthesizing why; having a scope and objectives, as discussed in Chapter 1, is not sufficient. You must know why these are of value both to you and to others, and you need to be able to articulate their importance.

The absence of concreteness bothers many people as they try to understand philosophy. Since concepts, feelings, and theories are more frequently the focal point of philosophy than are facts, understanding is somewhat difficult.

What is the worth of physical education to a school child? What is the value of learning a lifetime sport? What constitutes a healthy life-style? What is the role of play? These are just a few of the questions that a philosophy of physical education can help answer.

Developing a personal philosophy can improve teaching effectiveness, influence one's behavior, provide direction in program development, contribute to society's awareness of the value of physical activity, and encourage a feeling of commonality among co-workers. The discussion of the traditional philosophies that follows should help you in the formulation of your personal philosophy.

22

TRADITIONAL PHILOSOPHIES

This discussion focuses on five traditional philosophies: idealism, realism, pragmatism, naturalism, and existentialism. In addition to these, some educational philosophies (see Box 2–1) that will impact on your personal development of values, beliefs, and ideals are explained briefly.

BOX 2–1
EDUCATIONAL PHILOSOPHIES

Essentialism—An educational theory that states that a core of ideas and skills is essential for all students to learn and emphasizes that they be taught using traditional methodology and discipline.

Existentialism—A twentieth-century philosophy that centers on individual existence and advocates that truth and values are arrived at by each person's experiences.

Experimentalism—A philosophy that relies on experimental or empirical principles and procedures in establishing truth.

Humanism—A traditional philosophy that stresses an individual's worth and ability for self-realization through reasoning.

Idealism—A philosophical theory advocating that reality depends on the mind for existence and that truth is universal and absolute.

Naturalism—A belief that the scientific laws of nature govern life and that individual goals are more important than societal goals.

Pragmatism—An American movement in philosophy emphasizing reality as the sum total of each individual's experiences through practical experimentation.

Progressivism—A theory that applies pragmatism to education by focusing on the individual child rather than the subject matter, informality of classroom procedures, and problem-solving.

Realism—The philosophical thought that relies on belief in the laws and order of the world as revealed by science independent from human experience.

IDEALISM

Idealism centers on the mind as critical to understanding, since only through reasoning and mental processes can truth emerge. Never-changing ideals, not things, constitute the ultimate reality. Idealists since the Greek philosopher Plato have stressed that only the reflective and intuitive individual can arrive at truth (Wilson, 1984).

Ideals, values, and truths are universal and external and remain the same regardless of how individual interpretations may vary. As people develop and exercise their free will, they make choices through their intellectual powers. These decisions, whether right or wrong, do not alter the values integral to idealism.

The development of the total person is the objective of idealism as applied to physical education, too. The individual is important and should be nurtured through an emphasis on the mind and its thought processes. Since reality is spiritual rather than physical, sometimes physical activity is relegated to a secondary status, even though the mind and the body are supposed to be developed simultaneously.

Since the curriculum focuses on ideas, teachers, who are more important than the process, are free to use any methods that would help students achieve their optimal level of personality and character development. Outcomes of the affective domain, such as creativity and sportsmanship, are also values upon which idealism places emphasis.

REALISM

As a revolt against some of the tenets of idealism, the Greek philosopher Aristotle and today's advocates of realism state that the laws of nature, rather than existing truths, are in control (Barnes, 1982). The scientific method provides the realist with the process for acquiring and applying truth (i.e., the knowledge that originates in the physical world but emerges through experimentation). Scientific investigation examines the material things of the world when seeking truth.

The role of education, according to the realist, is to train the student to discover and to interpret the real things of life to ensure adjustment of the individual in the real world. Since the emphasis is on the whole individual, physical education has a vital contribution to make, including the traditional objectives of organic fitness, neuromuscular development, intellectual ability, and social and emotional development.

Inductive reasoning, an orderly progression in learning, extensive use of drills, and objective evaluation are important methodologies used by the

Realism advocates arriving at truth using the scientific method, as in a strictly controlled exercise
prescription research study.

realist teacher. Learning is subject-centered, rather than teacher-centered, as
is true for the idealist. The curriculum includes activities and experiences that
enable students to understand the laws of the physical world.

PRAGMATISM

Pragmatism states that experiences, not ideals and realities, provide the
key to seeking truth. Ultimate reality must be experienced and is not absolute.
Circumstances and situations constantly vary from person to person; thus,
pragmatism is characterized as dynamic and ever-changing.

In seeking knowledge, the pragmatist looks for truth that works in a given
situation. If it does, then it is true at that moment. Truth is a function of the
consequences of the time and even the social context and is considered good
if successful. Values are also relative and result from judgments about one's
experiences as long as they are evaluated in terms of the good of the group,

Participation in a variety of activities, such as a combination of roller skating and frisbee, can help individuals function more effectively in society, according to pragmatists. (Courtesy of Pamela G. Royal)

not selfishly. Pragmatists emphasize social responsibilities, since it is essential that every individual functions within and contributes to society.

The overall objective of a pragmatic education is the development of social efficiency in students, according to the most famous American pragmatist, John Dewey (1966). That is, students need to have opportunities to experience solving the problems of life and to learn how to become better-functioning members of society. Through the use of problem-solving, the teacher focuses on the needs and interests of the students. This student-centered curriculum encourages students to apply the scientific method and to experience a wide variety of activities. Team sports stress cooperation and the development of interpersonal skills, while movement activities provide opportunities for exploring numerous solutions to problems.

NATURALISM

The naturalist believes in things that exist within the physical realm of nature, which is itself the source of value. Since naturalism emphasizes that the individual is more important than society, education focuses on meeting each student's needs.

Stressing "everything according to nature," 18th-century philosopher Jean-Jacques Rousseau (1964) led in espousing this oldest known philosophy of the Western world. He advocated that education must use the physical world as the classroom and that teachers by example should guide students through inductive reasoning to draw their own conclusions. The laws of nature dictate to the teacher and to the student the logical pattern of growth, development, and learning. Rousseau also encouraged education of the mind and body simultaneously. Physical well-being should then enhance a readiness to learn mental, moral, and social skills.

Naturalism also declares the importance of individualized learning through self-education and self-activity. Exploration of one's capabilities and interests leads directly to greater skills and adjustments to nature. Non-competitive team, individual, and outdoor activities provide play opportunities that benefit students physically, psychologically, and, especially, socially. Through physical activities, the individual develops in an all-around way.

A natural setting provides an excellent learning environment for social, intellectual, and physical skills. (Courtesy of Pamela G. Royal)

EXISTENTIALISM

According to existentialism, human experiences determine reality. Emerging in the 1900s as a reaction against societal conformity, this philosophy subjugated everything to the individual as long as acceptance of responsibility for oneself is recognized. Leaders of existential thought include Jean-Paul Sartre (Silverman & Elliston, 1980) and Karl Jaspers.

Reality for the existentialist is composed of the experiences of humans and is determined by the choices they make. One's experiences and free choices result in truth and are uniquely personal. An individual's value system, while totally controlled by choice, must be tempered by an understanding of societal responsibility. No values are imposed by society; instead, each person is free to think and to act as personal desires dictate.

The self-actualizing person is the desired educational outcome, as each student is given freedom to choose. All students must accept the consequences of their actions. Within the curriculum, students are presented a wide variety of activities, especially individual ones, through which to develop creativity,

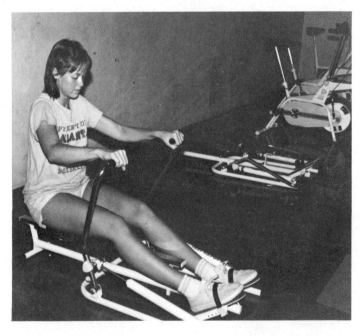

The existentialist teaches acceptance of individual responsibility, such as self-motivation in designing and implementing a personal fitness program.

self-awareness, self-responsibility, and realization of individual essence. The teacher raises questions and provokes reflective thinking but leaves students free to choose their own courses of action.

●   ●   ●

These five traditional philosophies offer diverse approaches to seeking truth as well as different methodologies for meeting physical education's objectives. Table 2–1 provides a general comparison of these five philosophies. Table 2–2 relates these and essentialism and progressivism to physical education.

BRANCHES OF PHILOSOPHY

Six branches of philosophy have also impacted physical education programs. *Aesthetics* deals with the principles of beauty and judgments concerning beauty and describes and explains artistic phenomena and experiences. The Greeks were zealous in their appreciation of the artistic beauty of the human body in motion.

Axiology is the study of the nature and criteria of values and value judgments in general terms.

Logic is a science based on the laws of validity of inference and the demonstration of the principles of reasoning. It is concerned with the relationship of ideas to each other.

Metaphysics, more abstract and difficult to comprehend, relates to the transcendent or supersensible and examines the principles underlying the nature of being and the kinds of existence. In essence, metaphysics studies the ultimate reality of everything.

Epistemology is the study of the nature of knowledge and how to learn its limits and to access its validity.

Ethics is the study of moral values. It deals with what is good and bad, with moral duty and obligation, and with principles of conduct. Since the Greeks, educators have been responsible for the development of ethical standards. Character, for example, has traditionally been a vital concern of educators and physical educators (Fraleigh, 1984).

How to teach ethical standards most effectively has been a dilemma for physical educators and coaches for a long time. Since fair play and sportsmanship are not inherent characteristics of physical activities, how do they result? When play, games, sports, and other physical pursuits are engaged in for their inherent pleasure, then no ethical problem emerges. When the outcome becomes so highly significant that some or all of the participants will employ whatever means possible to achieve success, then questionable behavior is readily evident, to the detriment of values. Ethics, or moral values,

TABLE 2–1
FIVE TRADITIONAL PHILOSOPHIES

	Idealism	Realism	Pragmatism	Naturalism	Existentialism
Source of truth	Ideas	Scientific reality	Human experiences	Nature	Human existence
Most important	People	Physical world	Society	Individual	Individual
How to arrive at truth	Reasoning and intuition	Scientific method	Experiencing changes	Laws of nature	Individual determination
Importance of the mind	Emphasized	Reasoning powers and scientific method used	Learning through inquiring, observing, and participating	Physical and mental balance for whole person	The individual's determination of the subject matter and the learning method
Importance of the body	Simultaneous development with mind	Emphasis on the whole individual	Variety of activities for effective functioning in society	Physical activity essential for optimal learning	Freedom to choose activity and to be creative

Curriculum focus	Teacher-centered through examples for students; qualitative	Subject-centered; quantitative	Child-centered; based on individual differences	Individual readiness to learn	Individual-centered; based on self-realization
Importance of the teacher	A model and example	Orderly presentation of facts; drills and scientific method used	Motivator, especially through problem-solving; co-learner	Guide and helper	Stimulator and counselor
Importance of the personality	Moral and spiritual values stressed	Learn for life adjustment	Development of social skills and meeting one's needs	Development of social skills also important	Learning self-responsibility and knowing oneself
Education	Self-development	To meet realities of life	For social efficiency	Natural process	Teaching acceptance of individual responsibility

TABLE 2–2
APPLICATION OF PHILOSOPHIES TO PHYSICAL EDUCATION

	Essentialism	Existentialism	Idealism	Naturalism	Pragmatism	Progressivism	Realism
Objectives	Adjustment of students to the social and cultural environment	Assisting students to become self-actualizing, independent beings	Development of personality and mind	Development of whole person	Helping students to become better-functioning members of society	Encouraging students to experiment and to gain experiences through democratic processes	Training students to meet realities of life
Subject matter	Core of knowledge, skills, and values	Wide selection of alternatives, especially individual activities	Utmost importance	Play; self-directed individual activity	Experiences in a wide variety of activities	Chosen by students	Required, and the focus of learning
Methodology	Traditional, with discipline important	Questions raised, thoughts provoked, and freedom of action encouraged by the teacher	Lecture, question/answer, discussions	Informal; problem-solving	Problem-solving	Child-centered approach (problem-solving)	Use of real world, drills, lectures, and projects

Teacher's role	Authoritarian and disciplinarian	Guide	More important than process	Guide; nature teaches	Guide	Permissive guide and facilitator	Selects knowledge to learn
Student's role	Self-discipline learned from authority	Focus of the program for self-realization	Development of total person	Individualized rate of learning	Focus of the program to learn about moral self	Focus of the program	Emphasizes the whole individual
Evaluation	Quantitatively linked with learning subject matter	Unimportant in the traditional sense	Subjective, qualitative	Based on attainment of individual goals	Subjective and self-evaluation	Individualized	Quantitative, using scientific means
Weaknesses	Not dynamic; students do not learn to think independently	Overemphasis on individuality precludes preparation for societal life	Resistance to change; development of the physical secondary to the mind	Too simple an education for the complex world	Lack of fixed aims to give students stability and direction	Deemphasis on subject matter; too permissive	Too narrow a view; everything must conform to natural laws or it is wrong

do not preclude seeking to perform to the best of one's ability, but doing so at the risk of impinging on what is good, one's obligation to others, or principles of proper conduct violates these values.

Can physical education teach ethics? In spite of our materialistic and pragmatic world, physical education has an obligation to teach and to perpetuate moral and ethical principles that are basic to our society. Among these principles are sensitivity to individual needs and differences, responsibility for our personal conduct, concern for others, and devotion to honesty, integrity, and fair play. Physical educators in all settings should exemplify ethical behavior and treat everyone fairly, so that others can be positively influenced. We must constantly be aware that our actions will teach character louder than our statements.

Since today many traits are modeled after athletes in professional and collegiate sports, physical education faces an even greater challenge. Sports heroes who are televised engaging in violence, abusive language, and rule violations are often mimicked by children and even by adults. Americans' compulsion for victory and the accompanying degradation of losing intensify the attitude of "winning is everything." Instead of teaching justice, equality, consideration of others, and respect for the rules, this attitude often results in the loss of ethical standards. Physical educators are challenged to reverse this trend and to work toward the attainment of the highest moral values possible. One way to help ensure this is to establish it as a priority as you develop your philosophy of physical education.

DEVELOPING A PERSONAL PHILOSOPHY OF PHYSICAL EDUCATION

Everyone who plans a career in physical education needs to develop a personal philosophy of physical education. This is important as a guide to your attitudes and actions. For example, if fair play is essential to your philosophy, you will stress this in your own behavior, your instruction of others, and the programs you lead. A personal philosophy forces you to think logically and analytically and to explain the worth and the value of physical education. This developmental process will help you relate physical education to general education and will enhance your professional growth. Too frequently physical educators have failed to develop definite personal philosophies, resulting in the loss of self-direction and career prestige. Therefore, it is essential that you formulate principles, guidelines, and directions for your career. If you do not know where or how you are going, it is unlikely that you will end up where you want to be (wherever that is!).

It is evident that many of the tenets of the philosophies discussed in this chapter conflict. For example, pragmatism advocates helping students become better-functioning members of society, while existentialism focuses on students becoming self-actualizing, independent beings. In light of this potential conflict in values and knowledge, you must proceed logically and critically. The first step in formulating a personal philosophy is to analyze and to determine your views about truth, knowledge, reality, and value. You may need to take a philosophy course or at least study what philosophers have written. You also should draw upon your own personal experiences as you develop a comprehensive philosophy.

Many educators and philosophers have adopted an eclectic approach rather than accepting all aspects of one particular philosophy. *Eclecticism* is a combination of theories and doctrines from several philosophies into a consistent and compatible set of beliefs. Based on your experiences and established values, an eclectic philosophy may emerge as the foundation for your personal philosophy. Again, the key is to realize the importance of examining what you believe, why you believe it, and what your values mean.

Regardless of your career choice, in the second step of this process you need to establish your educational aims, which are valuable because they provide a focus or direction for the subsequent activities that you will pursue. In other words, you need to decide what you want to accomplish while realizing that whatever you select must be logical and consistent with your previously chosen philosophy. During the third step, you should decide the functions for your school, business, or program as it exists in society. This process naturally follows the general aims you have already set and it specifies how these overall purposes can be achieved. Are individuals or outcomes the focal point? Do you stress the process or the product? It is essential that you answer these questions as you formulate your philosophy.

Based on your selected school, business, or program contributions, in the fourth step you need to specify practices and behavior patterns that you will use as a result of the attitudes and values that you espouse. Will you serve as a facilitator, authority figure, role model, friend, consultant, or boss? Will your program or curriculum focus on group or individual activities, team or individual sports, social games, play, or healthful, lifetime pursuits? How will you evaluate and motivate participants? The essentiality of answering these questions in harmony with your chosen philosophy cannot be overemphasized.

The fifth step is evaluation. General and specific aims and objectives should be compatible with your chosen values and knowledges. As you rethink various aspects of your philosophy, you may find conflicts in actual or planned practices. This necessitates a change in either philosophy or action to restore consistency. This step should be ongoing throughout your career.

These five steps apply to all careers in physical education as you develop a personal philosophy. You can start this process now as you learn more about philosophy and while you profit from your daily experiences.

To assist you further in the development of your personal philosophy and to show how it impacts on and interacts with many physical education careers, read the following situations and give your responses. A composite of your opinions should help you better understand your values and knowledge and how they provide the foundation for your personal philosophy.

Situation 1—During a basketball game, player 44 (team A) and player 12 (team B) both attempt to control a loose ball, but it goes out of bounds. As the official, you blow your whistle and award the ball to team A. Player 44 acknowledges touching the ball last. Do you change your call? If you were the player, would you have acknowledged causing the ball to go out of bounds?

Situation 2—During a recreation league softball game, you as the field supervisor learn that one of the teams is playing an illegal individual. That team is in last place in the league standing. What action, if any, do you take?

Situation 3—As a local sportswriter you were just given the facts about a 14-year-old who transferred to a private school because of promised financial benefits. This student happens to be an outstanding athlete. Do you write this story?

Situation 4—All funds for physical education at your school have been transferred to the athletic budget. As a teacher (not in physical education) and a coach, do you approve or disapprove, and why?

Situation 5—As a collegiate football player you are told by the coach to take anabolic steroids because they are supposed to help build muscle bulk. Do you take the drugs?

Situation 6—Your soccer team of 9- and 10-year-olds is in the last game of the season. If your team wins, it will capture the league championship. Your best player twists an ankle just as the first half ends. The player is in pain, but there is seemingly no fracture and only slight swelling. Do you allow that player to participate in the second half?

There are no right or wrong answers to these situations. Your responses simply indicate your beliefs and values and show what objectives and outcomes are important to you. Some especially relate to ethical judgments.

SUMMARY

As you progress in your education and enter your career, your philosophy may change. You may borrow concepts from idealism, realism, pragmatism, naturalism, existentialism, or one of the other philosophies, or you may adopt an eclectic approach. Regardless of the values chosen, having a philosophy is essential as your personal commitment to what you want to do and become. You can use your philosophy to help you think critically, to examine yourself, to resolve personal and professional issues, and to understand better your career.

LeROY T. WALKER

Chancellor
North Carolina Central University
Durham, North Carolina

EDUCATION

B.S., Biological Science, Benedict College (1940)
M.A., Physical Education, Columbia University (1942)
Ph.D., Physical Education/Administration, New York University (1957)

JOB RESPONSIBILITIES, HOURS, AND SALARY RANGE

LeRoy serves as the chief executive officer for one of the 16 campuses of the University of North Carolina system and thus carries out varied administrative responsibilities. Prior to his appointment to this position, he was a professor of physical education and track and field coach at the same institution. In addition to these duties, he has also served as President of the American Alliance for Health, Physical Education, Recreation and Dance and as the United States Olympic Games track and field coach. Like most university administrators, LeRoy typically works from 8:00 A.M. until the early evening hours Monday through Friday. Salaries for college and university administrators from presidents to deans range between $50,000 and $100,000, depending on the size of the institution, experience, and responsibilities.

SPECIALIZED COURSE WORK, DEGREES, AND WORK EXPERIENCES NEEDED FOR THIS CAREER

Individuals interested in this career must take specialized courses in administration, management strategies, and ethics and earn a Ph.D. Other background skills and knowledge that will contribute to a successful administrative career include strong interpersonal relations skills, good leadership qualities, and the ability to listen creatively. In preparation for this career, LeRoy recommends assuming community leadership positions, participating in counseling activities, and taking any required practicum in a management setting.

SATISFYING ASPECTS OF THIS CAREER

In achieving administrative positions, physical educators have enhanced the image and respect for this field and have helped it achieve greater acceptance in the academic community. From their leadership positions, these administrators can also promote the beneficial outcomes that can accrue from physical activities.

LeRoy especially enjoys noting the positive changes in the attitudes of faculty, staff, and students and in seeing an improving academic climate on campus. He also likes developing programs to celebrate his institution's 75th anniversary.

JOB POTENTIAL

Physical educators who have proven their administrative abilities while serving as chairs of departments or assistant deans are increasingly being chosen for upper-level administrative positions. Career advancement depends on demonstrated competence and, often, a willingness to relocate to gain experience in entry-level administrative careers.

ADVICE TO STUDENTS

In addition to developing a disciplined work ethic early in one's professional career, LeRoy stresses developing an understanding of management strategies, leadership characteristics, human organization demands, and a philosophy of leadership.

REVIEW QUESTIONS

1. What does philosophy mean?
2. Using the philosophy of idealism, contrast the role of the teacher with the role of the student.

3. How do realists seek truth?
4. Which philosophy seeks to help students become better-functioning members of society, and how is this accomplished?
5. Which philosophy focuses on self-realization for each student?
6. Which philosophies stress using a problem-solving approach?
7. How would naturalism emphasize attaining individual goals?
8. How can physical education teach ethics?
9. Why is a personal philosophy of physical education important?
10. What is an eclectic philosophy?

STUDENT ACTIVITIES

1. Select one of the five traditional philosophies and write a two-page paper explaining how it applies to both a traditional and a non-traditional physical education class.
2. Divide the class into five groups with each group adopting one of the five traditional philosophies. Ask each group to prepare and present a five-minute defense, based on their assigned philosophy, of the inclusion of required physical education classes in the schools.
3. Respond to each of the six situations and be prepared to discuss these in class. Be ready to justify your opinions.
4. Write your personal philosophy of physical education using the five steps presented in this chapter.
5. Make a chart showing the specific application of your personal philosophy of physical education in the categories of objectives, subject matter, methodology, teacher's role, student's role, evaluation, and weaknesses.

REFERENCES

Barnes, J. *Aristotle.* Oxford, New York: Oxford University Press, 1982.

Dewey, J. *Democracy and education: an introduction to the philosophy of education.* New York: Free Press, 1966.

Fraleigh, W. P. *Right actions in sport: ethics for contestants.* Champaign, Illinois: Human Kinetics Publishers, Inc., 1984.

Rousseau, J.-J. *Emile, Julie and Other Writings.* (Selections edited by R. L. Archer). New York: Barron's Educational Series, 1964.

Silverman, H. J., & Elliston, F. A. (Eds.). *Jean-Paul Sartre: contemporary approaches to his philosophy.* Pittsburgh: Duquesne University Press, 1980.

Wilson, J. F. *The politics of moderation: an interpretation of Plato's Republic.* Lanham, Maryland: University Press of America, 1984.

SUGGESTED READINGS

Figley, G. E., Moral education through physical education. *Quest, 36, (1)* 89–101, 1984. Physical educators are encouraged to revise teacher education curricula so that teachers can demonstrate greater concern and involvement with the goal of moral development.

Harper, W. The philosopher in us. *Journal of Physical Education, Recreation and Dance, 53,* 32–34, January 1982. Rather than just a college course or a useless statement, our wondering, analyzing, questioning, and judgment making define philosophy as an essential aspect of life.

Haper, W. A., Miller, D. M., Park, R. J., and Davis, E. C. *The philosophic process in physical education* (3rd Ed.). Philadelphia: Lea and Febiger, 1977. The authors help the reader learn more about how to think through active philosophizing and understanding the heritage of various philosophies.

Kretchmar, R. S. Ethics and sport: an overview. *Journal of the Philosophy of Sport, 10,* 21–32, 1983. In this review of the literature on ethics in sports, it is argued that because sports moralists have too often ignored the correct identification of "conditions of fact" and an analysis of "nonmoral good," a descriptive or metaphysical understanding of a sports ethic has not been established.

McKeag, D. B., Brody, H., and Hough, D. O. Medical ethics in sport. *The Physician and Sportsmedicine, 12,* 145–148, 150, August 1984. Two case studies illustrate the ethical dilemmas and conflicts facing physicians who treat amateur athletes.

McIntosh, P. *Fair play: ethics in sport and education.* London: Heinemann, 1979. In this historical-philosophical look at ethics in sports from the Greek athletes to competition, cheating, and violence in physical education, the author links an analysis of the ethics of sports with the description of educational theory and practice. He also describes the presence or absence of fair play and moral education in several contexts.

Miller, D. M. Ethics in sport: paradoxes, perplexities, and a proposal. *Quest, 32, (1)* 3–7, 1980. The author recommends a mobilization of professional forces, including professional preparation programs for coaches, schools, national governing bodies, and the media, to achieve ethics in sports.

Miller, D. M. Philosophy: whose business? *Quest, 36, (1)* 26–36, 1984. This essay states that philosophy is for everybody because it sharpens critical thinking, stimulates self-examination, helps resolve professional issues, provides for a better understanding of physical education, and elevates the wholeness of physical education's endeavors.

Shea, E. J. *Ethical decisions in physical education and sport.* Champaign, Illinois: Charles C Thomas, 1978. This text provides students with guidelines for the development of logical thinking relative to the principles of ethical judgments and their application.

Thomas, C. E. *Sport in philosophic context.* Philadelphia: Lea and Febiger, 1983. Written for students taking their first course in philosophy, this book provides a foundational understanding of various movement forms, philosophies, meanings of sports, and ethical considerations.

C H A P T E R

Three

Physical Education
as an Academic Discipline

KEY
CONCEPTS

- An academic discipline comprises a body of knowledge that is scholarly and theoretical and seeks to gain new knowledge.
- Physical education as an academic discipline has conflicted with its traditional identity as a profession.
- Twelve applied sciences contribute to the body of knowledge known as physical education.
- The allied sciences of health, recreation, and dance overlap in some programs and purposes with physical education.
- Nutrition and computer science also contribute to physical education's body of knowledge.

An emphasis on the theoretical and scholarly content of physical education rather than its practical aspects led in the thrust to rename this field the "art and science of human movement." The major question debated in the 1960s was whether physical education possessed a body of knowledge that was formally organized and that merited scholarly study. This chapter investigates the contributions of the applied sciences, allied sciences, and a few related fields to determine whether physical education deserves such a categorization. A description of the 12 applied sciences that contribute to this body of knowledge, other human movement areas, and related fields follows, because these bodies of knowledge all contribute to the content of the discipline of physical education.

WHAT IS AN ACADEMIC DISCIPLINE?

Franklin Henry, in 1964, defined an academic discipline as an "organized body of knowledge collectively embraced in a formal course of learning." (Henry, 1964.) The components of an academic discipline include:

1. A body of knowledge;
2. A conceptual framework;
3. Scholarly procedures and methods of inquiry;
4. Both the process of discovery and the end result.

If physical education merits the distinction of being called an academic discipline, then these criteria must be met.

A body of knowledge refers to an area of study that seeks to find answers to important questions. Participants in a field seek to gain information and to contribute to the knowledge available to others. Have physical educators discovered and reported information that is of value to researchers and practitioners in other fields? Examples of their contributions include studies about the effect of drugs on physical performance, the importance of feedback on learning, and the role of sports in developing cultures. In these and many other studies, the physical educator examines the physiological, psychological, historical, or sociological impact of physical activity on people.

Similarly, research studies in an academic discipline must ensure a conceptual framework. Proper hypotheses, experimental designs, strict controls, absence of bias, accurate reporting of findings, and interpretative analyses should characterize each attempt to gain new knowledge. This process requires stringent adherence to protocol while giving credibility to the results.

On this conceptual framework are placed scholarly procedures and methods of inquiry. For example, the sport historian must not rely on secondary, and often inaccurate, sources in examining changes or occurrences. Motor development specialists must evaluate the role of genetics and the environment in assessing readiness to learn. The exercise physiologist must control extraneous variables when analyzing the effect of one treatment, such as diet or drugs, on a training regimen.

In seeking knowledge, the process of discovery and the end result are equally important. How the researcher collected the data influences the findings, so accuracy in reporting and interpretation is vital. Also, replication studies should verify the results consistently. Other characteristics include a substantial history and tradition, a broad scope unique from other fields, and a specific language. Thus for physical education to qualify as an academic discipline, it must contribute to the body of knowledge by using conceptual frameworks, scholarly procedures and methods of inquiry, theoretical processes of discovery, and analyses of the end results.

THE DISCIPLINE-PROFESSION DEBATE

How do these characteristics compare with the traditional view that physical education is a profession? Chapter 4 discusses this in more depth, but it is important to realize here that since the 1960s, a debate has raged between advocates of both perspectives. Physical educators have long viewed themselves primarily as practitioners who taught knowledge, skills, and values. Just as they had studied the entire breadth of the field, they expected their students to become generalists who could apply the knowledge, skills, and values, usually as teachers and/or as coaches. In short, physical education defended its inclusion in schools and colleges because it taught an important subject in a practical way.

In contrast, the acquisition of knowledge for its own sake, rather than for any applied purpose, was the rallying cry of the academicians. They focused on researching, conceptualizing, and theorizing. Those who emphasized that physical education must defend itself through scholarly writings and publications seemed worlds apart from the practitioners in the gymnasium. As this chasm widened in the 1970s, the academicians formed numerous specialized organizations that provided outlets for their research in scholarly journals and through presentations at annual conferences. With universities demanding increased evidence of scholarship from their faculties in the 1980s, this splintering grew (Brooks, 1981).

The distinction between the researcher who sought new knowledge and the teacher who desired to know how to apply this information demonstrated dramatically the importance of both. However, tremendous changes and problems occurred before this grudging acceptance began. Generalists resisted what they viewed as an overspecialization. Those favoring scholarly productivity over teaching alienated colleagues who had long upheld the importance of the instructional field. Today, a greater tolerance is emerging, helped partially by the broadening of physical education careers and a recognition that both undergraduate and graduate students prefer to specialize. A more determined effort is being made to disseminate research findings written in clear language. At the same time, the specialists are realizing that physical education is still the "parent" discipline.

An outgrowth of this debate has been the emergence of new specialties. As they developed, many adopted "sport" as an identifying label because of some resistance to physical education as a teaching field and because of the tremendous popularity of and research interest in sports. As shown in

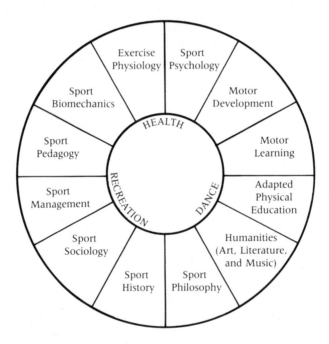

FIGURE 3–1. The discipline of physical education.

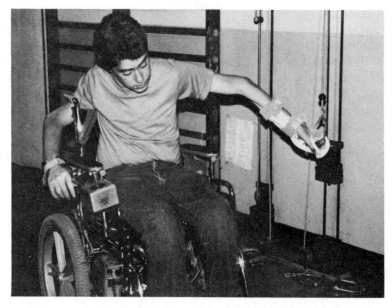

Through adapted physical education individuals with disabling conditions can develop physically by achieving their individual goals.

Figure 3–1, these specialties, or applied sciences, are important spokes in the well-rounded discipline of physical education.

THE APPLIED SCIENCES CONSTITUTING PHYSICAL EDUCATION

ADAPTED PHYSICAL EDUCATION

Adapted physical education provides specialized activity programs for individuals with unique and often limiting capabilities. Disabled individuals want their physical activity interests and needs met just as do all other populations. This may be accomplished by designing individualized programs or modifying activities when the disabled individuals are placed in classes with students without limitations. Public and private agencies with increased awareness provide a wide variety of choices for the disabled.

Physical educators are increasingly sharing their expertise with and borrowing from the various therapeutic fields. The value of exercise in retarding osteoporosis and other degenerative diseases carries broad implications for recreational activities for senior citizens. Physical therapists and athletic trainers are seeking the best programs for injury rehabilitation. Exercise physiologists are working with physicians in the prescription of exercises for cardiac victims. Recreational therapists and adapted physical educators together may provide appropriate activities for disabled employees and school children. In each of these cases, the medium of exercise is involved and, through consultation, the best activities are prescribed.

SPORT BIOMECHANICS

Sport biomechanics is the study of the effects of natural laws and forces on the body through the science and mechanics of movement. Biomechanists study the musculoskeletal system, the principles of mechanics, and activity analyses. They examine the force of muscular contractions; flexion, extension, pronation, and supination of the muscles during activity; the composition of muscle fibers; equilibrium, center of gravity, and base of support; transfer of momentum; and projection of the body or an object. Their findings have contributed to improved performances and have been used to prevent injuries, which is of special interest to physical therapists and athletic trainers. For example, through biomechanical analysis, minor flaws in throwing technique for the discus or stride length of a sprinter can be isolated and corrected to enhance distance or reduce time.

Biomechanists and kinesiologists explain movement in relation to acceleration, energy, mass, power, torque, and velocity (Cooper, 1980). Mechanical principles focused on are force application and absorption, leverage, and stability. Use of cinematography, motion-picture photography, has become common among coaches and teachers for the analysis of performance. Electromyography measures electrical discharges from a muscle to study the action potential and the sequence of muscular activity. An analysis of the position and movements of joints is possible with electrogoniometry. Biomechanists and kinesiologists also measure muscular forces using a force platform, determine speeds or frequencies using stroboscopy, and record movements and electrical responses, such as the heart rate, using telemetry. Computer-assisted analyses have helped them isolate components of physical skills that then can be corrected or changed to improve efficiency. Researchers in the Eastern bloc countries are leading the way in the use of these techniques to enhance performance.

EXERCISE PHYSIOLOGY

The study of bodily functions under the stress of muscular activity is called exercise physiology. The anatomic bases for human movement include the 206 bones in the human skeleton; the joint structure, which includes cartilage, ligaments, and muscular attachments; the muscular system; the nervous system; and the circulatory/respiratory systems. More than 400 muscles, through a system of levers in conjunction with the skeletal system, provide the physiological key and guide to human movement. This potential for motion is released through the initiation of the neural system and the biochemical reactions that supply muscles with energy. Exercise physiology also draws vital information from nutrition, psychology, and biochemistry.

Exercise physiologists measure the training effects of exercise on the body's systems through various endurance, flexibility, and strength programs. In these projects, they may examine changes in stroke volume, pulse rate, blood composition, and other physiological adaptations. Others test how the body utilizes carbohydrates, fats, and proteins during exercise, the effects of diet, smoking, and temperature on performance, and differences between trained and untrained individuals based on a variable such as sleep, diet, sex, or body type.

Exercise physiologists, because of their expertise in understanding bodily functions under the stress of muscular activity, often are consulted on or given

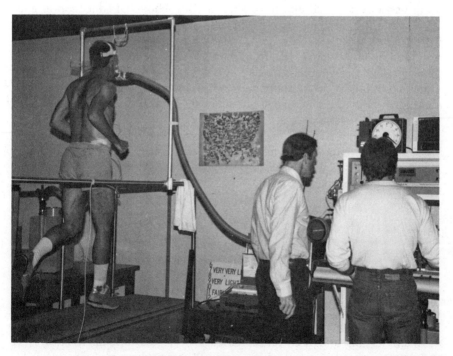

Measuring oxygen uptake and heart response factors during exercise is one example of exercise physiology research.

the responsibility of prescribing and monitoring exercise programs for post-cardiac patients. Biomechanists and exercise physiologists often work together to design the most appropriate training programs for elite athletes, such as that of the United States Olympic Training Center in Colorado Springs.

Researchers in exercise physiology often use treadmills when prescribing workloads to monitor oxygen uptake, expired carbon dioxide, and heart rate and function measurements and to analyze the chemical activities of the body. Interfacing some of these measures with computers has furnished accurate and immediate results. Exercise physiologists also conduct joint research projects with athletic trainers concerning the prevention and rehabilitation of injuries and with physicians in the areas of muscle biopsies and blood lactate analyses.

SPORT PEDAGOGY

Sport pedagogy, an emerging area of research interest, is probably the oldest of the applied sciences constituting physical education. For longer than a century teacher training programs have stressed both the knowledge and the skill bases of this field and have aligned with schools of education to apply practically the most effective methods of teaching in the schools (Cheffers, 1980).

Traditionally, teachers taught as they had been taught or experimented to find instructional methods and approaches that proved most appropriate to their situations. More recently, researchers have recognized the existence of a void in both the knowledge about what is effective teaching and how it can be implemented.

Studies now examine analyses of teachers' interactions with students, methods and frequency of feedback, and administrative, instructional, and evaluative skills. The sport pedagogist also monitors students' behaviors relative to teacher behavior, the class atmosphere, and peer interactions. Through observation of their teaching and the use of behavior checklists, teachers can learn how to improve instruction. Chapter 7 elaborates on teaching skills.

SPORT HISTORY

Sport historians examine the past by seeking to explain the how, what, when, where, and why of physical education and sport. Descriptive history explains events and occurrences based on artifacts, original writings, eyewitness accounts, and secondary sources. The first three of these are primary sources, or firsthand information, that are judged to be reliable and accurate. Based on the facts, events, individuals, and developments often are described through a narrative approach. More difficult, but vital to an understanding of why events happened as they did, is the interpretive, or analytical, perspective, which explains the significance of each event while comparing it with other developments. Events must be interpreted in the context of the time frame and other societal happenings, rather than the researcher's value system. Historians examine changes and progress as they record biographies, examine organizations and their activities, describe trends and movements, and analyze how and why societal events occurred when and as they did.

MOTOR DEVELOPMENT

Motor development is the maturation of the neuromuscular mechanism that permits progressive performance in motor skills. Although frequently associated with children, motor development actually continues throughout life; thus, research studies frequently are longitudinal, or lasting several years. This is also important because of the genetic limitations, which predispose each individual's body type, posture, and body mechanics, and environmental experiences that further impact on development over time. Age and experiences correlate with a person's developmental readiness, as do height, weight, and other growth indices. Motor development depends on the interactions of all of these factors.

MOTOR LEARNING

The conceptualization of cognitive processes underlying motor acts and performance associated with skill acquisition describes motor learning (Schmidt, 1982). This field also can be defined as an area of psychology dealing with human performance and behavior. Information processing, which is essential to motor learning, includes input of information from various sources, decision-making, output by the respondent, and the feedback received. Feedback in activity settings including intrinsic, extrinsic, terminal, concurrent, visual, verbal, constant, and interval may enhance or impede performance.

The learning curve, developmental readiness to learn, knowledge of results, overlearning, and perceptual interpretation of stimuli combine to influence the concept of learning progressions. Methods of practice and skill development situations impact on learning progression as well as motor control. Skill development, depending on the skill desired, uses knowledge about open versus closed skills, self-paced versus externally paced, body stability versus body transport, and no-manipulation versus manipulation. The method of practice, such as speed or accuracy, whole or part, massed or distributed, and physical or mental, helps determine the degree of learning that occurs. Motor learning also examines the degree of transfer of training, or specificity versus generality of tasks, from activity to activity.

HUMANITIES

Humanities, encompassing the areas of art, literature, and music, are noteworthy from both a historical and current perspective. Archaeological discoveries from early civilizations verify the significance attached to physical

"American Dream Machine"
Steel, 16 Feet Tall
Pat Monk

Pat Monk's *American Dream Machine* in an unusual yet lifelike manner depicts one type of sport. (Courtesy of Pat Monk)

activity for survival, group affiliation, religious worship, and enjoyment. From Myron's "Discobolus" during the Greek zenith to R. Tait McKenzie's "The Joy of Effort" to a wall fresco of Olympic marathon champion Joan Benoit, art has vividly shown the beauty of human movement. The Sport Art Academy of the National Association for Sport and Physical Education encourages continued expression, through displays of paintings, photographs, sculptures, and other works, of the efforts and pleasures inherent in physical education. Homer's *Iliad* and *Odyssey* verify the importance of athletics in Greek times. According to several presenters at conferences of the North American Society for Sport History, some literature in the United States today as well as that of earlier times affirms the socialization role expected of sports. Music provides the rhythm for movement experiences for all ages. The Greeks exercised to the music of the lyre. Music became a vital component of German school gymnastics in the 1800s. Children in elementary physical education today frequently experiment with and explore movement to the accompaniment of their favorite songs. In the 1980s, the addition of music to exercise routines resulted in a boom in popularity for aerobics. Athletic team practice sessions, weight-training workouts, and daily jogs often include music. Thus art, literature, and music can help focus on the development of a fit body, the socializing nature of sport, and the free experimentation of movement, thus facilitating the application of physical education's body of knowledge.

SPORT PHILOSOPHY

Sport philosophy is the search for truths and values and the interpretation of these, thus being both the process and the product. Every person has a philosophy, although it may be unstated. Philosophy dictates thought patterns, behaviors, and aspirations. Sport philosophers analyze concepts, make normative statements that guide practical activity, and speculate or extrapolate beyond the limits of scientific knowledge. Within the schools, how physical education contributes to educational objectives and societal values delimits philosophy as it explains the nature, import, and reason for programs. Meeting peoples' needs, relating physical activity to human performances of all kinds, and enhancing the quality of life are the roles of philosophy outside the schools.

SPORT PSYCHOLOGY

Sport psychology is the study of mental processes as they relate to human sports performance. Theories and laws of learning, the importance of reinforcement, and the linking of perceptual abilities with motor performance contribute to this body of knowledge. Sport psychologists utilize this information when studying topics such as achievement motivation, arousal, attribution, and personality development. Achievement motivation research examines how to fulfill the higher needs of esteem and self-actualization. Excitement and relaxation, as well as tension reduction, are among the parameters of arousal studied. Causal attribution weighs the importance placed on ability, effort, luck, and task difficulty relative to contest outcome. Aggression, competitiveness, anxiety, independence, extroversion, and self-confidence are among the personality traits researched. Sport psychologists also examine group affiliation, exercise addiction, and enhanced body image relative to their impact on people who are physically active.

SPORT SOCIOLOGY

The study of the origin, development, organization, and role of sports in human society describes sport sociology. This field seeks an understanding of why people play and what activity does for people while providing opportunities for recreation, relaxation, self-expression, and wish fulfillment. The dynamics of socialization may result in integration, competition, conflict, rivalry, and cooperation within the sporting context (Young, 1984). As a member of a group or team, one may learn sportsmanship, cooperation, leadership, and affiliation skills. On the negative side, loss of identity, violence, ego-centeredness, and a win-at-all-costs mentality can evolve from activity participation. Sociology examines sport as a game and as an institutional game, as a social institution, and as a social situation. It looks at the concepts of social mobility, stratification, status, acceptance of all races and creeds, and understanding social consciousness and values. The key to understanding sport sociology is that it deals with the relationship between sports and other social institutions—the group perspective on social life.

SPORT MANAGEMENT

Recently sport management has emerged as a popular specialty because of the pervasiveness of sports. Because management tasks relative to facilities, budgets, programs, and personnel demand specialized training and experiences, physical education curricula at both the undergraduate and graduate levels have been developed (Vander Zwaag, 1974).

While it is not as research-oriented as exercise physiology or sport psychology, sport management faculty think it is important to expand the knowledge base of this applied science. For example, they seek to know how to develop better leadership qualities, how to motivate personnel, how to plan efficiently and effectively, and how to incorporate computer capabilities into their operations.

•   •   •

All of the applied sciences contribute to the greater whole. They certainly are not mutually exclusive (Figure 3–1); each interacts to some extent with all others. In addition, each relates to the allied sciences of health, recreation, and dance.

THE ALLIED SCIENCES OF PHYSICAL EDUCATION

Health, recreation, and dance are often allied in purposes and programs with physical education.

HEALTH

Many of the early (1800s) school and college physical education programs emphasized health benefits as their primary justifications. For example, at Amherst College, beginning in the 1860s, the president supported a physical education program to help the students become and stay healthy. As was the case with many other institutions, the person charged with directing this program was a medical doctor. In the twentieth century, the dual role of the health/physical educator divided as colleges prepared physical education teachers for jobs that focused on teaching physical activities, especially in alignment with educational objectives rather than health objectives. In 1937, health was added to the title of the national organization, today's American Alliance for Health, Physical Education, Recreation and Dance, in keeping with the importance placed on health within the educational system. Since then, health has struggled for its own identity as a field of study. Because of the shared health outcomes of physical activity programs and the reality that school health classes often are assigned to physical educators who at best have minimal academic preparation in this field, acceptance of health as a separate discipline has been gradual.

Soundness of body, mind, and soul, or one's general well-being, is health. Examples of knowledge from health that contribute to the quality of life are disease control, preservation of the environment, avoidance of the abuses of tobacco, alcohol, and drugs, promotion of mental health and proper nutrition, and maintenance of physical fitness. Obviously, there is overlap between the interest areas of health and physical education.

In the 1980s, the popularity of health concepts has gained momentum as a fitness mania has affected almost everyone in some way. Depending on the study, from one-third to two-thirds of the people in the United States participate in physical activity on a regular basis. Of course, how "regular basis" or "physical activity" is defined varies widely. Upper-class adults, in particular, have joined health clubs, begun jogging, or tried to change their nutritional habits and inactive life-styles. Corporations have encouraged their employees to exercise regularly by providing equipment, trained personnel, and incentives. The popularity of the healthy-looking body has led to a mania to get fit, to dress to accent fitness, and to enjoy the social atmosphere of the weight room or a 10-kilometer run. Others rely on programs such as those offered by holistic health clinics to replace their bad habits with fitness-oriented ones. Health has become a life-style commitment to well-being rather than to the traditional absence of disease.

RECREATION

The renewing or refreshing of one's strength and spirits after work and a diversion that occurs during leisure hours constitute recreation. In 1938, recreation became a part of the national organization, joining physical education and health. This reflected the important role of recreational activities for people of all ages. Schools, businesses, communities, and families increasingly offer activities for fitness and pleasure as each of these groups accepts some responsibility for educating for leisure. The popularity of home fitness programs and home equipment illustrates how some adults have decided to use their own resources during leisure hours. Schools teach courses such as camping, canoeing, and skiing as lifetime activities. The multiplicity of recreational programs for children through senior citizens meets the fun and fitness needs of large numbers of people. Businesses provide work site fitness centers, sponsor teams, and offer a variety of fitness activities for their employees and their families. The similar objectives of physical education and recreation programs are evident.

DANCE

Bodily movement of a rhythmical and patterned succession usually executed to the accompaniment of music is dance. Both as physical activity and as a performing art, dance varieties include aerobic, ballet, ballroom, folk, jazz, modern, square, and tap. Dance can provide the participant the opportunity for aesthetic expression whether in a beginners' class or on stage. People

Dance, an allied science of physical education, is a popular activity in schools, colleges, and private studios.

of all ages can dance for fitness and for fun. Although for numerous years a vital component of school and college programs, it was not until 1979 that dance officially became a part of the title of the national organization. Some schools and most colleges have dance specialists, yet many dance classes are still taught by physical educators who have had minimal preparation in this field.

•   •   •

Overall, health, recreation, and dance are allies of physical education in promoting healthy life-styles, leisure-time activities, and movements that appeal to all groups.

CONTRIBUTIONS FROM OTHER FIELDS

In addition to the applied and allied sciences, other fields contribute vital knowledge to physical education. Nutrition, often studied by exercise physiologists, encompasses the understanding of how the body utilizes its food intake relative to energy output. Numerous factors, such as sleep, drugs, work, and stress, influence how the body reacts to a specific diet or an exercise paradigm. Biochemical and physiological tests isolate those nutritional factors that most dramatically affect performance. Studies include the effects of marathon training on nutritional needs, the risks or benefits of vitamin supplementation, and the effects of caffeine on various heart parameters. Nutritional information is also vital for weight maintenance for the athlete in training, for the physically disabled individual who is minimally active, and for the senior citizen whose metabolic rate has slowed.

Physical education, like most other fields of endeavor, has joined the computer age. The speed, accuracy, and efficiency of computer-generated results enable researchers in most disciplines to spend more time designing studies and analyzing the data rather than tediously compiling findings. Physiological and biomechanical research rely extensively on computers to compile and to compute test variables. Storage of data for historical or psychological studies is both time-saving and helpful in the interaction of factors or developments. The capability to interface with a mainframe computer and thus have access to all of its resources, the availability of the increasing number of statistical and other software packages, and the option to develop a program especially designed for a research project make the use of computers a necessity rather than a luxury. Using computers for basic word processing, record keeping, and filing is a more efficient use of support staff time than traditional methods allowed.

SUMMARY

The 12 applied sciences, the 3 allied sciences, and the 2 other contributing fields enhance physical education. Each seeks through scholarly inquiry to expand its body of knowledge. Physical education depends on each of these for theoretical knowledge and for ways to disseminate this information to others.

JOHN A. LUCAS

Professor of Physical Education
Pennsylvania State University
University Park, Pennsylvania

EDUCATION

B.S., Physical Education, Boston University (1949)
M.S., Physical Education, University of Southern California (1950)
Ed.D., Physical Education, University of Maryland (1962)
M.A., History, Pennsylvania State University (1970)

JOB RESPONSIBILITIES, HOURS, AND SALARY RANGE

John, like most college and university professors, teaches both undergraduate and graduate students and conducts research. John's usual work hours of 8:00 A.M. to 1:00 P.M. Monday through Friday and 7:00 P.M. to 10:00 P.M. three nights a week are illustrative of the flexible scheduling permitted individuals in this career. Entry-level assistant professors in colleges and universities earn around $20,000, while university professors like John earn between $35,000 and $45,000.

SPECIALIZED COURSE WORK, DEGREES, AND WORK EXPERIENCES NEEDED FOR THIS CAREER

John recommends that students who have an interest in sports history take courses in physical education and sport history, American and non-American history, history of antiquity, and philosophy. Although bachelor's, master's, and doctor's degrees are essential for university professional rank, John states that his master's degree in American history was the catalyst that convinced him to pursue sport history with vigor. In preparation for a university position, John recommends that students teach and coach in the public and/or private schools and in the colleges while constantly, never-endingly trying to better themselves intellectually.

SATISFYING ASPECTS OF THIS CAREER

University professors are expected and encouraged to become productive researchers, to enhance the quality of their teaching as an outgrowth of their scholarly efforts, and to offer their expertise for the benefit of society or some aspect of it. This trilogy of research, teaching, and service comprises both the responsibilities and the rewards of this career. More specifically for John, he especially enjoys teaching, overseas travel, research, publishing, and public speaking.

JOB POTENTIAL

The availability of university faculty positions depends on each institution's needs and each individual's expertise and specialization. A willingness to relocate is imperative, as is a willingness to start at an assistant professor's level after completion of a doctor's degree. While the job market in the 1980s is tight, by the year 2000 many of today's tenured university faculty will have retired, leaving numerous vacancies.

ADVICE TO STUDENTS

Becoming a college or university faculty member best begins with gaining a strong liberal arts education. On this base is added a major in physical education and possibly a second major in psychology, chemistry, business, history, or some other area. Specialization in an allied science may begin at the master's degree level but becomes more focused at the doctoral level. Developing research skills is essential to future success in this career. John stresses that attendance at professional meetings is even more important than he had realized earlier in his career. In addition, he states that in a dramatic or a subtle way, annual attendance at four or five professional meetings can alter the direction of a young person's career.

REVIEW QUESTIONS

1. What are the characteristics of an academic discipline?
2. What is the basis for the conflict between the profession of physical education and the academic discipline approach?
3. What is biomechanics?
4. What is the difference between narrative and interpretative history?
5. What is the difference between motor development and motor learning?
6. Within which applied science would research studies on mental practice be conducted?
7. Describe how any three of the applied sciences in physical education interrelate in their research interests.
8. Name four topics within health that interrelate with knowledge in physical education.
9. What applied science in physical education conducts research studies in conjunction with nutritionists?
10. Is physical education an academic discipline? Why or why not?

STUDENT ACTIVITIES

1. Select 1 of the 12 applied sciences and describe how it contributes to physical education's body of knowledge.

2. Write a one- to two-page summary of how dance, health, or recreation contributes to the attainment of similar objectives with physical education.

3. Volunteer to help a faculty member or a graduate student conduct a research project specific to 1 of the 12 applied sciences.

4. Read two research articles that contribute to the body of knowledge of physical education. Summarize their conceptual frameworks, scholarly procedures, and methods of inquiry and the process and end result of each study.

5. Develop a 5-minute defense of physical education as an academic discipline. Be prepared to present your defense in class.

REFERENCES

Brooks, G. A. *Perspectives on the academic discipline of physical education.* Champaign, Illinois: Human Kinetics Publishers, Inc., 1981.

Cheffers, J. T. F. Pedagogy. *Journal of Physical Education and Recreation, 51,* 50–52, November-December 1980.

Cooper, J. M. Biomechanics. *Journal of Physical Education and Recreation, 51,* 43–44, November-December 1980.

Henry, F. M. Physical education: an academic discipline. *Journal of Health, Physical Education and Recreation, 35,* 32–33, 69, September 1964.

The promise of sport history: progress and prospects. *Journal of Sport History, 10, (1)* 1983.

Schmidt, R. A. *Motor control and learning.* Champaign, Illinois: Human Kinetics Publishers, Inc., 1982.

Vander Zwaag, H. J. *Sport management in schools and colleges.* New York: John Wiley and Sons, 1974.

Young, T. R. The sociology of sport: a critical overview. *Arena and the Institute for Sport and Social Analysis Review, 8, (3)* 1–14, 1984.

SUGGESTED READINGS

Fox, E. L. *Sports physiology.* New York: Saunders College Publishing, 1984. This extensive book describes the physiological functions of the body as they apply to sports and includes discussion about topics such as weight training and sprint and endurance training methods and effects, nutrition, and heat-related problems.

Henry, F. M. The academic discipline of physical education. *Quest, 29,* 13–29, Winter 1978. Physical education is a justifiable academic discipline provided it is organized as a cross-disciplinary structure drawing from fields such as physiology, psychology, motor learning, and history.

Lawson, H. A., and Morford, W. R. The cross-disciplinary structure of kinesiology and sports studies: distinctions, implications, and advantages. *Quest, 31, (2)* 222–230, 1979. The scholarly and scientific analysis of human involvement in physical activity draws from a cross-disciplinary integration rather than a vertical orientation of traditional disciplines.

The man behind the computer of the u.s. olympics sports medicine committee. *Scholastic Coach, 52,* No. 6, 31–32, 78–80, and No. 7, 26–28, 58–60, February 1983. This interview with Gideon Ariel, the guru of computerized biomechanical analysis, speaks candidly about using computer analysis of films in scouting opponents, drug abuse by Olympic athletes, improving athletic performances, and computerized exercise machines.

Park, R. J. Research and scholarship in the history of physical education and sport: the current state of affairs. *Research Quarterly for Exercise and Sport, 54, (2)* 93–103, 1983. This essay reviews the current status of historical research and suggests that future studies would be enriched by casting them in broader social, cultural, and intellectual contexts and by focusing on analytical history.

Parkhouse, B. L., Ulrich, D. O., and Soucie, D. Research in sport management: a vital rung of this new corporate ladder. *Quest, 34, (2)* 176–186, 1982. This article reviews traditional research trends in sport management and discusses behavior research opportunities for future study in this emerging field.

Ryan, E. D. Synthesis: how the profession could try to reunify. *The Academy Papers, 15,* 51–57, April 1981. To reunify the splintering within physical education today, it is imperative that faculties become more involved in applied as well as basic research, that students learn the relevance of this research to practical problems, and that all work together to understand the individual in physical activity.

Sage, G. H. Growth of sport sociology. *The Academy Papers, 14,* 24–30, December 1980. Three issues facing sport sociologists are which paradigm best explains social reality, what is the appropriate research methodology for sampling social phenomena, and which research is most appropriate—basic or applied.

Siedentop, D. Recent advances in pedagogical research in physical education. *The Academy Papers, 16,* 82–94, April 1982. Two research studies illustrate the two major methodological features of the natural science of teaching, and the programs from which these emanated show the achievement of generality through systematic replication.

Silva, J. M., and Weinberg, R. S. (Eds.). *Psychological foundations of sport.* Champaign, Illinois: Human Kinetics Publishers, 1984. Thirty-two contributors discuss personality, anxiety, arousal, exercise and well-being, and other sport psychology topics in this comprehensive text.

The Profession of Physical Education

KEY CONCEPTS

- Physical education and its many diverse careers are characterized by the four components of a profession.
- The American Alliance fulfills its objectives through the programs of its six associations and through conventions, publications, and other activities that benefit its membership and the people it serves.
- Many professional organizations promote the study of and involvement in sports, leisure activities, fitness programs, and other physical education–related pursuits.
- Teaching tracks prepare students through academic, professional, and pedagogical course work for state certification.
- Non-traditional tracks prepare students for diverse physical education careers following the completion of specialized course work.

Physical education has long been recognized as a part of the teaching profession, evidenced by its affiliation with the National Education Association since 1937. Even earlier, in 1885, a group of teachers and other interested individuals formed the Association for the Advancement of Physical Education to encourage the exchange of program and instructional ideas. The American Alliance for Health, Physical Education, Recreation and Dance today, along with a multiplicity of affiliated organizations, promotes physical education, sports, leisure, and fitness. This chapter describes many of these associations along with their purposes, publications, and services. To understand physical education as a profession, it is important to know the requisite educational background needed to enter many physical education careers; therefore, some teaching and non-traditional tracks are described.

IS PHYSICAL EDUCATION A PROFESSION?

Before looking specifically at physical education, we need to define what a profession is. A profession requires an extensive period of training, has an intellectual component that must be mastered, offers opportunities for communication among its members, and provides an important service that is recognized by society. Physical educators usually have at least a bachelor's degree and frequently have advanced study and training in an extensive body of knowledge that takes considerable time and effort to learn. Colleagues in related careers share research findings and new ideas while serving people in all aspects of society. The following overview of the structure and activities of the American Alliance demonstrates that physical education qualifies as a profession.

NATIONAL ORGANIZATION AND SERVICES

The American Alliance for Health, Physical Education, Recreation and Dance (AAHPERD, or the Alliance) has enjoyed a century of service and growth (from 49 to more than 37,000 members). According to Executive Vice President Jack Razor,

No other organization in America can match the scope of our efforts and the impact we are having. We can be proud of all that we do. The breadth of our services and the many lives that we touch indirectly and directly serve together as an essential catalyst for our continuing viability and a foundation upon which to build.

One reason for the widespread influence of the AAHPERD is the many professional groups that have merged into its structure. In 1937, as a department of the National Education Association, the former American Physical Education Association became the American Association for Health and Physical Education. (It became an alliance in 1974.) Recreation was added to its title in 1938, and dance was added in 1979.

The Alliance's missions are to improve the quality of school programs and to enhance positive life-style changes for all Americans. It is headquartered in Reston, Virginia. Its objectives are as follows (AAHPERD By-laws):

1. Professional growth and development—to support, encourage, and provide guidance in the development and conduct of programs in health, leisure, and movement-related activities which are based on the needs, interests, and inherent capacities of the individual in today's society;

The American Alliance for Health, Physical Education, Recreation and Dance serves the needs of its professional members from its headquarters in Reston, Virginia. (Courtesy of the American Alliance for Health, Physical Education, Recreation and Dance)

2. Communication—to facilitate public and professional understanding and appreciation of the importance and value of health, leisure, and movement-related activities as they contribute toward human well-being;
3. Research—to encourage and facilitate research which will enrich the depth and scope of health, leisure, and movement-related activities; and to disseminate the findings to the profession and other interested and concerned publics;
4. Standards and guidelines—to further the continuous development and evaluation of standards within the profession for personnel and program in health, leisure, and movement-related activities;
5. Public affairs—to coordinate and administer a planned program of professional, public, and governmental relations that will improve education in area of health, leisure, and movement-related activities.

The services provided by the Alliance are also varied. For example, in 1958 the Alliance developed the Youth Fitness Test, the first of its kind with national norms and fitness standards for boys and girls aged 10 to 17 years. In 1980, the Alliance launched its Health Related Physical Fitness Test, which measures cardiorespiratory function, body composition, strength, and flexibility. Other services include holding an annual convention; publishing brochures, research abstracts, books, conference proceedings, and other information pertinent to its fields of interest; positively influencing public opinion and legislation; and providing consultant services.

Three periodicals are published by the Alliance. The *Journal of Physical Education, Recreation and Dance* includes articles of a broad and practical nature, while the *Research Quarterly for Exercise and Sport* reports research findings. *Update*, in newspaper format, keeps the membership apprised of current events and legislation.

The following discussion describes the six associations that constitute the Alliance (*Journal of Physical Education*, 1985).

The American Association for Leisure and Recreation promotes leisure services at the local and national levels and recreation education in the schools. Areas of concern and services include leisure education in higher education, the place of recreation in American society, continuing education workshops, bicycle education, and legislative support for outdoor recreation resources.

Programs of health education in schools, communities, and colleges are the purview of the Association for the Advancement of Health Education. Health issues are vigorously promoted by this association through position papers; leadership for projects such as the drinking/driving problem is provided; and health education legislation is actively supported.

The Association for Research, Administration, Professional Councils and Societies is composed of 10 special-interest groups, including the Aquatics

Council, the College and University Administrators Council, the Council of City and County Directors, the Council on Outdoor Education, the Therapeutics Council, the Council on Facilities and Equipment, the International Relations Council, the Measurement and Evaluation Council, and the Physical Fitness Council. Among the varied professional services these groups provide is co-sponsorship of the FITNESSGRAM with the President's Council on Physical Fitness and Sports, the Institute for Aerobics Research, and the Campbell Soup Company. The project provides parents with a computerized fitness report card (see Figure 4–1) of their child's test results on the AAHPERD Youth Fitness Test or on the Health Related Physical Fitness Test.

The Student Action Council, the tenth special-interest group, has served student members of the Alliance and has worked with collegiate majors' clubs since 1969. Because the future of the profession and its organizations depends on today's students, it is essential that students become actively involved in professional activities. The objectives of the Student Action Council include improving local, state, district, and national student programs, providing opportunities for student leadership experiences, supporting and promoting youth service projects, and serving as an advocate for maximum involvement of students in all Alliance associations. This group also promotes the active involvement of students in local physical education majors' clubs as avenues for leadership and enhanced professional preparation.

The National Association for Girls and Women in Sport seeks to improve and to expand sport opportunities for girls and women at all levels of competition. One major effort has been the training of officials through its Affiliated Boards of Officials. The National Association for Girls and Women in Sport and the National Association for Sport and Physical Education share leadership in the National Council of Athletic Training and the National Intramural Sports Council.

The largest of the Alliance associations, the National Association for Sport and Physical Education, promotes physical education and sports for all people through its numerous substructures and activities. Its Physical Education Justification Packet helps colleagues whose programs are threatened by economic cutbacks and lack of community support by providing materials such as documented research, survey results, and statements relative to the importance of physical education in the daily lives of students. Physical Education Public Information (PEPI) actively spreads the word about physical education through print ads, pamphlets, public service announcements, and the observance of the annual National Physical Education and Sport Week. Ten academies (Adapted Physical Education, Curriculum, Exercise Physiology, History, Kinesiology, Motor Development, Philosophy, Psychology, Sociology, and Sport Art) play an integral role in enhancing research.

Five special-interest councils are also a part of the National Association for

TOTAL PHYSICAL FITNESS SCORE	
EXCELLENT	352 +
ABOVE AVERAGE	316–351
AVERAGE	287–315
BELOW AVERAGE	251–286
WELL BELOW AVERAGE	0–250

DATE	HEIGHT	WEIGHT	TOTAL FITNESS
SEM–YR	FT–IN	LBS	SCORE
Fa 83	4-07	69	297
Sp 84	4-08	73	309

These activities are recommended:

To improve your cardiorespiratory endurance: jogging swimming, rope jumping, walking, and cycling.

To improve your agility: rope jumping and activities which call for sudden change of direction (racquet sports and soccer).

*WALK/RUN TYPE
600 = 600 YARD (MIN:SEC)
1 mi = 1 MILE (MIN:SEC)
1.5 = 1.5 MILE (MIN:SEC)
9 = 9 MINUTE (YARDS)
12 = 12 MINUTE (YARDS)

Dear Parent:
We are pleased to send you this FITNESSGRAM® to provide information on your child's level of physical fitness as indicated by his/her performance in the AAHPERD Youth Fitness Test recently administered in our school. This test was developed by the American Alliance for Health, Physical Education, Recreation and Dance.

Your child participates in the test at least once a year. The FITNESSGRAM® will show you any progress in his/her growth and development over the school years.

The FITNESSGRAM® provides the following information:

1. A total physical fitness score for your child based on assessments of
   - upper body strength and endurance—measured by flexed-arm hang or pull-up test;
   - abdominal strength and endurance—1 minute sit-up test;
   - speed with change of direction—shuttle run test;
   - explosive power—standing long jump test;
   - speed—50 yard dash;
   - cardiovascular fitness—600 yard, 1-mile, 1.5-mile, 9-minute, or 12-minute walk/run.

2. A percentile rank (% RANK) for each test item is computed based on a national norm developed over the last 20 years. You can see both your child's score and the national average (50%) of students of his/her age who have taken the test.

3. An exciting feature of the FITNESSGRAM® is the recommendation for activities which can help improve your child's individual scores.

4. The FITNESSGRAM® reflects past performances which will allow the monitoring of improvement from test date to test date!

We hope you will find the FITNESSGRAM® a useful tool to assess your child's fitness level, height and weight development—and to encourage your entire family to enjoy the benefits of an active lifestyle.

Mrs. Pam Long
Physical Education Instructor
Westside Elementary

NAME William J. Clark   GRADE 05   SECTION 01
SCHOOL Westside Elementary   INSTRUCTOR Long

Pull-up		Sit-up		Shuttle		Standing Long Jump		50 Yard Dash		Walk/Run		
no.	% RANK	no.	% RANK	sec.	% RANK	ft-in	% RANK	sec.	% RANK	MIN: SEC. OR YARDS	% RANK	*TYPE
2	55	36	55	11.4	30	5-01	40	8.3	40	2:30	45	600
4	75	44	80	10.9	40	5-05	50	7.6	60	2:39	20	600

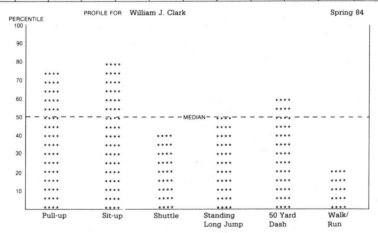

PROFILE FOR William J. Clark   Spring 84

FIGURE 4–1. FITNESSGRAM.

Sport and Physical Education; these are the Council on Physical Education for Children, the Secondary School Physical Education Council, the College and University Physical Education Council, the College and University Physical Education Department Administrators Council, and the National Council of Secondary School Athletic Directors.

The National Dance Association, the only association serving dance as education, promotes dance through conferences, workshops, publications, research, and liaisons with numerous groups, such as the Kennedy Center for the Performing Arts' education program and the National Endowment for the Arts. It cooperates with Dance USA to promote National Dance Week.

The Alliance is divided into six district associations that share the goals and activities of the Alliance while providing leadership opportunities and services within each region. Memberships in the Alliance and in a district are combined, thus enabling professionals to attend their district's and the Alliance's annual conventions. Non-convention workshops, clinics, seminars,

For more than 100 years the American Alliance for Health, Physical Education, Recreation and Dance has led and served professionals in physical education-related careers. (Courtesy of Bob Blackburn)

and other learning opportunities provide Alliance members with the latest research findings, innovative activities, and teaching approaches and provide opportunities for personal enrichment and growth. Most state associations, state departments of education, and other physical education-related organizations also provide year-round programming.

Each state also provides professionals the opportunity to learn different coaching techniques, to acquire new skills, and to interact and exchange information with other members at its annual convention. Students, especially you, should take advantage of state conventions, because not only will you learn from these experiences, but you also may make contact with many individuals who later may hire you or help you to get a job. The aims of the North Carolina Alliance for Health, Physical Education, Recreation and Dance, like those of other state organizations, are consistent with the purposes of general education and relate specifically to the areas of athletics, dance, health education, intramural programs, physical education, and recreation. These aims include the following (Constitution of the North Carolina Alliance):

1. To awaken and stimulate wide and intelligent interest in its areas of concern;

2. To acquire and disseminate accurate professional information;

3. To promote adequate programs in the areas of concern and to advance the standards of teaching and performance in these areas;

4. To cooperate with the American Alliance for Health, Physical Education, Recreation and Dance, the Southern District Association for Health, Physical Education and Recreation, and other state and national education associations interested in the growth and development of children and adults.

Physical education provides enrichment opportunities to its members as they prepare themselves to serve others. They are joined in their efforts by related groups who seek to share knowledge for the benefit of all.

AFFILIATED ORGANIZATIONS

While the AAHPERD is the largest organization associated with physical education and its related fields, it shares its interests with numerous other groups. The discussion that follows briefly describes some of these organizations.

HIGHER EDUCATION

In 1978, the National Association for Physical Education in Higher Education (NAPEHE) was formed by a merger of the National Association for Physical Education of College Women and the National College Physical Education Association for Men. Since the merger, NAPEHE has continued the publication of *Quest* and its conference proceedings.

Since 1930, the American Academy of Physical Education has been the highest honorary group in health, physical education, and recreation. Its more than 100 members have contributed scholarship and professional service, especially in colleges and universities. Some of their research studies are published annually in *The Academy Papers*. Illustrative of its leadership, the Academy, in 1981, identified the following contemporary social problems of import to the profession: that physical educators need to help their clientele in all sectors to discriminate between fact and myth in the development of fitness, diets, exercise equipment, and health programs; that if moral and ethical values are to result from physical education and athletic programs, teachers and coaches must emphasize them; and that physical educators should share their knowledge with others involved in sport programs for youths to help ensure quality experiences (Park, 1983).

HEALTH

Since 1926, the American School Health Association has sought to improve health instruction, healthful living, and health services in the schools. Although originally only for physicians, membership is now open to anyone engaged in school health work. This association publishes the *Journal of School Health*.

RECREATION

Development and expansion of programs and services along with environmental concerns constitute the primary work of the National Recreation and Park Association. It is also dedicated to having trained personnel conduct community recreation programs. The *Journal of Leisure Research* and *Parks and Recreation* are its publications.

The National Intramural-Recreational Sports Association was begun in 1950 to provide an opportunity for college intramural directors to meet annually to exchange ideas and information. With the expansion of college programs into recreational services of all kinds, the Association assumed its present name in 1975. Sharing innovative program ideas, reporting research, and discussing policy and procedures highlight its annual convention and the *NIRSA Journal.*

SPORTS MEDICINE

The need to establish professional standards and to disseminate information led to the establishment of the National Athletic Trainers' Association in 1950, which publishes *Athletic Training* for its membership.

The American College of Sports Medicine was founded in 1954 by individuals drawn from medicine, physiology, and physical education. Among its objectives are advancing scientific studies dealing with the effects of physical activities on health and well-being; encouraging cooperation and professional exchange among physicians, scientists, and educators; initiating, promoting, and correlating research in sports medicine; and maintaining a sports medicine library. It encourages research publications in injury prevention and rehabilitation, and in environmental effects of exercise, nutrition, and other factors through its *Medicine and Science in Sports and Exercise.*

PSYCHOLOGY, HISTORY, PHILOSOPHY, ANTHROPOLOGY, AND SOCIOLOGY

Psychologists, psychiatrists, and physical educators founded the North American Society for the Psychology of Sport and Physical Activity in 1965 to promote this increasingly popular field of study. Since 1973, the North American Society for Sport History has encouraged scholarly research in all aspects of this discipline of sport, conducted an annual conference, and published the *Journal of Sport History.* The Philosophic Society for the Study of Sport, founded in 1972, encourages scholarly investigation of the philosophical aspects of sport through its *Journal of the Philosophy of Sport.* Other specialized associations are the Association for the Anthropological Study of Play, the North American Society for the Sociology of Sport, and the Association for the Advancement of Applied Sport Psychology.

FITNESS

The Association for Fitness in Business, since 1974, has led in the expansion of employee fitness programs through its approximately 2000 members. These exercise-testing technicians, exercise physiologists, recreation specialists, and program directors conduct exercise testing, prescribe exercise programs, promote healthful life-style changes, and administer programs for corporate executives and employees.

ATHLETICS

In the realm of college athletics, the regulatory bodies include the National Collegiate Athletic Association (founded in 1906), the National Association of Intercollegiate Athletics (founded in 1952), and the National Junior College Athletic Association (founded in 1938). The National Collegiate Athletic Association, with 644 members, promotes competition through 22 championships in 12 sports for women and 42 championships in 19 sports for men. The 520 members of the National Association of Intercollegiate Athletics represent smaller institutions and provide 15 women's and 17 men's championships. The National Junior College Athletic Association conducts championships in 9 sports for women and 12 sports for men. Other athletic organizations that encourage the exchange of ideas include the College Sports Information Directors of America, the College Athletics Business Managers, the National Association of Collegiate Directors of Athletics, and the National Strength and Conditioning Association.

The Amateur Athletic Union (AAU) was founded in 1888 to promote amateur sports and to check the spread of the problems associated with professional sports. Using more than 300,000 volunteers at the local, regional, and national levels, this organization conducts sports events for competitors of all ages.

The National Federation of State High School Associations (founded in 1920) and the 50 state high school athletic and/or activities associations work to protect the activity and athletic interests of high schools, to promote the growth of educational interscholastic athletics, and to protect high school students from exploitation.

Many states also have coaches' associations that either are specific to one sport or have coaches from all sports in their memberships. These groups usually sponsor statewide or regional workshops or clinics about specific coaching techniques or strategies, rule changes, values and ethics in school athletics, and sport psychology.

YMCA-YWCA

The Young Men's Christian Association, since 1851, and the Young Women's Christian Association, since 1866, have promoted physical activities and sports as well as the development of values. Today, both groups offer a wide range of fitness and sports activities that target all skill and age levels.

•   •   •

The basic objectives for all professional groups are to exchange information, to learn, and to serve. To enhance both your knowledge about and commitment to your chosen career, you should seek opportunities through these organizations to grow professionally. By exchanging program ideas and instructional and motivational techniques, members can improve their abilities to serve others and to learn how to communicate their goals and activities to colleagues and to the general public. Through the sharing of experiences and research, many ideas for further study are generated. Therefore, as a young professional, you are encouraged to join your college, state, and national associations and one or more of those in your interest area. You also should begin to read physical education periodicals, as listed in Box 4–1, to help you more fully understand your profession.

BOX 4–1
SELECTED PERIODICALS

Periodical	*Publisher and/or Organization*
Applied Sciences	
Adapted Physical Activity Quarterly	Human Kinetics
American Journal of Sports Medicine	American Orthopedic Society for Sports Medicine
Athletic Administration	National Association of Collegiate Directors of Athletics
Athletic Training	National Athletic Trainers Association
Journal of Motor Behavior	Heldref Publications
Journal of Sport and Social Issues	Arena, Inc.
Journal of Sport History	North American Society for Sport History
Journal of Sport Psychology	Human Kinetics
Journal of Sports Medicine and Physical Fitness	International Federation of Sportive Medicine
Journal of Teaching in Physical Education	Human Kinetics
Journal of the Philosophy of Sport	Human Kinetics

(continues)

(*concluded*)

Medicine and Sciences in Sports and Exercise	American College of Sports Medicine
Perceptual and Motor Skills	Box 9229, Missoula, Montana
The Physician and Sportsmedicine	McGraw–Hill Publishing Company
Sociology of Sport Journal	Human Kinetics

Allied Sciences

American Journal of Public Health	American Public Health Association
Dance Magazine	Donad Publishing Company, Inc.
Health Education	American Alliance for Health, Physical Education, Recreation and Dance
Journal of Leisure Research	National Recreation and Park Association
Journal of School Health	American School Health Association

Professional

Periodical	Publisher and/or Organization
The Academy Papers	American Academy of Physical Education
Journal of Physical Education, Recreation and Dance	American Alliance for Health, Physical Education, Recreation and Dance
NIRSA Journal	National Intramural-Recreational Sports Association
The Physical Educator	Phi Epsilon Kappa Fraternity
Quest	National Association for Physical Education in Higher Education
Research Quarterly for Exercise and Sport	American Alliance for Health, Physical Education, Recreation and Dance
Update	American Alliance for Health, Physical Education, Recreation and Dance

PROFESSIONAL PREPARATION PROGRAMS

Assuming that you are considering physical education as a career, the second section of this chapter introduces you to the various tracks or majors that exist in many colleges and universities. This will prepare you for Chapter 5, which describes many careers related to physical education, and Chapter 6, which explains many specific programs and certifications.

Professional preparation programs in physical education traditionally have been oriented toward teacher education with a secondary track or option sometimes available for those interested in physical education in other settings. Until the demand for teachers decreased dramatically in the late 1970s, most students completed the first option in case they ever wanted to teach. Seldom does this occur today due to a surplus of teachers. The tight job market, however, is only one factor in this change. Colleges and universities, in response to the decreasing number of teaching positions, have revised their curricula to include non-traditional tracks. Simultaneously, the popularity of and resultant expansion in fitness, leisure, recreation, athletic, and sports-related activities have created a boom in the diversity and availability of careers. Since qualified individuals are needed for these positions, several nontraditional tracks offer specialized course work, internships, and certifications.

TEACHING TRACK

Teacher certification following graduation from an accredited 4-year institution is the goal of the teaching track. This preparation may occur throughout the undergraduate years or may be concentrated in just 2 years following the completion of general course work taken at a junior or community college or at a 4-year institution. Certifications that can be obtained include those of physical education for kindergarten (K) through grade 6; grades 7 through 12; K through 12; health education; and dance.

The National Council for the Accreditation of Teacher Education (NCATE) now allows "learned societies," such as the American Alliance for Health, Physical Education, Recreation and Dance, to recommend guidelines for the professional studies component of its standards. These guidelines, containing all the attitudes, knowledge, and skills required of a physical education teacher, have been subdivided into three elements: academic, professional, and pedagogical. Aquatics, dance, exercise, games, sports, and other leisure pursuits are components of the unique academic content of physical education. The applied sciences of motor development, sport management, sport pedagogy, motor learning, sport philosophy, sport biomechanics, adapted physical education, exercise physiology, sport history, sport psychology, sport sociology, and the humanities of art, literature, and music, as discussed in Chapter 3, provide the intellectual and theoretical bases for studies in physical education. The professional aspect of the undergraduate program develops an awareness of and commitment to the various educational, research, and service activities of physical education. These include studies in curriculum models, organizational structures, diagnostic and evaluative procedures, and problem solving. Knowledge about the teaching and learning of physical skills constitute the pedagogical element. Abilities to plan, implement, and evaluate learning are observed in a supervised student teaching experience.

According to the Council on Physical Education for Children, the curriculum for the prospective elementary physical educator should develop competence in:

1. Understanding child growth and development, with an emphasis on motor development;
2. A knowledge of and appreciation for the structure and function of human movement;
3. Observing and assessing children and their movements;
4. A knowledge of learning processes, teaching strategies, and factors that affect motor learning;
5. Developing curriculum with emphasis on curriculum designs and strategies appropriate for elementary school programs;
6. Assessing and working with children who have special needs;
7. Personal skills and teaching skills in the content areas of fundamental movement patterns, games/sports, dance, gymnastics, and aquatics to meet the needs and interests of children in kindergarten through grade six (Essentials, 1981).

Following completion of a program that includes learning and developing these competencies and a supervised student teaching experience in grades K through 6 students receive their certification.

Similarly, all prospective teachers seeking certification in grades 7 through 12 must complete course work in academic, professional, and pedagogical areas, although specific requirements vary by state as they do for elementary school certification. Students often must complete fieldwork experiences, such as class observations, beginning as early as the first year in college in some programs. These are often used to help students decide whether they wish to pursue a teaching track. A part of this commitment of teachers at all levels is the belief in and advocacy of the essentiality of physical education in the schools. Box 4-2 is one example of a position paper that states the important components of quality physical education programs. Health education and

Physical education is an integral part of the development of the total student. An appropriate physical education program encompasses the cognitive, affective, and psychomotor domains, thus promoting the physical, psychological, and social development of the student. It is the position of the Physical Education Association that such a program shall be available to all students regardless of age, sex, or disability.

Consistent with the above statement, the NCAHPERD supports the following concepts:

1. It is essential that all students from kindergarten through grade twelve engage in an appropriate physical education program. This program shall be sequential in nature, emphasizing movement activities, basic skills, and fitness activities at the elementary level and progressing to lifetime sports and development of healthy lifestyles at the secondary level. Health-related concepts shall be taught and emphasized in all classes.

2. The length of the structured physical education program shall be no less than 150 minutes per week at the elementary level and no less than 250 minutes per week at the secondary level. The time allotted for physical education shall be in excess of the time allotted for activities such as intramurals, recess, and free play. At the secondary level, the time allotted for physical education shall be consistent with the time allotted for other academic classes.

3. The size of the physical education class shall be consistent with that of other academic classes offered at the school.

4. An individualized adapted physical education program shall be available whenever appropriate or necessary.

5. Physical education classes at all levels shall be taught by certified physical education teachers. Funding for physical education instructors and administrators should be consistent with that of other academic areas.

6. Physical education teachers shall be both encouraged and supported to participate in ongoing professional development activities.

7. Facilities shall be adequate to meet the goals of physical education programs at all levels.

8. Funding for equipment and supplies shall be adequate to meet the needs of the program and consistent with that of other areas.

9. Periodic evaluation of students' fitness levels, skill achievement, and knowledge shall be ongoing.

(continues)

(concluded)

> **10.** Because of the developmental nature of the physical education pro-
> gram and its expected outcomes, no course substitutions for phys-
> ical education shall be made.

dance majors have similar requirements, but their academic bodies of knowledge differ from those of the physical education student.

NON-TRADITIONAL TRACKS

Non-traditional tracks or course work options vary widely in colleges and
universities as each seeks to meet the interests of its students. Six of the most
common curricula are listed below.

Athletic Training

Athletic training is currently offered as a undergraduate major in 63 colleges
and universities. This curriculum specifies 11 courses emphasizing the sciences and at least 800 hours of clinical experiences for completion (Kauth,
1984).

Sport or Exercise Science

A sport or exercise sciences option focuses on courses in chemistry, biology
or zoology, anatomy, physiology, biomechanics, and exercise physiology. This

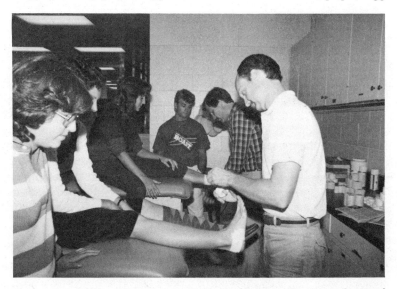

Careers in athletic training are available in schools, colleges, professional
leagues, and public clinics.

Coaching and teaching are often combined careers in schools and colleges.

background prepares graduates for advanced studies in one of these scientific fields as well as for careers in which understanding the scientific bases of exercise and sport is vital.

Coaching

Coaching emphasis or certification programs are becoming increasingly popular as junior and senior high schools and youth sport leagues want individuals who are trained specifically to work with this population. The need for coaches of interscholastic teams exceeds the supply due to increased numbers of girls' teams, the hiring of fewer new teachers, and the resignation of tenured physical educators from coaching but not from teaching. Coaching curricula most often include first aid and care and prevention of athletic injuries, anatomy, physiology, coaching theory and techniques, human growth and development, sport administration or management, sport psychology, exercise physiology, and sport pedagogy (Noble & Sigler, 1980).

Health and Fitness or Fitness Specialist

A health and fitness or fitness specialist track combines a scientific foundation, such as in biomechanics and exercise physiology, with business and management courses for physical education-related careers in the public and private sectors. In this option, some emphasis is placed on the teaching of various physical activities.

Sport Communication or Management

Sport communication seeks to merge knowledge in physical education and sports with skills in English, speech, journalism, and broadcasting. Similarly, sport management combines business and management course work with selected physical education courses. A diversity of courses selected to meet each individual's interests and needs, combined with independent studies emphasizing practical application of knowledge, is the best preparation for careers in these two fields.

•   •   •

These six tracks are not the only ones available, but they are illustrative of the emphasis on professionally preparing yourself for a career. Chapter 5 will help you in making that choice.

SUMMARY

A part of becoming a professional is the adherence to the highest ethical standards. This is especially essential for the educator because of the magnitude of the trust and responsibility inherent in the teaching process. Educators must believe in the worth and dignity of all students and must seek to help them realize their potential as effective members of society. Students are encouraged to inquire, to acquire knowledge, and to formulate and to achieve worthy goals. As a student aspiring to a particular career, you need to understand the significance of your commitment when you join a career.

This chapter is focused on being a professional, not on joining a profession. While physical education is characterized by extensive training in a body of knowledge and service, communication among colleagues is also essential. The services provided by the Alliance will enhance development of each of these component parts; involvement starting while you are a student is important in this process, too. Similarly, you need to participate in conferences, attend workshops, and read publications of physical education–related organizations to prepare for your chosen career. As a young professional, you can make a significant contribution to the quality of life of those you serve as either a teacher, a researcher, or a program leader. You have the opportunity to become a role maker by planning and implementing effective programs that meet the activity needs of diverse groups. Rather than reacting, you can become proactive by promoting the values of physical education and by implementing beneficial programs.

NANCY SMITH McNEIL

Elementary Physical Education Specialist
Winston–Salem, North Carolina

EDUCATION

B.S., Physical Education, Wake Forest University (1976)

JOB RESPONSIBILITIES, HOURS, AND SALARY RANGE

Nancy teaches elementary physical education in two schools and sees approximately 1,000 students weekly. She also helps classroom teachers with special programs and assignments as well as furnishing them with lesson plans for days when they are responsible for physical education. Minimal hours for school teachers are 8:00 A.M. to 3:45 P.M. Monday through Friday, although frequently other duties extend the work day. Beginning teachers may start around $12,000, depending on the degree held and the school system, and experienced teachers with advanced education may earn up to $32,000.

SPECIALIZED COURSE WORK, DEGREES, AND WORK EXPERIENCES NEEDED FOR THIS CAREER

Nancy specifies that elementary physical education course work emphasizing games, gymnastics, dance, fitness, special events, psychology, and child development is essential. At least a bachelor's degree is essential for teaching to meet state requirements, and also so the teacher has an understanding of how the body works. Graduate study is extremely beneficial, so that the teacher never stops growing and learning. In preparing for this career, students should work at any jobs dealing with children, such as summer camp, recreation programs, lifeguarding, child care, YMCA/YWCA classes, scouts, youth organizations, and church groups.

SATISFYING ASPECTS OF THIS CAREER

Individuals who choose a teaching career in the schools are usually intrinsically motivated to help children and adolescents learn. Tremendous satisfaction is realized when young people discover the joys of physical activity and develop a personal commitment to lifetime fitness. Winning adherents to the concept of wellness during these formative years is easier and more lasting than addressing the same issues with adults. Nancy especially loves children and enjoys seeing the sparkle in their eyes when they are learning.

JOB POTENTIAL

Depending on the state and the school system, elementary physical education teachers may be in demand, or there may be an oversupply. As with secondary physical educators, relocation may be essential for the elementary specialist to find a position. Being diligent in the job search is also important. Nancy believes that there are jobs for good teachers, but they have to be willing to work hard to find them.

ADVICE TO STUDENTS

Nancy emphasizes that students must be sure they love people. Elementary physical education specialists must constantly "sell" their programs and ideas to parents, teachers, principals, and children. The children deserve the best physical education time possible and positive feedback. Being physically fit and setting an example is a great way to teach, according to Nancy. She encourages teachers to go to every relevant workshop and to read every appropriate book and then to use the information that gels with their philosophies of teaching and about children. Nancy asks that teachers remember that every child they teach is a special little person who deserves their best every day.

REVIEW QUESTIONS

1. What are the characteristics of a profession?
2. How has the American Alliance for Health, Physical Education, Recreation and Dance sought to achieve any one of its objectives?
3. How can you justify that physical education is a profession?
4. What is the FITNESSGRAM?
5. What is the Student Action Council, and what are its objectives?
6. What types of services are provided by the National Association for Sport and Physical Education?
7. What are the purposes of the American College of Sports Medicine?
8. What national association has led in the expansion of employee fitness programs and how has it accomplished this?
9. According to the National Council for the Accreditation of Teacher Education, in what three elements of physical education must a prospective teacher gain knowledge?

10. What is the difference between teaching tracks and non-traditional tracks in physical education?

STUDENT ACTIVITIES

1. Write to the American Alliance for Health, Physical Education, Recreation and Dance (1900 Association Drive, Reston, VA 22091) to obtain information about its services and student membership.
2. Write to one physical education organization that interests you (other than the AAHPERD) and request information about possible careers.
3. Read at least one article from any two of the periodicals listed in Box 4–2.
4. Write a one-page statement defending the proposition that physical education is a profession.
5. Attend at least one professional workshop or clinic during this school year.

REFERENCES

American Alliance for Health, Physical Education, Recreation and Dance. By-Laws, Article III.

Constitution of the North Carolina Alliance for Health, Physical Education, Recreation and Dance.

Essentials of a quality elementary school physical education program. Reston, Virginia: Council on Physical Education for Children of the American Alliance for Health, Physical Education, Recreation and Dance, 1981.

Journal of Physical Education, Recreation and Dance, 56, 97–123, April 1985.

Kauth, B., The athletic training major. *Journal of Physical Education, Recreation and Dance, 55,* 11–13, 80–83, October 1984.

Noble, L., and Sigle, G. Minimum requirements for interscholastic coaches. *Journal of Physical Education and Recreation, 51,* 32–33, November-December 1980.

Park, R. J. Three major issues: the academy takes a stand. *Journal of Physical Education, Recreation and Dance, 54,* 52–53, January 1983.

Razor, J. Annual report of the American Alliance for Health, Physical Education, Recreation and Dance. *Update, 5,* April 1984.

SUGGESTED READINGS

Arason, L., et al. Teaching/coaching: where it is and where it's going. *Scholastic Coach, 53,* 62–68, February 1984. Six top administrators answer questions about hiring coaches, nonstaff coaches, merit pay, coaching certification, community pressures to win, budgeting, equipment purchase, and the status of athletics in high schools.

Broekhoff, J. Physical education as a profession. *Quest, 31, (2)* 1979. Physical education should describe itself in terms of how the members of this profession meet the expectations of its students and other clientele. Its importance is based on its value to people rather than its applied or academic knowledge.

Cobb, R. S. Health education . . . a separate and unique discipline. *The Journal of School Health, 51*, 602–603, November 1981. While health education and physical education share the common goal of development of high-quality health in each individual, each is distinct in its instructional content and requires unique professional preparation.

Corbin, C. B. Status: what the profession is like now. *The Academy Papers, 15*, 29–31, April 1981. After listing eight characteristics of a profession, this author proposes five descriptors of the status of the profession of the physical educator today.

Dimondstein, G. Moving in the real and feeling worlds: a rationale for dance in education. *Journal of Physical Education, Recreation and Dance, 54*, 42–44, September 1983. Dance can help students interpret and express ideas and emotions symbolically through movement while developing a kinesthetic perception about themselves.

Jable, J. T. The AAHPERD: professionals proudly promoting physical education. *The Physical Educator, 38*, 205–211, December 1981. Since 1885, the American Alliance for Health, Physical Education, Recreation and Dance has promoted physical education, especially through public information and publicity, professional preparation and teacher certification, physical fitness, and state and federal physical education legislation.

Lawson, H. A. Paths toward professionalization. *Quest, 31, (2)* 231–243, 1979. Due to the schism between the discipline of pedagogy and the discipline of sport studies, physical educators must work to improve the chances of becoming completely professionalized.

McBride, R. E. Some future considerations in the professional preparation of physical education teachers. *The Physical Educator, 41*, 95–99, May 1984. It is imperative that teacher education in the future focus on the criteria of a profession, such as demanding high-caliber candidates in its training programs through selective admissions and improving teacher quality in interpersonal communication skills and through demonstrated competencies.

Pearson, K. Applied futurism: how to avoid professional obsolescence. *The Physical Educator, 39*, 170–175, December 1982. The author superimposes the four branches of Toffler's futures tree on physical education to show how they affect specialists versus generalists, experimental research and objective grading procedures, intercollegiate athletics, and movement in space.

Welsh, R. Sharpening our professional focus. *Journal of Physical Education, Recreation and Dance, 54*, 13–15, November/December 1983. The author examines important issues in physical education, such as what business we are in and we should be in, whether high technology will alter what we do, what it means to be physically educated, and whether there is a need for a new synthesis in physical education.

Selecting
a Career Pathway

KEY
CONCEPTS

- Self-assessment inventories help identify individuals' characteristics and desired life-styles that influence career choices.
- Traditional and non-traditional settings foster the teaching-learning process yet differ in clientele, work hours, salaries, and related responsibilities.
- Programs for the development of fitness and to regain fitness offer careers for those interested in helping others incorporate healthful habits and practices into their life-styles.
- Schools, colleges, non-school agencies, and professional leagues expect coaches, administrators, trainers, officials, and other personnel to direct and to provide quality athletic programs.
- Many schools and public and private organizations need individuals with sport management knowledge to direct their programs.
- Sport marketing has grown to be a multimillion dollar business as it capitalizes on the nation's enthusiasm for fitness.

Career choices today are more complex decisions than they used to be because of the obsolescence of some jobs, the burgeoning of technology, the shifts in population, the acceptance of women in more jobs in the work force, and economic necessity. Men seldom continue with their initial career choices; they change jobs several times during their working years. Women, once expected to learn domestic skills for their roles as homemakers, now educate themselves for careers; more than 50% of today's women have careers outside the home.

The preceding chapters described the broad spectrum of physical education laying the foundation for the career options presented in this chapter. You should now be prepared to assess objectively your future in the field. This is not a one-time event, but rather an ongoing process. Your initial career choice is not necessarily a lifetime commitment but one that should be reevaluated periodically. As you read this chapter and assess your interests, abilities, and goals, remember that you are choosing a career pathway, not necessarily a single job.

Before embarking on this process, list your attitudes and expectations. Your attitude toward a career greatly influences whether you will be successful and happy. A major characteristic is your self-concept. How do you evaluate your abilities? Are you willing to listen to the advice of teachers, coaches, parents, and others? Can you objectively assess your personal strengths and weaknesses? Are you people-oriented? Are you motivated to do your best?

Before considering the available careers, analyze the relative importance of some personal and job-related factors. Two self-assessment inventories are provided in Boxes 5–1 and 5–2. Your responses to both of these will help you determine which physical education career best meets your needs and aspirations.

FACTORS INFLUENCING CAREER CHOICES

Family influences relative to a career choice can be positive, negative, or both. Parents may overtly or subtly persuade you to pursue a career on which they place a high value. Many times parents have forbidden their children

BOX 5-1
FACTORS INFLUENCING CAREER CHOICES

Using the scale below, indicate how you value each of the following relative to your selection of a career:

5	4	3	2	1
Most highly valued	Strong influencing factor	Average consideration	Weak influencing factor	Not valued at all

_____ Influence of your family and significant others
_____ Identification with role model(s)
_____ Knowledgeable about many aspects of this career
_____ Would personally enjoy this career
_____ Enjoy working with people
_____ Desire to serve others
_____ Ease of entrance into this career
_____ Monetary and other benefits from this career
_____ Time compatibility (work hours versus leisure time) meets your desires
_____ Job security available in this career

From the list above, select the five that you think are most important to you in your career choice and write them (in descending order of importance) in the spaces below.

1. _____
2. _____
3. _____
4. _____
5. _____
Other factors influencing your career choice
_____
_____

to major in physical education because they viewed it as frivolous, nonacademic, or not prestigious enough. On the other hand, parents may push their children into a physical education-related career because of their own rewarding past experiences. Regardless of situation, remember that your family will not be going to work for you each day or fulfilling the responsibilities of your chosen career. Parents, siblings, and significant others, while they can express their opinions and share their experiences, should not decide for you.

BOX 5–2
LIFE-STYLE PREFERENCE ASSESSMENT

1. Where would you prefer to live (state or region)? _____
2. Would you prefer an urban, small-town, or rural work environment? _____
3. Do you prefer to work for yourself or for others? _____
4. Do you prefer a large or small work environment? _____
5. What ages of people (if any) would you prefer to interact with daily? _____
6. Do you prefer an outdoor or indoor work environment? _____
7. Do you prefer a sedentary or an active job? _____
8. How much travel (if any) would you want as a regular part of your work? _____
9. What days of the week would you prefer to work? _____
10. What hours of the day would you prefer to work? _____
11. What salary would you need now? _____ in 10 years? _____
12. How much vacation time would you want each year? _____
13. What fringe benefits would you want as part of your job? _____
   _____
   _____
14. How important to you is career advancement? _____
15. What other job characteristics do you think would be important to your job satisfaction? _____
   _____
   _____

Whether consciously or not, many people select a career because they respect and admire someone who is in a particular position, a role model whom they wish to emulate. This may be a parent, sibling, coach, teacher, or friend who has demonstrated enjoyment of and dedication to a career that you wish to share. One precautionary note is that you may not be able to find the same type of position or may not possess the same abilities. Remember, you need to develop your own niche rather than trying to mimic another person.

The skills, knowledge, abilities, and experiences that you bring into your career will influence whether or not you are successful. This is not to imply that all prerequisite preparation precedes employment; certainly there is considerable learning while on the job. Your confidence in accepting an initial position is based on two factors, only one of which is prior preparation. Always remember the importance of gaining experiences, even voluntary experiences, that may enhance your chances of career advancement or change.

An important criterion for continuation in a job is the level of personal fulfillment and satisfaction. If you dread going to work, hate the day-to-day routine, and think the negative aspects far outweigh the positive gains, then it may be time for a change. It is not disastrous to sacrifice job security and material benefits and to start a career that enhances self-worth and pleasure. One way to make a career change less traumatic is to prepare yourself for a broad physical education career pathway that can offer you numerous alternatives.

Some people prefer a solitary setting; others need to interact frequently with people. If you are people-oriented, then you need to identify the ages of those with whom you find the greatest enjoyment and you need to seek a career that includes these opportunities. It is also important for you to identify which aspects of working with people you enjoy the most. Do you prefer to work with large groups, small groups, or one-on-one? Do you prefer constant or periodic interactions? Can you make decisions with others and about them?

Sometimes interaction with others is so highly valued that your personal needs become secondary to those of others. This characteristic is known as altruism. Teachers in traditional and nontraditional settings often focus on helping their students develop healthy life-styles, even though their material benefits seem small compared with the hours spent in instruction.

With high unemployment, a major concern for individuals making their first career choice is: are there any jobs? The answer is always "yes" in physical education-related jobs, because your expertise is needed by people due to their increased leisure time, higher standards of living, and the emphasis on fitness. Your ideal job in the exact location with the dreamed-for salary may not be available. After realizing that jobs are available for those who actively seek them, you must be willing to accept the probability of starting at the bottom. As a young professional, you probably can expect to work hard, to volunteer for extra duties, to learn new ideas, to gain experiences, and to accept less desirable responsibilities as a test of commitment to your field. If you do so successfully, you will advance.

You must determine the importance you place on monetary and other material benefits as you choose a career. Your response on the Life-style Preference Assessment indicated the value that a certain salary has for you and how it relates to other aspects of your life, such as family, status, location, and travel. The importance that salary has for you is also shown in the hours and days that you prefer to work as well as your desired vacation time. Money, however, is only one type of remuneration. Other benefits, including health insurance, retirement benefits, expense account, travel, club membership, and prestige, may offset a lower salary. Only you can decide the importance to you of money and other benefits, but you must do so honestly, since it frequently is a pivotal factor in career selection.

The 5-day, 8-to-5 work week is no longer the required norm. Your career choice could result in working any number of hours a week, nights, holidays, and weekends, and anywhere from 9 to 12 months a year. Only you can weigh your personal preferences versus each job's characteristics. Begrudging time spent working often results in negative feelings toward that task. How important is the amount and scheduling of leisure time for you? How do work hours relate to monetary benefits in importance?

Job security varies dramatically in physical education-related careers. Competent fulfillment of job responsibilities in some careers results in retention of positions based on merit; careers in education require earned tenure for job security. Some careers carry no guarantee of future employment other than the demand for your services. Inherent within the concept of job security is also the potential for advancement. Challenge and stimulation are important to many people for continuation in a career, as is recognition for a job well done and increased material benefits.

As you decide on a career, review and weigh all these factors. Only after evaluating the most influential considerations and your own personal life-style preferences can you select objectively a career pathway. Regardless of your choice, the key is your commitment to and motivation for it. Box 5–3 previews the next section of this chapter, which presents broad categories of careers and describes some alternatives within each. Educational preparation, salary ranges, job availability, and positive and negative aspects are presented.

BOX 5–3
CAREER OPPORTUNITIES FOR PHYSICAL EDUCATORS

Teaching

Traditional

A. Elementary school (K–6)
B. Middle school (5–8)
C. Secondary school (7–12)
D. Junior/community college
E. College/university
F. Adapted physical education

Non-traditional

A. Sports club
B. Health club
C. Sports camp or school
D. Recreation department
E. YMCA/YWCA program
F. Corporate fitness
G. Geriatric program
H. Military

(continues)

I. Dance studio
J. Resort
K. Peace Corps and VISTA

Fitness

Development

A. Private sports club
B. Recreation department
C. Dance studio
D. YMCA/YWCA
E. Corporate fitness
F. Protective services (police and fire)
G. Industrial recreation

Corrective

A. Physical therapy
B. Corrective therapy
C. Recreation therapy
D. Occupational therapy
E. Cardiac rehabilitation
F. Sports medicine
G. Weight-control center
H. Stress management clinic
I. Massage clinic
J. Fitness and nutrition counseling
K. Holistic health clinic
L. Wellness clinic

Athletics

School

A. Team coaching
B. Athletic administration
C. Athletic training
D. Sports officiating

College/University

A. Team coaching
B. Athletic administration
C. Athletic training
D. Business management
E. Facility management
F. Sports information
G. Sports promotions
H. Academic counseling
I. Sports officiating
J. Ticket sales
K. Strength and conditioning coach
L. Sport psychology

Sport Management

Business/Industry

A. Sports club
B. Health club
C. Sports camp and school

School

A. Program/department head
B. Intramurals/campus recreation

(continues)

(*concluded*)

D. Corporate fitness	C. Research
E. Theme park and resort	
F. Sports hall of fame and museum	
G. Public fitness and recreation	
H. Facility management	

Sports Marketing
A. Clothing sales
B. Equipment sales
C. Club membership sales
D. Book sales

Sports Communication
A. Sports broadcasting
B. Sports journalism
C. Sports photography

TEACHING

TRADITIONAL

Employment for college graduates with a major in physical education has traditionally been in the public and private schools (Dougherty, 1983). This remains a viable career choice: schools are still hiring first-year, state-certified teachers at a salary range of $12,000 to $20,000. This wide range in pay is due to variance in state base salaries and differences in local supplements. Since jobs are not as plentiful as they formerly were, graduates may have to move to smaller communities or different states. In the latter situation, a reciprocal agreement may exist between the certifying state and the new state, or additional course work may be required before full certification is granted. Many states also require the National Teachers Examination for certification.

Junior high and senior high physical educators in their first years sometimes teach classes outside their major field. Willingness to accept these teaching assignments may lead to full-time physical education positions in subsequent years. The physical educator, while perhaps not prepared to teach or interested in teaching health, frequently is assigned classes in this area, too. Some schools hire certified health educators and others have health consultants, but because of budget constraints most health classes are taught by physical educators in the secondary schools. Physical education teachers work at least 7 hours at school, which usually includes one planning period and at least five classes. In addition, the teacher is expected to plan classes, grade papers, monitor the halls, lunchroom, and buses, and complete administrative reports. Some secondary teachers are faced with discipline problems, apathetic students, drug abuse, inadequate facilities and equipment, and lack of administrative and community support. On the other hand, professional involvement and educational enrichment are sometimes encouraged by supportive administrators. Low salaries deter some good candidates, while student interactions, retirement and health benefits, summer vacations, and job security once tenure has been achieved are attractive job characteristics.

Adapted physical education specialists are hired most frequently by large systems and state departments of education so that many schools may share the expertise of one individual. This specialist helps classroom teachers and physical educators meet the needs of disabled students who have been placed into regular classes, or they may individualize instruction for students with special needs. Educational background and experience emphasizing adapted physical education is essential for this career. Hours and salaries correspond with those of other teachers.

In some states, elementary school physical educators are in demand; in others, jobs are scarce. Their responsibilities vary from teaching daily classes for children at one school to conducting ten 30-minute classes at a different school each day of the week. Student interactions and the intrinsic satisfactions of watching students learn and develop are the rewards cited by these teachers. Positively impacting on children's attitudes toward movement skills and encouraging healthy life-styles are often weighed against inadequate facilities and equipment and limited administrative support.

Teaching physical education in junior or community colleges or in 4-year colleges and universities requires education beyond the bachelor's degree. Faculty with master's degrees in smaller institutions are expected to teach pre-major or major courses. Most institutions also require sports and activity instructors to have master's degrees. Since university activity instructors and small college teachers spend much more time teaching than researching, job security or tenure is based on teaching and service rather than scholarly productivity. (These same teachers often are expected to advise students and to serve on departmental and university committees.) Beginning salaries range from $15,000 to $25,000, with benefits including health insurance, retirement programs, and summer vacations. In their activity and theory classes, these teachers enjoy helping adult students learn healthy life-styles and relish the generalist approach to teaching physical education 3 to 6 hours per day and 4 or 5 days a week. Teaching facilities and equipment are usually good, and problems are minimal in most colleges.

In larger institutions, physical educators with doctorates specializing in biomechanics, exercise physiology, sport psychology, or other applied sciences teach undergraduate and graduate courses in addition to conducting research. Both teaching and research, to varying degrees, are required for tenure, which is granted in 5 to 7 years. Starting salaries range from $20,000 to $30,000. For university professors, conducting research, writing manuscripts for professional journals, and giving scholarly presentations is a prerequisite for job security. Lack of time for research and class preparation is cited frequently by university teachers as a problem. While their hours are somewhat flexible, committee meetings, student advising, and other departmental responsibilities besides teaching, research, and service extend the work week well beyond 40 hours.

NON-TRADITIONAL

Opportunities abound for those who want to teach fitness and sports skills outside a school environment (Fordham & Leaf, 1978). Dance studios provide instruction in aerobic, jazz, ballet, and modern dance for children as well as for adults. Individuals with dance majors or physical education majors with some course work and experience teach dancing to customers for fees at these studios. Classes may be scheduled throughout the day and evening as well as on weekends. These instructors are paid either by the class or by the hour or with an initial salary of $15,000 to $18,000 and have few other responsibilities.

Sports clubs focus on individual sports, such as tennis, swimming, or racquetball, and need instructors for private and group lessons. Other clubs, which usually have expensive membership fees, may cater to several sports, such as the country clubs that offer swimming, golf, and tennis. Vacation resorts are increasingly providing sports instruction for their guests. Health clubs usually offer fitness programs in aerobic conditioning, weight training, sports instruction, such as racquetball, and possibly classes in stress management and weight control. Because of the tremendous variety in clubs, salaries depend on location, clientele, instructional expertise, and assigned responsibilities.

Sports camps have become booming businesses related to commercial recreation. Children, as well as adults, attend these highly successful ventures in the summer and on weekends and holidays. For young physical educators, sports camps provide excellent opportunities for gaining teaching experience and for making valuable contacts that may lead to permanent positions. For school teachers looking for summer employment related to physical education and sports, sports camps abound. Expertise in teaching one or more activities is important for employment, as is a desire to work with various age and skill

Teaching racquetball, weight training, aerobics, and other activities in health clubs, private settings, and community programs are increasingly popular careers for physical educators.

levels. Responsibilities, such as those of instructor or program director, determine salaries, which may vary widely.

Concomitant with the increasing life span in the United States is the critical need for professionals trained to provide recreational and leisure activities for senior citizens. By the year 2000, approximately 20% of this country's population will be 65 years of age or older. Federal programs, as well as private agencies, increasingly must provide health, physical education, recreation, and dance services in retirement homes, day-care centers, and senior citizens' apartment complexes. The job potential, with starting salaries of $15,000 to $18,000 for individuals trained to prescribe and to direct activities for this clientele, will expand rapidly in the years ahead.

The military provides additional opportunities for physical educators. Fitness training is highly valued by the various branches of the armed services, as are competitive sports. Frequently, civilians instruct at the service academies, on military bases, and at special training facilities. As an employee of the federal government, one's pay depends on classification, but benefits are usually excellent.

Corporations and businesses continue to expand the fitness programs for their executives and, to a lesser extent, for all of their employees. Their classes and programs require exercise leaders, salaried initially around $18,000 to $20,000, to motivate out-of-shape and poorly skilled individuals to set and reach fitness goals.

YMCAs and YWCAs provide a wide variety of fitness and sport classes as well as facilities for individual workouts. Some of these organizations cater to the rich, and others focus on the involvement of families from all socio-economic classes. Youth camps, gymnastics, basketball, aerobics, racquetball, scuba diving, canoeing, and swimming for toddlers to senior citizens are among their popular programs. Salaries for instructors start around $12,000 to $15,000 for full-time work; sometimes program leaders are paid for classes by the hour. The Y's also have good opportunities for advancement into the directing and other administrative positions.

While still sponsoring the traditional leagues and providing facilities for use by anyone at their leisure, recreation departments today offer a broad spectrum of instructional classes. This diversity may include water aerobics, massage, disco dancing, slimnastics, and cross-country skiing. Similar to YMCA/YWCA classes, hours are usually in the early mornings, afternoons, and evenings. Salaries range from $12,000 to $15,000.

The Peace Corps was established as an independent federal agency to provide services to underdeveloped nations and people in South and Central America, Africa, the Caribbean, Asia, and the Pacific. Today, more than 5,000 volunteers live with and help these people with problems in agriculture, forestry, rural development, engineering, health and nutrition, and education. Among these volunteers, who serve for 2 or more years, are physical educators who teach fitness and sports skills. Another government agency, VISTA, is one of nine agencies in ACTION, which mobilizes citizens for voluntary service in the United States, Puerto Rico, the Virgin Islands, and Guam. During their 1-year service, the volunteers, who live and work with the poor, develop programs to meet basic human needs and to support self-help efforts.

FITNESS AND LEISURE SERVICES

PROGRAMMING AND INSTRUCTION

The private sector currently provides approximately 5 million jobs in commercial recreation, with a projected addition of more than 1 million by 1990. Many physical education and recreation graduates obtain their first jobs in one of seven subclusters of career opportunities delineated by the U.S. Office of Education:

1. Lodging—Management, operation, and programming for housing services, such as hotels, motels, resorts, convention centers, cruise lines, and camps.

2. Recreation—Planning, management, and operation of recreational programs, facilities, and areas for agencies such as commercial/private, governmental, volunteer, industrial, outdoor, and therapeutic institutions.
3. Entertainment services—Management, operation, and programming for entertainment services, such as theaters, theme parks, racetracks, night clubs, and toy and game manufacturers.
4. Cultural services—Management, operation, and programming for institutions that deal with the fine arts, such as museums, zoos, aquariums, and historical sites.
5. Sports—Management, operation, and programming for athletic areas and facilities, such as racquetball and tennis complexes, health and fitness clubs, and professional athletic organizations.
6. Food and beverage services—Management and operation of food establishments, such as restaurants, school cafeterias, snack bars, and catering services.
7. Travel services—Management, operation, and programming for tourist organizations, such as travel agencies, tours, and chambers of commerce (Priest & Summerfield, 1983).

Of this list, probably the sports subcluster appeals to most individuals in physical education, with instruction and program planning being the major types of jobs available. Racquetball, tennis, golf, and swimming are among the popular types of specific sports clubs, and multisport complexes also exist. Health and fitness clubs, YMCAs and YWCAs, and aerobic salons are examples of both general and specific types of leisure services. All of these activity-related clubs or businesses require membership, thereby excluding a segment of the population. Most individuals who work at these are encouraged, if not required, to sell memberships as one of their responsibilities. Hours vary by club, but are usually in the afternoons, in the evening, and on weekends, since these are the leisure hours of those who join. Starting salaries range from $15,000 to $20,000. Job security varies with each person's expertise, yet potential for advancement into management and even ownership is good. Benefits include working with people and seeing their improvement as well as the opportunity for maintaining your own healthy life-style in these settings. Social skills, sales ability, and sports expertise are more important than a college degree, although being knowledgeable about the components of physical fitness and having expertise in skill analysis are quite helpful. The American College of Sports Medicine now offers national certification in exercise testing for those who administer and analyze stress and fitness tests in these clubs.

The lodging subcluster includes resorts, hotels, condominium complexes, and camps, which are increasingly hiring specialists in golf, tennis, swimming, and other sports to organize and to instruct groups and individuals. For these recreation directors, hours vary to meet the needs of the guests, but the pleasant work environment and beginning salary ($12,000 to $20,000) may compensate.

Many large industries and corporations, such as Levi-Strauss, Xerox, and Campbell Soup Company, provide fitness centers for their executives. Concerns about work efficiency and loss of time and money from absenteeism have resulted in elaborate facilities for daily aerobic, strength, and flexibility workouts. Exercise physiologists, with certification in exercise testing, design individually prescribed programs, and physical educators instruct and motivate executives in their workouts. The starting salaries range from $18,000 to $20,000.

Some companies are extending this fitness concept through recreational services to include all of their employees. Although they are not as elaborate as the programs for executives, management has realized the interrelationship of exercise and work efficiency; thus physical educators are needed to provide the supervision and instruction for these programs. Working with people in a non-structured setting appeals to many people in spite of the hours, which are scheduled frequently during the workers' leisure time.

Corporate fitness program participants often cycle to enhance their cardiovascular conditions. (Courtesy of W. Bertsch from H. Armstrong Roberts)

Related to both industry and job-site fitness is the need for professionals to design and to implement training programs for workers in the protective services (public safety officers). Physical educators, especially those with training in exercise physiology, are being hired to test the fitness levels of these workers and to prescribe exercise programs to meet their individual needs and to prepare them to meet the demands of their jobs. Salaries exceed those in the public schools, and security is based on job performance. Satisfaction in observing positive life-style changes is rewarding; frustration may result when public safety officers fail to achieve their goals.

CORRECTIVE

An outgrowth of the desire for a healthy life-style is the proliferation of specialized clinics and counseling centers. These include those for weight control, massage, nutrition, holistic health, wellness, and stress management. The weight-control centers sometimes promote a particular diet or system, and sometimes provide generic information about nutrition and encourage proper exercise. In massage, a method of tension release and relaxation, one manipulates the body with various stroking, kneading, rubbing or tapping motions. Holistic health and wellness programs emphasize the development of nutritional, exercise, and attitudinal life-style changes through counseling and participatory sessions. The proliferation of stress management classes, clinics, seminars, workshops, and counseling centers indicates the popularity and need for information in this area and in preventive and corrective strategies. Since these are fee-based businesses, salaries vary dramatically.

A physical education major may wish to continue to study in one of the therapeutic fields to seek employment in hospitals, retirement homes, private clinics, or special schools. Occupational therapists work with individuals trying to regain work skills following accidents or illnesses. National certification in physical or corrective therapy allows use of various modalities to help rehabilitate people and to help them develop new skills. Recreational therapists use sports, games, arts and crafts, and social activities to assist individuals' development, self-confidence, and acceptance of physical limitations. Clients served by therapists are of all ages and abilities. The rewards of seeing physical, mental, emotional, and social enhancement far surpass the $20,000 to $25,000 starting salaries.

Cardiac rehabilitation programs have grown out of the need to help heart attack and disease victims regain their health and develop fitness life-styles. Programs at YMCAs and YWCAs, hospitals, private clinics, and many other settings provide the exercises and activities prescribed by physicians.

Sports medicine clinics on college campuses and in hospitals provide the settings in which physicians, physical therapists, and athletic trainers treat and rehabilitate sports-related injuries. Team physicians for professional, college, school, and community teams must have earned medical degrees before specializing in this field. Physical therapists must be certified.

Athletic trainers are critical to athletes' successful performance because they, in conjunction with team physicians, prevent, treat, and rehabilitate injuries. Certification by the National Athletic Trainers' Association is required for positions in colleges and sports medicine clinics. In colleges and universities, athletic trainers may hold staff positions in athletics departments, combine training with teaching in physical education, health, or sports medicine, or work as trainer-physical therapists in conjunction with student health services. Salaries reflect responsibilities. Hours are long and usually include afternoons, evenings, weekends, and frequently holidays. Travel with teams and the pleasure derived from helping athletes return to competition following injuries may compensate for the heavy time commitment. Increasingly, schools are being required to have among their faculty someone serving as an athletic trainer; therefore, there may be as many as 10,000 to 20,000 jobs in this career at present. Since many schools cannot afford to hire full-time, certified athletic trainers, they often use the talents of individuals who also teach physical education.

ATHLETICS

SCHOOL

A second career aspiration of many secondary school and some elementary school physical educators is coaching the numerous teams for boys and girls. Many schools have coaching vacancies but no teaching positions in physical education, due to the resignations of some physical educators from coaching but not from teaching and due to increased numbers of girls' teams. If certified in and willing to teach in a second area, the physical educator-coach is automatically more marketable. Coaching positions in the more visible sports of basketball and football are not as easy to obtain as those in other sports, and more openings exist for coaches of girls' sports than for boys'. In many schools coaches are expected to work with more than one team and may sometimes have to work with as many as three teams. Some states allow non-teachers to coach; in others, only employees of the school system can be hired. Supplements of $500 to $5000 are minimal when compared with the long hours and the innumerable demands on coaches. Job security for football and basketball coaches in some high schools does not exist unless winning teams are consistently produced. Victories are not as critical to job retention for coaches of other sports.

Other athletic opportunities within the schools include athletic training, sports officiating, and administration. High school sports officials normally work at other jobs, including those related to physical education, and only umpire or referee as a hobby or as a second job. A former coach or current coach usually serves as the school's athletic director. This individual coordinates team schedules, budgets, and facilities, and supervises the overall athletic program.

COLLEGE AND UNIVERSITY

Athletic programs vary dramatically depending on the size of the institution. In junior or community colleges and small 4-year colleges and universities, almost all coaches teach in physical education or in other departments, and coaching remains a secondary responsibility, providing a supplementary salary with less teaching. Most sports at these institutions are non-revenue-producing, although for some teams recruiting is expected, since athletic grants-in-aid are awarded. At larger universities, coaches of non-revenue-producing sports may hold full-time positions in athletics by coaching more than one sport or team or by carrying out additional administrative responsibilities. Other coaches at larger institutions teach or coach only part-time. Coaches of non-revenue-producing sports are paid initially between $2000 and $40,000 for the coaching aspects of their jobs. Head and assistant football and basketball coaches at major universities receive salaries ranging from $25,000 to well over $100,000.

The teacher-coach, administrator-coach, part-time coach, or full-time coach frequently works day and night because of the increasing competitiveness of intercollegiate athletics (and the rewards that accrue to the victorious). Seldom is there an off-season or free time. While most college coaches have earned master's degrees, this is not a prerequisite, and the major field does not have to be physical education, although it often is. Ways of gaining entrance into college coaching vary. For example, you may volunteer to serve as an assistant or to serve as a graduate student assistant coach, you may earn an assistant coach's position after a successful high school coaching career, or you may win a job because of outstanding collegiate or professional play. In most cases, future head coaches, even those at small institutions and for non-revenue-producing sports, must get experience serving as successful assistant coaches. Once jobs are obtained, most coaches, although not guaranteed tenure, retain them as long as they abide by the rules, keep their athletes happy, maintain their own desire to coach, and develop a successful program. In larger institutions, most football and basketball coaches have job security only when they win and show that they can handle the pressures of the job without cheating. For these coaches, the long hours and pressures are compensated by the material benefits and the prestige. Most coaches take satisfaction in helping their athletes improve their skills and in seeing them mature as individuals.

In small colleges, coaches are also the administrators of athletics. As larger universities' athletic programs grew, they expanded into businesses and required administrators to direct them. Athletic directors, associate and assistant directors, fund raisers, ticket managers, and others often have earned master's degrees in sport management to prepare them for these careers. Money and people management skills are crucial, as is public relations, since skyrocketing budgets have made fund raising vital. When skillfully achieved, all of these factors mesh into a successful athletic program that brings prestige and lucrative benefits to its director. Security is based on the institution's overall program rather than on one team's performance, although the successes of the revenue-producing sports are certainly most important.

Associated with intercollegiate athletics and vital to their programs are

Management and computer skills are important for careers in athletic administration.

Sports information, an integral part of college athletics, offers careers for individuals with good writing skills.

numerous career options. Assistant and associate athletic directors assume responsibility for facility management, concessions, grants-in-aid, business affairs, fund raising, and coordination of non-revenue-producing sports. These positions may be filled by coaches, former athletes, or people trained in sport management. Starting salaries range from $20,000 to $50,000, depending on experience and expertise. Job security is not guaranteed: continuation is based on successful completion of assigned duties. A major benefit is the association with a successful athletic program and its reflected glamour.

For individuals who wish to combine writing skills with athletics, there is sports information. This vital component of the athletic program is responsible for compiling statistics and personal information about the players and teams to publicize upcoming events and to provide post-contest data. Press releases and team brochures further publicize the intercollegiate program. A degree in journalism or sports communication would be appropriate, but volunteer experience and the willingness to start at the lowest level and work upward may be necessary to gain entrance into this athletic career. Travel, personal contacts with players and coaches, and contributing to the success of a program are benefits surpassing the starting salaries of $15,000 to $20,000.

Sports promotions specialists are responsible for filling the stadium and the coliseum through advertising and various promotional schemes. At a small college, one person may handle both sports information and sports promotions, or each coach may have to accept these additional responsibilities. Larger institutions have promotions specialists who frequently share in fundraising activities for grants-in-aid and capital improvements. Public relations skills are usually more important than a particular educational degree. Since this person's efforts bring a lot of money into the athletic department, salaries up to $50,000 are realistic.

Strength and conditioning coaches design and implement training programs for all athletes. Frequently, these positions are filled by physical educators with strong exercise physiology and biomechanics backgrounds. Helping athletes reach their athletic potentials is the greatest reward for these individuals, who are initially paid between $15,000 and $30,000.

Another emerging career is that of sport psychology within both college and professional sport. These specialists apply the principles of behavior as they help athletes understand themselves, handle the pressures of competition, and achieve their potentials (1983 *Women's Sports Careers Guide*).

NON-SCHOOL

More than 20 million children participate on youth sports teams sponsored by recreation departments, YMCAs and YWCAs, private clubs, community service organizations, national sport associations, and churches. In most cases, the coaches are volunteers; officials and league, program, and association directors are paid. Many of these same groups also provide athletic competition for adults, such as softball and basketball leagues, master's swimming events, and road races. Experience gained as a volunteer coach, program administrator or assistant, or official may lead to a full-time job in a recreation-related career.

PROFESSIONAL

Prior playing experience in college and as a professional is an asset for coaches of professional teams, although not necessarily a prerequisite. Coaches are hired based on demonstrated success with high school, college, or professional teams and are fired for not producing winning teams. Lucrative salaries help compensate for the pressures to win and the constant media bombardment.

Professional sports require hundreds of people working behind the scenes to ensure that the events take place as scheduled. A commonality of many of these positions is the need for experience in college athletics, business, and

Hours of practice and competition are necessary for highly skilled athletes to develop and to refine their talents, which may help qualify them for coaching careers later in life. (Courtesy of UNC Sports Information Office)

promotions. Responsibilities of the ticket sales staff include season ticket packaging, selling tickets for individual events, and arranging for complimentary seating. Correspondence and direct contacts with fans are extensive, with the greatest challenge always remaining that of trying to satisfy as many fans as possible. No formal educational background is required, but a sport management degree is desirable. Salaries for starting ticket sales managers range from $15,000 to $30,000.

Business managers are responsible for planning budgets and administering the expenditures of all monies for the program. While accountants and secretaries actually may handle the daily transactions, business managers oversee multimillion-dollar budgets and the many personnel who work in this area. A business background is helpful, but on-the-job training in a small program or as an intern may be equally as valuable in obtaining this job, with an initial salary of $30,000 to $50,000.

Promotions directors serve varied functions, depending on the situation. With a team struggling to gain fan support, their primary responsibility focuses on public relations efforts to increase ticket sales. Radio or television commercials, newspaper advertisements, an exciting upcoming event or opponent, or a winning record are used to generate greater spectator interest. Season ticket sales are the next promotional effort, since these stabilize income and indicate increased and consistent fan support. Promotions directors also may help market team emblems or merchandise. Salaried at $40,000 to $100,000, these promotions specialists are hired for their proven abilities to fulfill the job responsibilities rather than for any educational degree.

Sports officiating provides many part-time and a few full-time (mostly in baseball and basketball) careers. No specific educational background is required, but years of experience are necessary. As early as possible, such as in recreational youth leagues, anyone interested in officiating should start learning the rules and the techniques while gaining experience and expertise. There may be some reflective glamour and prestige, but officials often are the villains and are only begrudgingly accepted as vital to the games. After success in the high school and college ranks and completion of training programs, the best-qualified officals make it to the pros. While earning $10,000 to $50,000 as officials, most hold other jobs and officiate as a hobby or as a second career. Unusual hours and travel are inherent characteristics.

SPORT MANAGEMENT

BUSINESS AND INDUSTRY

Golf courses, bowling lanes, gymnastics schools, tennis camps, swimming centers, racquetball clubs, and health spas all require administrative skills in addition to knowledge about physical skills. Directors in each of these settings must possess budgetary skills, personnel management abilities, planning knowledge, and supervisory capabilities (Lopiano, 1984). While they are primarily interested in producing profits and thus maintaining high enrollments or large attendance, they must hire qualified instructional staff.

Corporate fitness programs also demand management, motivational, and supervisory skills. Abilities of these sports professionals in public relations and in promotions may supersede their knowledge of fitness, since their employers want maximal participation to enhance worker productivity.

Theme parks and resorts have become multimillion-dollar ventures that provide leisure for people of all ages. A recreation administration and sport management background is essential for handling the massive budgetary and personnel aspects of these businesses.

More than 150 sports halls of fame and museums each year host millions of people who examine the memorabilia and the statistics and recall the stars of the past. These tourist attractions highlight the past and annually elect new enshrinees, and some host events to promote their respective sports. Sport historians and administrative curators are needed for these careers.

The fitness mania pervading this country has led to a proliferation of public facilities and programs promoting life-style changes for all groups. Directors and program coordinators may start at salaries of $10,000 to $30,000. They organize and implement fitness programs, sport teams, and various social activities. Job security is good, yet few advancement opportunities exist unless management skills learned in this setting are transferred to another career. The minimal wages earned in many part-time positions in public recreation are offset by the invaluable experience gained.

Facility managers are associated with arenas and stadiums at a few universities, in communities, and with professional teams. To be cost-efficient, large facilities must be multipurpose because audiences must be attracted to several different sporting events as well as to concerts, speeches, and conventions. Facility managers must have planning and organizational abilities foremost, as well as personnel management skills. There are some specialized facilities, such as an aquatic arena, but most facility managers work for either a university or a professional team and then schedule events around the major team(s) or work for a municipality that rents time to teams. Facility managers initially earn $30,000 to $50,000.

SCHOOL

Administration is another career possibility for physical educators in the schools. This may be as a department head who accepts management responsibilities resulting in a reduced teaching load or through appointment as a principal, headmaster, or superintendent. Such promotions result from successful service to the school, advanced education, or interest in and competence for these positions. In these jobs, salaries increase with time, but so do the hours and the responsibilities.

COLLEGE AND UNIVERSITY

Colleges and universities have many administrative positions, ranging from program director to department head to college dean. These careers are open to individuals with doctoral degrees, years of experience, expertise in working with people, and management skills. Competition for these positions is high.

Salaries range from $30,000 to $60,000. Administrative hassles, such as personnel problems, tight budgets, and day-to-day operational demands, are countered by the opportunities to effect program change, to lead faculty in the attainment of their professional goals, and to impact positively on students' education.

Intramural and campus recreation programs are popular components of collegiate life. Directors, assistant directors, facility supervisors, and program coordinators constitute the staff. Job responsibilities vary from publicity to facility management and from personnel to programming. Beginning salaries range from $15,000 to $30,000. These programs are administered either through the physical education department or the office of student affairs. In the first paridigm the staff may also teach; in the second they seldom do. Most intramural or campus recreation professionals have earned at least master's degrees in physical education or recreation. Increasingly, the trend is to make these positions non-faculty with job security based solely on fulfillment of assigned responsibilities. Rather than the usual school-day hours, these programs operate in the afternoons, evenings, and weekends, the leisure hours of the students they serve. Student interactions in non-academic activities and the opportunities to administer programs attract people to these positions.

SPORTS MARKETING

Sports attire is popular for all, whether the wearer is exercising, going out on the town, or working. From jogging shoes to tennis shorts to designer warm-up suits, everybody is wearing sports clothing. In 1982, athletic and sports clothing sales were at $3.18 billion. Regardless of skill level, seemingly only oversized tennis rackets, custom-made golf clubs, and autograph baseball gloves are good enough for aspiring athletes, as retail sporting goods sales reached $11.84 billion in 1982. Therefore, jobs are and will continue to be plentiful in the sales and marketing of sporting goods. Expertise in sports is an advantage for people in sales, marketing, and management. Individuals choosing sales may enjoy flexible hours, good salaries ($10,000 to $100,000), travel, rapid advancement, and job security if they are good at what they do.

Most administrators and many instructors in health clubs and sports clubs are expected to sell memberships. Those who are especially adept at this frequently advance into management positions and can earn $30,000 to $40,000.

The design of new equipment and improved facilities requires a great deal of research. Safety and improved performance motivates these efforts to produce the best ball or surface. Inventors or innovative designers may reap

Sporting goods sales provide numerous career opportunities for individuals interested in combining business skills with expertise about sports equipment and clothing.

financial benefits, providing their products gain the same kind of wide acceptance that the makers of oversized tennis rackets, for example, have seen.

SPORTS COMMUNICATION

The interdependency of the media and sports has created numerous opportunities in the glamour careers of sports broadcasting, sports journalism, and sports photography. Broadcasting opportunities vary from prime-time, national telecasts to special events coverage to sports reporting for a local network. On-the-air experience, experience with play-by-play announcing, an aptitude for interviewing, and a smooth delivery in reading sports news overshadow an educational degree. Willingness to start in small markets, where salaries average between $16,000 and $18,000, is a key to advancement. Cable networks provide another avenue for aspiring sports broadcasters.

Since sports sell newspapers and magazines and increase television ratings, thereby selling commercial time, professional and college teams are especially sensitive to the media. The sportswriting field attracts a large number of people; the percentage who succeed in it is small. Many sportswriters have earned college degrees in journalism, but some secure newspaper or magazine jobs because of their past experiences in college sports information offices, their own sports careers, or their background in physical education. Sportswriters must possess an inquiring mind, a desire to talk with people, the ability to listen, and the willingness to work unusual hours while under the pressures of deadlines and space limitations. Salaries vary dramatically depending on expertise.

A sports photographer may start by taking pictures for a college newspaper and then progress to assignments with a major publication. A thorough understanding of the intricacies of various sports provides a photographer with the insight necessary to capture the essence and meaning of sports as well as the outcome of a particular event. Generally, long hours, low compensation, and little glamour may eventually be rewarded with $25,000 salaries or more and extensive travel for a major publication.

OTHER RELATED CAREERS

In addition to the aforementioned broad categories of jobs open to physical education majors, several other specific careers are also available. Many of these, however, require specialized education, training, or certification. For the medical doctor with an interest in sports, there are specializations in exercise physiology, orthopedic surgery, and sports podiatry as well as the option to serve as a team physician. Sports nutrition and sports psychology are growing fields for both private practice and consultation with college and professional athletes. Lawyers may choose to emphasize the ever-expanding area of sports law.

Besides the performing artists with national and regional companies, dance careers include those of artistic directors, managing directors, development officers, public relations agents, booking agents, dance journalists, and dance photographers. Many of these positions are held by former dancers who understand the world of dance and can better market and promote it as an art form. Limited jobs, minimal salaries, ($15,000 to $30,000) and long hours deter some people from pursuing careers as a dancer or in one of the dance-related jobs. No educational degree is required for these positions or for those of studio teachers, yet all who pursue them have spent years developing their expertise.

•   •   •

Rather than viewing the sky as falling, a young professional should view the sky as the limit. Box 5–3 provides an overview of the careers discussed. Knowing these alternatives should help you focus on one or more broad areas of interest as you choose a career pathway.

SUMMARY

In this rapidly changing, technological world, career changes as often as every 10 years may become the norm rather than the exception. Instead of looking at one specialty, you need to become a multispecialist who can make different applications of your knowledge. Young people entering the work force need to bring creativity and imaginative reasoning to their jobs as well as an adventuresome willingness to accept risks and failures while bouncing back to try again. Your first challenge is to assess your preferences and interests. Then you can select a career pathway from the more than 50 careers in teaching, fitness, athletics, sport management, sports marketing, and sports communication. After matching your aspirations and abilities with the career characteristics, you can select one or more as the focus for your college preparation and life's work.

RICHARD WILLIAM FAIR

General Manager
Lifestyle Health Spa and Fitness Center
Raleigh, North Carolina

EDUCATION

B.A., Physical Education, Catawba College (1980)
M.A., Physical Education with an emphasis in Sport Administration, University of North Carolina, Chapel Hill (1984)

JOB RESPONSIBILITIES, HOURS, AND SALARY RANGE

Rick recruits new members through various marketing and sales approaches and promotes their adherence to the Nautilus and aerobic exercise programs that he oversees. In administration, he is responsible for budgeting, advertising, personnel, and the publication of a monthly newsletter. Work hours for this career range between

9:00 A.M. and 9:00 P.M. Monday through Friday with the exact hours varying daily. Salaries range between $20,000 and $30,000.

SPECIALIZED COURSE WORK, DEGREES, AND WORK EXPERIENCES NEEDED FOR THIS CAREER

Individuals interested in this career need to take exercise physiology, business management, human behavior, and organizational behavior. Degrees in both business and physical education are important, because the fitness industry is a business with fitness as the product. Second, the individual must understand the product to promote or to sell it. Rick recommends obtaining part-time instructor positions in a fitness facility. These can provide opportunities to gain a strong knowledge of total fitness and its related components, an understanding of sales and marketing strategies, and management training with an emphasis in organizational and communicative skills important for success in this career.

SATISFYING ASPECTS OF THIS CAREER

Physical educators who choose this non-traditional career can positively influence adults who, through exercise, may develop healthy lifestyles. By having well-equipped and aesthetically pleasing exercise environments and opportunities to meet and to work out with others having similar interests, these adults are often motivated to maintain their fitness patterns throughout their lives. Once these adults have been personally convinced of the lasting benefits of fitness, they may in turn influence their families and co-workers. Rick enjoys helping people to understand and to regard physical fitness as a part of their lives. As a manager, he also takes pleasure in seeing the implementation of ideas into long-term successes for the program.

JOB POTENTIAL

This career offers good potential for promotion, especially if the individual is willing to move to where the jobs are open, usually in urban areas, although most cities with a population greater than 40,000 have at least one health club. Since security may be directly proportional to the results of continual new member recruitment, sales skills are imperative for success in this career.

ADVICE TO STUDENTS

Rick suggests that individuals interested in this career get experience prior to graduation to develop an understanding of the business. He cautions not to allow the salary potential to have too great an influence on deciding whether or not to choose this career. In addition, he recommends that students be extremely goal-oriented by setting high but realistically attainable goals, to believe in themselves, and never to give up.

REVIEW QUESTIONS

1. What are several factors that may influence one's career choice?
2. What factors may outweigh the importance of one's salary?
3. What are several non-traditional careers that involve teaching?
4. What are several careers in professional sports?
5. What are the responsibilities of the sports promotions specialist?
6. What are three careers related to the media and sports?
7. What is the job potential for careers in recreational services for senior citizens?
8. What are two types of industrial fitness and recreation programs?
9. What is the availability of coaching positions in the schools?
10. What are the major differences between the responsibilities of athletic directors at small colleges and at large universities?

STUDENT ACTIVITIES

1. Complete the self-assessment inventories in Boxes 5–1 and 5–2.
2. Write a three- to five-page essay describing your professional and personal goals.
3. Make a list of your strengths and weaknesses as they relate to your career aspirations.
4. Compile a list of the abilities and characteristics needed for success in your prospective career.
5. Talk with one person in a career that (1) you think you definitely would like to pursue; (2) you think you might like to pursue; (3) you know little or nothing about.

REFERENCES

Dougherty, N. J. (Ed.). *Physical education and sport for the secondary school student*. Reston, Virginia: American Alliance for Health, Physical Education, Recreation and Dance, 1983.

Fordham, S. L., and Leaf, C. A. *Physical education and sports: an introduction to alternative careers*. New York: John Wiley and Sons, 1978.

Lopiano, D. A. How to pursue a sport management career. *Journal of Physical Education, Recreation and Dance*, 55, 15–19, September 1984.

Priest, L., and Summerfield, L. Careers in commercial and private recreation. *ERIC Clearinghouse on Teacher Education*, February 1983.

1983 Women's sports careers guide. Women's Sport Foundation and Women's Sports Magazine.

SUGGESTED READINGS

Baun, W. B., and Landgreen, M. A. Tenneco health and fitness: a corporate program committed to evaluation. *Journal of Physical Education, Recreation and Dance, 54*, 40–41, October 1983. The key to the attainment of the Tenneco Health and Fitness program's six objectives lies in employees' individually measured and analyzed results as personal improvement leads to exercise adherence.

Clayton, R. D., and Clayton, J. A. Careers and professional preparation programs. *Journal of Physical Education, Recreation and Dance, 55*, 44–45, May/June 1984. Careers in education, fitness, medical specialties, rehabilitation, and therapy, sales, management, performance, and communication are available to students graduating with health, physical education, recreation, and dance degrees.

Hopps, D. S. What can I do and where can I go? adventures in student employment. *NIRSA Journal, 7*, 18–20, Spring 1983. Students seeking to earn a little pocket money while learning skills and gaining experience may choose to work in intramurals in five levels of job responsibility.

Lambert, C. Career directions. *Journal of Physical Education, Recreation and Dance, 55*, 40–43, 53, May/June 1984. The author provides data about and insights into a variety of careers that currently exist or that will become available for physical educators, and offers strategies for career planning, assessing interests and attitudes, and obtaining a job.

Lopiano, D. A. How to pursue a sport management career. *Journal of Physical Education, Recreation and Dance, 55*, 15–19, September 1984. Before embarking on a sports management career, students need a properly focused education, work experiences, including voluntary jobs, interactions with various employers, and to develop "people" skills.

Samuels, J. B. JOBS in unexpected places: a pattern for the 80s. *Parks and Recreation, 17*, 53–54, 58, May 1983. The number of job opportunities is increasing in recreation and leisure services for candidates who will gain experience through internships after learning programming, management, and interpersonal skills.

Shyne, K. David Costill: human performance is his business. *The Physician and Sportsmedicine, 11*, 185–187, 191, March 1983. David Costill, director of the Human Performance Laboratory at Ball State University and leader in exercise physiology research as applied to athletics, always tries to interpret the results of his meticulous research for athletes and the general public.

Sylvester, N. Marketing fitness: sell the imagery not the agony. *Athletic Business, 8*, 8, 10, 12, 14, 16, July 1984. Fitness, a rapidly expanding business, should not take its successes for granted but needs to use the image of happy customers to create future membership sales.

VanderZwaag, H. J., and Sheehan, T. J. *Introduction to sport studies.* Dubuque, Iowa: Wm. C. Brown Company Publishers, 1978. In acknowledgement of the increasing interest in the study of sports, this book describes what sports are, how they should be studied, using sociological, philosophical, historical, psychological, and physiological perspectives, and how this understanding of sports can be applied in various careers.

Wicks, B. Physical fitness programs in business and industry. *NIRSA Journal, 7*, 31–36, Winter 1983, Increasingly, physical fitness programs emphasizing cardiovascular fitness, strength, and flexibility are being offered to all company employees, rather than just to executives.

Preparation for a Career

KEY
CONCEPTS

- Establishing short-term and long-term goals directs career development.
- Course work required for a liberal arts education with a physical education major varies by institution and career.
- Extracurricular activities and volunteer work in physical education-related jobs offer important learning experiences and preparation for careers.
- Certification in athletic officiating, aquatics, first aid, exercise testing, and/or coaching improves professional credentials for employment.
- Graduate programs provide opportunities for advanced study in specialized areas.
- Leaders need certain qualities that will contribute to their effectiveness.
- Getting a job after preparing academically and experientially involves writing a resume, learning about job openings, interviewing, and convincing the prospective employer that you are the person to hire.

Behavior is based on knowledge. Thus far, you have learned about physical education's objectives, disciplinary content, and professional structure. Now, with a career pathway selected, you are getting ready to learn more about your work. The information in this chapter should help you get the most out of your college years. As you grow in knowledge about physical education, experience varied activities in the field, obtain certifications, and develop leadership qualities, you are not just joining a profession; you are becoming a professional. This will demonstrate itself by your commitment to learning and your desire to develop your capabilities to their fullest.

THE CHALLENGE

Everyone's existence depends on self-worth. All of us have varying degrees of this basic need that relate directly to our personal levels of happiness. Goal-setting helps us to assess abilities and interests and establishes immediate and future expectations.

Short-term goals are changes or accomplishments that can be brought about within a day, week, month, or other not-too-distant time period. Examples include attending a weekend workshop, starting a personal exercise program, or joining a professional association. It is important that short-term goals are readily achievable, positively reinforcing, and related to or leading to the attainment of long-term goals.

Short-term goals that are realistic and achievable motivate without creating stress and frustration. Long-term goals, by definition, usually take longer to accomplish and often are larger in scope than the short-term goals that constitute them. Essential within goal-setting is continual self-assessment and reestablishment of goals as interests and aspirations change.

What are your career goals? What can you learn and do *now* to promote the attainment of your goals? Use Box 6–1 to assist you in answering these questions.

BOX 6–1
GOAL-SETTING

Example

Career objective: To become a soccer coach at a large university; to build and maintain the team as one of the top 10 squads in the nation.

Long-term goal: 1) To become a high school soccer coach

Short-term goals: 1) To volunteer to coach a youth soccer team
                    2) To read two books about coaching soccer
                    3) To attend a weekend coaches' clinic
                    4) To attend two college soccer games and write analyses of the offensive and defensive strategies employed

Career objectives:

Long-term goals	Short-term goals
1)	1)
	2)
	3)
2)	1)
	2)
	3)
3)	1)
	2)
	3)
4)	1)
	2)
	3)
5)	1)
	2)
	3)

EDUCATIONAL BACKGROUND

Academic success in college can greatly facilitate the achievement of goals and the response to the challenge of enhancing our self-worth as a contributing member of society. Try to benefit from these chances to learn. That does not mean that all you need to do is to study, although this certainly is vital.

Everyone needs to develop the basic academic competencies of reading, writing, speaking, listening, mathematics, reasoning, studying, and computer literacy (*Academic Preparation*, 1983). Basic academic competencies and general education course work constitute most liberal arts programs through which institutions provide students a broad knowledge base for their lives and careers. Advocates of a liberal arts education think that all students should be educated to function effectively in a diversified and ever-changing society regardless of their career choice. Such an education potentially helps the research scientist interact with the practitioner, assists the coach in understanding family backgrounds and pressures on athletes, provides insights about other people and their languages in our multicultural society, and develops appreciation for the arts, history, and philosophy.

Some students may fulfill these core requirements by taking a conglomeration of easy or recommended courses without much thought or direction. Whether general education courses are taken during the first 2 years at a junior or community college or throughout a 4-year college program, you should seriously consider your selection and sequence of course work to maximize career preparation.

Your major or specialized studies normally hold greater interest, because they seem to relate more directly to your chosen career. You still need to make a serious commitment to learning the most that you can from each class. Box 6-2 illustrates the typical course work in physical education, although institutional requirements vary.

Other valuable aspects of career preparation are internships and field work. Some majors' programs require students to spend time each week observing in the schools, to participate in a summer cooperative education program, to design practicum experiences for their career choices through independent study courses, or to take a laboratory course that offers practical experiences. Usually, education courses for the prospective teacher require observations and mini-teaching experiences, some as early as the first year in college.

Several curricula allow students to secure paying jobs, such as a recreation leader for a community, a camp counselor, or a sports club instructor, that provide learning experiences and for which college credit is earned. The independent study option allows students to earn college credit for developing a research project or for work experience specific to their areas of interest. Other curricula have experiential courses as a part of their requirements. Each

BOX 6–2
EXAMPLE OF PHYSICAL EDUCATION MAJOR COURSE WORK

Human Anatomy
Human Physiology
History and Principles of Physical Education
Measurement and Evaluation in Physical Education
Motor Learning
Sport Psychology and Sociology
Elementary Physical Education
Biomechanics
Administration of Physical Education and Athletics
Adapted Physical Education
Emergency Care of Injuries and Illnesses
Exercise Physiology
Analysis and Teaching of Sports Skills, such as basketball, volleyball, soccer, softball, track and field, badminton, tennis, weight training, and gymnastics
Coaching Sports

of these options allows students the opportunity to gain valuable experience while they are selecting and preparing for their careers.

RELATED EXPERIENCES

Not every waking hour needs to be spent studying, since some people advocate that more learning occurs during the college years outside the classroom than inside. Whether this hypothesis is factual or not, learning from experience is invaluable. For example, by serving as a team manager, sports official, or event coordinator in intramural and recreational sports, you can learn about personnel management, scheduling, and rules. With a sports club you may get an opportunity to coach and to manage the club's financial affairs. Of course, you can learn many things just by participating in various activities or in athletics.

Officiating opportunities abound in intramurals, within recreation leagues, and in the junior high schools; some colleges offer classes in officiating. These learning experiences may result in advancement into the high school, collegiate, and professional ranks. The National Federation of State High School Associations, through its state associations, requires clinic attendance and written and practical examinations for prospective officials in various sports in its certification process. Following successful completion of these requirements, individuals earn ratings that enable them to officiate high school athletic contests through a booking agent who assigns officials and rates them during games. The most proficient receive the top rankings, earn the honor of calling in championships, and may get an opportunity to move up to the colleges and even to the professional leagues. The Affiliated Boards of Officials of the National Association for Girls and Women in Sport conduct clinics and rate officials for some high school and college sports. Several single-sport organizations, such as the United States Volleyball Association, also train and certify officials for their sports.

Volunteer work merits reemphasis (Henderson, 1985). (See Chapter 5.) Sometimes all the course work possible in a certain subject is not as valuable as experience. Take advantage of as many opportunities as possible by working as a student athletic trainer, a team manager, a youth sport coach, a church-league official, a college newspaper reporter, an usher at an athletic event, a teacher's aide, a timer at a community fun run, an assistant for Special Olympics for handicapped individuals, or a subject in a research study. Any of these experiences may help in selecting a career or in confirming interest in an area. While serving others, these volunteers learn and develop their own abilities. Each time you volunteer to help in a career-related activity, add this to a list of extracurricular activities or record of your experiences.

Officiating is a popular part-time job for both students and physical education professionals.

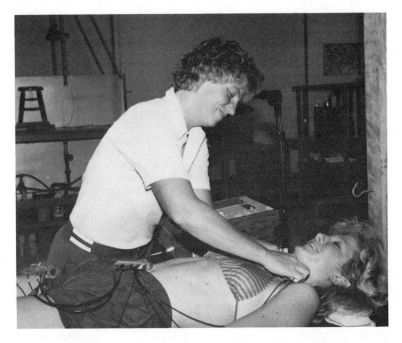

Students can learn about the various applied sciences by volunteering to serve as subjects in research projects and by assisting with data collection.

Later, when you apply for a job, you can include each of these experiences, which may distinguish you from the other candidates, resulting in your selection.

BEGINNING YOUR CAREER INVOLVEMENT

Even while a student, get involved in career-related activities. Most colleges and universities have a Physical Education Majors Club or a similar group that provides this opportunity (Kennedy, 1985). Majors often sponsor faculty-student colloquia, invite leaders in the profession to give presentations, and interact academically and socially. These organizations also frequently organize trips to state, district, and national conventions, where students learn about the profession, hear about current developments, and listen to research reports. Service projects, such as working with Special Olympics, holding Jump Rope for Heart programs, and officiating at sporting events to raise money for charities, are also popular ways for young professionals to help

Conventions offer opportunities for professional enrichment and growth as well as settings for learning about the latest developments in equipment and facilities. (Courtesy of the American Alliance for Health, Physical Education, Recreation and Dance)

others by sharing their expertise, and, at the same time, they gain valuable experience.

An important aspect of professional growth is obtaining one or more certifications. For those who choose a career in athletic training, certification is strongly recommended, if not required. The National Athletic Trainers' Association (NATA) grants certification in two ways (*Certification Information for Athletic Trainers*). The first requires completion of an approved undergraduate (see Box 6–3) or graduate athletic training curriculum, presentation of a competency evaluation checklist from a certified athletic trainer, certification in standard first aid and cardiopulmonary resuscitation or emergency medical technician equivalent, and passing the NATA Certification Exam. The internship method requires completion of specified course work (in the absence of an approved curriculum), fulfillment of the other requirements as stated above, and letters of recommendation from the supervising NATA-certified trainer and the team physician following a minimum of 1800 hours of on the job training with them during a period of 2 to 6 years. Some states require only a minimal amount of academic course work, practical experience, and attendance at clinics to qualify as an athletic trainer in a high school.

The American Red Cross offers the Water Safety Instructor's program to

---

BOX 6-3
UNDERGRADUATE ATHLETIC TRAINING CURRICULUM

Human Anatomy
Human Physiology
Physiology of Exercise
Applied Anatomy and/or Kinesiology
Psychology
First Aid (including cardiopulmonary resuscitation)
Nutrition
Adapted Physical Education
Personal, Community, or School Health
Basic Athletic Training
Advanced Athletic Training
Clinical Experience (800 clock hours) distributed over a period of at
    least 2 academic years under the supervision of a qualified clinical
    instructor in an acceptable clinical setting.

---

individuals who currently hold an Advanced Lifesaving certificate and who attend class for at least 35 hours. This certification enables a person to lifeguard and to teach swimming classes. The American Red Cross also offers certifications in first aid and cardiopulmonary resuscitation and in lifeguarding.

The American College of Sports Medicine offers Exercise Testing Technologist, Exercise Specialist, Program Director, and Fitness Leader certification programs (*Certification Programs*). The first of these, for example, requires a 6-hour written test on exercise physiology, graded exercise testing, and knowledge of basic electrocardiography. The practicum exam in six stations measures knowledge about case studies and standards of the graded exercise test, patient orientation and preparation for exercise electrocardiography, blood pressure monitoring and operation of the graded exercise test mode, electrocardiographic recording and monitoring of graded exercise test responses, emergency preparedness and responses, and electrocardiogram interpretation. Some colleges and universities offer certification in fitness, too, as shown in Box 6-4.

Coaching certifications, such as the American Coaching Effectiveness Program (ACEP), are currently available in some colleges and through nonschool agencies. In ACEP's level 1 clinic, prospective and current youth sport coaches are provided an overview of coaching philosophy, sport pedagogy, sport psychology, sport physiology, and sports medicine. Completion of the 10-hour clinic and a written test and attendance at a 6-hour sport-specific clinic lead

BOX 6–4
PUBLIC/PRIVATE FITNESS CERTIFICATE

The Public/Private Fitness Certificate incorporates basic knowledge of business and management with the scientific and clinical knowledge of exercise physiology, human chemistry, psychology, and nutrition. These graduates work in a wide range of enterprises, including public, private, and corporate fitness programs and various wellness and rehabilitation programs.

Computers and Computing
Programming for Leisure
Introduction to Human Relations in Business
Principles of Management
Survey of Organic Chemistry
Biochemistry
EKG Principles and Interpretation
Life-style Management
Nutrition for Fitness and Sport
Test and Exercise Prescription for Fitness Specialists
Directed Field Work

to certification. The level 2 program provides a more in-depth exposure to these same topics and sports law and time management.

Minors focus on minimal course work taken in a particular area in addition to the major. For school teachers this may be in math, science, or history, thus improving credentials for obtaining a job.

For the non-traditional teacher, minors may include course work in exercise science, nutrition, or business. Often, minors can help prepare a student for advanced study; for example, a student might complete a major in physical education with a minor in business, prior to seeking a master's degree in sport management.

GRADUATE EDUCATION

Your career objective may require advanced study in physical education or one of its allied sciences at an accredited institution. Master's degree programs usually take 1 to 2 years to complete; doctoral degree programs require 2 to 4 years beyond the master's degree. A Master of Science (M.S.), Master of

Arts (M.A.), Master of Physical Education (M.P.E.), Master of Education (M.Ed.)., and Master of Arts in Teaching (M.A.T.) are the typical offerings. They normally require 30 to 36 semester hours for completion, although the actual course work taken varies from institution to institution. The M.S., M.A., and M.P.E. degrees generally emphasize more discipline-oriented study and may allow for specialization in exercise physiology, athletic training, sport management or another emphasis, as shown in Box 6–5. Completion of these degrees requires a master's thesis, an original research project, or an internship in addition to a comprehensive examination. Oriented toward education and teaching, the M.Ed. and the M.A.T. degrees lead to advanced certification for individuals working in the schools and usually require a practicum experience. Many institutions offer certifications in advanced study beyond the master's degree in special education, supervision, counseling, and administration.

BOX 6–5
*MASTER'S DEGREE SPECIALIZATIONS**

Athletic Training
Human Anatomy for Athletic Trainers
Management of Athletic Injuries
Sports Medicine Analysis: Special Problems Related to Sports
Clinical Methods in Athletic Training
Practicum in Athletic Training
Physiology of Exercise
Data Analysis in Physical Education
Research Techniques in Physical Education
Thesis (6 hours)

Exercise Physiology

Physiology of Exercise
Assessment of Physiological Functions in Exercise or Adult Fitness/Cardiac Rehabilitation
Seminar in Exercise Physiology
Practicum in Exercise Physiology
Data Analysis in Physical Education
Research Techniques in Physical Education
Electives (6 hours)
Thesis (6 hours)

(continues)

(concluded)

Human Performance

Sport Psychology
Motor Learning
Physiology of Exercise
Analysis of Human Motion
Data Analysis in Physical Education
Research Techniques in Physical Education
Electives (6 hours)
Thesis (6 hours)

Motor Learning

Sport Psychology
Motor Learning
Information Processing and Motor Control
Analysis of Human Motion
Adapted Physical Education
Data Analysis in Physical Education
Research Techniques in Physical Education
Electives (3 hours)
Thesis (6 hours)

Sport Administration

Administration of Physical Education and Sports
Organizational and Personnel Issues
Practicum in Sport Administration
Social Issues in Physical Education and Sport
Data Analysis in Physical Education
Research Techniques in Physical Education
Electives (6 hours)
Thesis (6 hours)

Sport Psychology

Sport Psychology
Applied Sport Psychology
Motor Learning
Social Issues in Physical Education and Sport
Data Analysis in Physical Education
Research Techniques in Physical Education
Electives (6 hours)
Thesis (6 hours)

* University of North Carolina at Chapel Hill

One important component of graduate education is participation in research projects.

The highest academic degrees are the Doctor of Philosophy (Ph.D.), the Doctor of Education (Ed. D.), and the Doctor of Physical Education (D.P.E.). The Ph.D. is oriented toward research in a specialty such as exercise physiology, sport history, sport management, teacher education, sport psychology, motor development, or adapted physical education, but it also can be awarded for studies in curriculum and instruction, educational administration, or educational psychology. The focus of most Ed.D. course work is education with physical education, health, or another field of study being only one segment of the program. General course work in physical education, combined with an area of specialized research, is the focus of the D.P.E.

Before deciding whether to enroll in a prospective graduate program, determine whether advanced education is needed in your career. If so, then you may want to find out which accredited universities offer the type of program that meets your needs. For example, only eight institutions offer a specialization in athletic training at the master's degree level. Although some institutions require an area of specialization for a master's degree, others offer a general physical education program.

Most admission requirements include an undergraduate degree in physical education or at least specific course work, a minimum of a 3.0 (on a 4.0 scale) grade point average, and a better-than-average score on the Graduate Record Examination (GRE). Since institutions are free to set their own admissions' standards, review the institutions that offer the program desired. Libraries house catalogs of most leading institutions, or you may write for information. Applications should be completed during the middle of the senior year or at least 6 months prior to the expected entrance date. Required admissions materials include college transcript(s), letters of recommendation, application forms, and test scores, such as GRE results.

For careers that do not require an advanced degree, additional and ongoing training is beneficial. Employers sometimes provide this on the job; otherwise, employees need to attend workshops, conferences, or continuing education classes. Keep current with and stimulated by career changes and developments. These often result in greater job productivity and can lead to career advancement.

LEADERSHIP QUALITIES

In addition to a career choice and a commitment to continual job training and enrichment, leadership qualities, if incorporated into the job performance, can benefit both you and those you serve (Blanchard & Johnson, 1982).

The idea that "the buck stops here" refers to who decides and who is responsible for a decision—that is, *accountability*. A leader must examine the pros and cons in each situation and then make the decision that is best for all concerned or appropriate in that situation. Leaders accept responsibility for their decisions, whether correct or incorrect. Employees who are unwilling to take risks and to assume responsibility but who are willing to give orders are quickly judged as ineffective. Likewise, individuals who fail to weigh all the necessary factors prior to making a decision receive poor evaluations. Exercise leaders in a corporate fitness program must assess the physical limitations and capabilities of participants prior to prescribing activity because they will be held responsible if an inappropriate program leads to injury. Coaches must be accountable to their athletes, as described in the "Bill of Rights for Athletes" in Box 6–6.

Related to accountability is *decisiveness*. Good leaders realize that the moment of absolute certainty may never occur when faced with tough decisions; therefore, they must be willing to act, state, or direct based on the information they have. Lack of decisive judgment may result in a disaster, such as failing to start cardiopulmonary resuscitation after a near-drowning or moving an athlete following a neck injury before medical help arrives. Preventing a par-

---

BOX 6–6
*BILL OF RIGHTS FOR ATHLETES**

1. Right to participate in sports regardless of age, sex, or ability level;
2. Right to participate in sports that promote safety and health;
3. Right of participants to share in the leadership and decision-making of their sport;
4. Right to be treated with respect contingent on reciprocal attitudes toward others in sport;
5. Right to an equal opportunity to strive to attain their personal aspirations through sport;
6. Right to have fun through sport.

---

ent-official confrontation at a Little League game may result from a recreation leader's decision to train better officials and to educate parents during the preseason. This, too, is decisive behavior.

Commitment and dedication are critical in career selection and job fulfillment. For example, you may emphasize how much you enjoy working with children or with senior citizens, yet have no experience to verify this. Volunteer work as a youth sport coach or in a retirement home would reinforce the stated desire to work with these groups. Other illustrations of dedication are willingness to accept part-time jobs to prove interests and capabilities and agreement to attend workshops and clinics to develop further skills and to improve knowledge.

Enthusiasm for a job, about one's abilities, and for life in general is an infectious quality. Every career demands a degree of this; those that include personal interactions between leaders and followers benefit from an abundance. Enthusiastic individuals believe in the product, whether it is a fitness program, a tennis racket, or employees. Through positive reinforcement and constant interaction with personnel, clients, patients, and students, participants share their leader's excitement. The greatest resource for every leader is people, and enthusiasm promotes their greatest involvement.

Leaders should be secure in their roles and not feel threatened by others. If a threat does exist, *friendliness* is often lost or never demonstrated. Effective leaders can make decisions and give orders without appearing bossy, dictatorial, uncaring, rigid, or snobbish. School teachers, YMCA and YWCA directors, coaches, health club instructors, and others in physical education-related careers must realize the essentiality of communicating with the individuals they serve to meet their needs. Friendliness to groups of senior citizens, to overweight corporate executives, to elementary school children, and to athletes in the Special Olympics shows a genuine respect for individual capabilities and a willingness to help others reach their unique goals.

Many leaders possess a readily evident charisma. Since they look *healthy* and actively pursue fitness for themselves, others may simply follow them. Their practices speak louder than words. The teacher who never leads exercises or demonstrates skills earns little respect from program participants. The vibrant individual is able to handle the pressures of decision making and usually is also more patient with the foibles of others.

Integrity is a must when serving others. Coaches who forbid their athletes to question officials, yet who constantly berate and argue with those same officials are not demonstrating the same behavior they are expecting. "The YMCA Youth Sports Philosophy" (see Box 6–7) is an excellent example of integrity related to this association's programs for youth. Athletic trainers must honestly assess injuries regardless of the pressures of the competitive situation and the wishes of the athlete and the coach. When selling memberships, health club employees should never mislead people about the services and facilities available.

Several of the qualities already discussed relate to *respecting others*. Individuals who disregard or are insensitive to the feelings of people are assured

---

BOX 6–7
THE YMCA YOUTH SPORTS PHILOSOPHY

The essential elements of good competitive sports philosophy for coaching young players:

Know your motives for coaching. Think about what you expect to gain from your coaching experience. Make sure your principles of coaching are compatible with the philosophy of the total program.

Make your own education a priority. Take advantage of every opportunity available to learn more about coaching techniques, teaching skills, and helping players set personal goals and reach for them.

Work with every player on your team. The most highly skilled and least skilled members of your team should be given equal attention. It is more important that all athletes participate and have fun than that a few good athletes dominate the action.

Work on basic skills and teach good physical fitness habits. Teach the skills and concentrate on the basics. Help athletes become conscious of the importance of proper execution without interfering excessively.

Demonstrate the importance of fitness habits such as warm-up and

(continues)

conditioning exercises. ·Talk to your players about diet, rest, and involvement in other sports and activities.

Use positive reinforcement as often as possible. Early successes are essential for developing self-confidence. Peer recognition and acceptance are very important.

Teach fair play. Competing fairly is an essential part of competitive sports. It is a set of attitudes which include:

- Respect for oneself; taking responsibility for one's own behavior and learning.
- Respect for one's teammates; working to become a team member who unselfishly contributes to the good of the whole team.
- Respect for the other team; considering the other team as an essential partner in competition.
- Respect for the rules and the officials who uphold them.

Emphasize both learning skills and sportsmanship, accepting both winning and losing, respecting the officials, cooperating, always giving one's best effort, and having fun.

Help players set and evaluate individual goals. Competing against oneself is perhaps the best way to improve skills. Help players measure their skills, set goals for the future, and work to reach their goals.

Keep winning in perspective. Winning games and matches is one of the many important goals in sports. Help competitors (and parents) become aware of other important goals: learning skills; becoming more fit; being a good leader sometimes, a good follower other times; dealing with the emotions of sport; and having fun.

Encourage lifetime involvement in sports and physical activity. More importantly, regular cardiovascular exercise is essential to continued physical well-being.

Work with the whole person: body, mind, and spirit. Physical fitness is important, but so are mental attitudes and spiritual growth. Youth sports programs should emphasize holistic individual development.

Make sure that equipment and facilities meet safety standards and are appropriate to the age of players. Emphasis should be given to safety in teaching techniques and elements of play.

Involve the whole family. Parents should be viewed as participants rather than as spectators. They should be included as coaches and officials, in special activities, and encouraged to get involved in the sport as a family.

Encourage skilled volunteer leadership by all participants. Volunteers are crucial to youth sports programs. Players, parents, and others should be encouraged to share responsibility for sports programs and to get involved in service opportunities in other community programs as well.

of failure. The best way to show respect for others is to listen to their concerns. This does not require following their suggestions, but it does necessitate a sensitivity to their ideas. Aerobics instructors will lose students rapidly if they provide workouts for themselves rather than for their frequently unfit participants.

Successful leaders need to be *self-directed* or *self-motivated*. If you must constantly receive instructions about how and when to fulfill your responsibilities, you are a follower, not a leader. Self-discipline helps the leader separate the trivial from the significant. The self-motivated person observes the situation, sees the need for action, decides on the course to pursue, and ensures the proper outcome. For example, an intramural coordinator notices that participation is decreasing. A meeting of sport managers is called to assess the reasons for the decline. They recommend a change from trophies to T-shirts for winners of events. The coordinator publicizes the change, and immediately the entries increase. By respecting the opinions of others and taking action, the coordinator was able to correct the problem. A leader must also take action even when that action will be unpleasant. This may mean firing an unproductive employee, insisting that a youth coach play all the team members every game according to league rules, or suspending an athlete because a team rule was violated.

The leader must also possess a *technical mastery* of the program being directed. This does not mean knowing how to do each job better than those being supervised, being a superior athlete, being more fit, or being a better salesperson. Rather, it implies that the leader understands each individual's responsibility and how these responsibilities work together to accomplish group goals. For example, athletic directors seldom collect tickets, sell concessions, or manage facilities, yet they must know the duties of the people they hire and must see that all fulfill his or her responsibilities.

Leaders emphasize high performance, communicate the consequences of high and low performances, and concentrate on improving their personal performances. They recognize and reward, both personally and tangibly, high performances. Goal-setting on personal and group levels is an imperative for successful leaders. Creative thinking, such as developing new ideas and encouraging risk-taking, is another leadership characteristic. Leaders also delegate responsibility and decision-making authority, solve conflicts, and coordinate group efforts.

GETTING A JOB

While you are still a first- or second-year college student, it is important to investigate the job market by talking with older students, faculty members, or individuals in the career(s) you are considering, maybe by asking them the questions listed in Box 6–8. Reflect on their responses as you continue to narrow or to broaden your career possibilities. Quite helpful in this endeavor is maximizing your education. By carefully selecting your elective courses, you may be able to obtain a minor, or a double major, or be able to specialize in some area, such as adapted physical education or business. Through certain courses you may qualify for an internship, a summer field work experience, or a part-time job or have an opportunity to gain valuable experience as a volunteer in sports information, sports medicine, or athletics.

Be sure during your college years to take advantage of your institution's resources. Most college libraries have materials on market trends, career guidance, and opportunities for advanced education. Counseling or guidance personnel offer career aptitude testing, assistance in resume writing, and hints for interviews. Files of available jobs are available at placement centers, and the career counselors there often schedule interviews with prospective employers.

As a junior or senior taking primarily major courses, you need to emphasize learning as much as possible about your career while maintaining quality

---

BOX 6–8
POSSIBLE QUESTIONS TO ASK ABOUT YOUR PROSPECTIVE CAREER

1. What is the educational background required?
2. How much prior experience is needed?
3. What are the typical hours?
4. What are the starting and average salaries?
5. How much vacation time is provided?
6. What are the fringe benefits?
7. To what extent will this job affect my personal life?
8. What are the requisite skills and knowledge for this job?
9. What personal characteristics, such as creativity, problem-solving ability, or enthusiasm, are necessary for this job?
10. What is the potential for employment in this career?
11. In what regions or states is this job available?
12. What is the potential for advancement in this career?
13. Is on-the-job training or advanced education required to maintain employment or to advance in this career?
14. What are the specific work responsibilities of this type of job? How much time is spent doing each?
15. How and on what criteria is job performance evaluated?
16. What are the most satisfying aspects of this job?
17. What are the most frustrating aspects of this job?

BOX 6-9
SAMPLE RESUME FOR A PROSPECTIVE TEACHER
Lewis Ray Knight

School Address:	**Permanent Address:**
1234 Drake Lane	567 Swinging Bridge Boulevard
Columbus, Florida 38281	Norlina, Texas 72802
Phone: (915) 437-4921	Phone: (173) 548-2183

Career Objectives: To teach physical education in a junior high school and to coach basketball

Education: University of Miami, Miami, Florida, May 1986
Bachelor of Arts in Physical Education

Experience: Student Teacher, East Junior High School, Miami, Florida (Spring 1986)
Teacher's Aide, West Junior High School, Miami, Florida (Fall 1985)
Miami Boys' Club volunteer basketball coach (1982–1986)
Counselor at Norlina, Texas, summer sports camp (1983–1985)

Honors and Awards: Residence Hall Intramural Manager of the Year (1985)
Dean's List (Fall 1983)

College Activities: Chairperson of the Social Committee of the Physical Education Majors' Club (1984–1985)
Intramural and Boys' Club basketball official (1982–1986)
Intramural participant in basketball, touch football, softball, and tennis (1982–1986)

Personal Data: Student member of the American Alliance for Health, Physical Education, Recreation and Dance
Hobbies include water skiing, video games, and reading
Available for employment June 1986

References: Available from the Placement Office, University of Miami

BOX 6–10
SAMPLE RESUME FOR A PROSPECTIVE CORPORATE FITNESS LEADER
Mary Ann Smith

School Address:
88923 Amigo Drive
Northridge, California 90324
Phone: (482) 901-4413

Permanent Address:
12-7421 Langley Road
San Antonia, California 97181
Phone: (433) 821-0431

Career Objective: To develop or to implement a corporate executive fitness program, utilizing skills in exercise prescription

Education: California State University, Northridge, California, May 1986
Bachelor of Science in Physical Education (with an emphasis in exercise science)

Experience: Intern as an exercise leader with Johnson & Johnson Company in Newark, New Jersey (Summer 1985)
• Designed an aerobics program for 125 employees
• Organized a family-oriented fun run
• Initiated a company-wide incentive program for weight reduction

Volunteer at Redwood Convalescent Center, Northwest, California (1983–1984)
• Developed a recreation program for non-ambulatory patients

Salesperson, The Sports Shop, Northwest, California (1984–1985)

College Activities: Vice-President of University's Racquetball Club (1985–1986)
Member of Physical Education Majors' Club (1983–1986)
Volunteer assistant in department's exercise physiology laboratory (1983–1986)

Special Skills: Certified as an Exercise Testing Technologist (American College of Sports Medicine)
Certified in first aid and cardiopulmonary resuscitation

(continues)

(concluded)

Affiliations:	Student member of the American College of Sports Medicine
	Student member of the American Alliance for Health, Physical Education, Recreation and Dance

References:

Mr. Robert L. Sams
Director of Fitness
Johnson & Johnson
  Company
Newark, New Jersey
  07508

Ms. Patricia S.
  Wheeler
Director of Patient
  Services
Redwood
  Convalescent
  Center
Northwest, California
  97181

Dr. Raymond W. Allen
Director of Exercise Physiology Laboratory
Department of Physical Education
California State University
Northridge, California 90324

BOX 6–11
SAMPLE JOB INTERVIEW QUESTIONS

1. What type of job are you seeking?
2. Why did you choose your major and your college or university?
3. How has your education prepared you for work in this career?
4. What are your long-term and short-term career goals?
5. What opportunities do you see for yourself in this career?
6. In what type of environment are you most comfortable?
7. What are your experiences and skills relevant to the job you are seeking?
8. What are your greatest strengths?
9. What are your weaknesses?
10. What motivates you to put forth your best effort?
11. What leadership skills do you have?
12. What kind of salary do you expect to receive?
13. Do you work well under pressure?
14. What do you see yourself doing in 5 years?
15. Why do you think you might like to have this particular job?

work. With competition for some jobs intense due to the large number of applicants, many recruiters refuse to interview anyone who has a low academic average (less than a 3.0). Extracurricular activities can strengthen your social, intellectual, and physical abilities as well as impress employers. The most desirable background is an internship in your prospective career. This may be as a part-time job, an independent study for college credit, or work as a volunteer, but it is vital.

During your senior year, you need to go to your institution's placement office and establish a file. This placement file includes a resume such as those illustrated in Boxes 6–9 and 6–10 and letters of recommendation. A resume emphasizes strengths, such as academic performance and honors, all work experiences with career-related ones highlighted, extracurricular activities, and personal information. It should be prepared in a professional manner and updated as needed. At least three letters of recommendation should be obtained: one or more from teachers, one or more from former employers, and one from a person who knows you personally or who has observed you in some extracurricular activity. You should send your placement files to all prospective employers, even when you inquire about only a possible job opening.

It has been said that "it's not what you can do, but who you know," since many good jobs are obtained because of personal contacts. Why not let this happen to you? Notify friends, relatives, former employers, and other people that you have met that you are looking for a job. Follow up on all leads, because it also is said that sometimes getting a good job results from "being in the right place at the right time." This includes initiating contact with anyone you think can help you.

Prior to an interview, find out all you can about the job. This may include learning about the employing organization, the boss, the job responsibilities, or the job's special needs. In other words, let your knowledge about the job impress the person conducting the interview that you want the job and that you are the best applicant. It is helpful to prepare for the interview by formulating answers to the often-asked questions listed in Box 6–11. Since first impressions are critical, dress professionally for the appointment, and arrive well ahead of the scheduled time. During the interview, project a positive image by showing that you believe in your abilities and have something to offer. Sell yourself without being aggressive.

SUMMARY

As a young professional, begin now to set short-term and long-term goals to help focus career aspirations. Make a personal commitment to getting the most out of your college education, both general and major courses. Choose several activities that you can participate in, even as a volunteer, to gain valuable experience. Work to attain certifications in your area(s) of interest. Commit yourself to advanced study if this will enhance your job qualifications. Seek to develop the qualities that will contribute to your success. Let these suggestions help you get a job.

FRANCES M. JENKINS

Teacher/Athletic Trainer
Steamboat Springs High School
Steamboat Springs, Colorado

EDUCATION

B.A., Physical Education, Seattle University (1972)
M.A., Physical Education with an emphasis in Athletic Training
University of North Carolina at Chapel Hill (1984)

JOB RESPONSIBILITIES, HOURS, AND SALARY RANGE

Frani teaches high school physical education classes and works with all of her school's teams as an athletic trainer. Normal work hours for professionals who combine these two careers are 8:00 A.M. to 6:00 P.M. Monday through Friday plus evening competitions. Depending on state, school system, years of experience, and educational background, salaries for individuals in similar positions range from a beginning salary of $12,000 to $32,000 for those with master's degrees and many years' teaching experience in affluent school districts.

SPECIALIZED COURSE WORK, DEGREES, AND WORK EXPERIENCE NEEDED FOR THIS CAREER

In addition to specialized sports medicine classes and a physical education undergraduate degree, Frani recommends taking courses in sport psychology, chemistry, and nutrition and keeping up-to-date on research. Depending on an individual's career goals, a master's degree may be required for advancement. A physical therapy degree would also enhance marketability. Experiences in recreation settings may help prepare students for teaching physical education, and work in physical therapy is valuable for future athletic trainers. Frani stresses that the ability to get along with people is essential in this career. She does not believe that a person has to excel at sports to teach them to others and to analyze another person's performance.

SATISFYING ASPECTS OF THIS CAREER

Athletic trainers take personal satisfaction in helping athletes and other sports enthusiasts recover from injuries and participate again as soon as possible. They also enjoy counseling about fitness training and injury prevention. With increased numbers of first-time through world-class athletes, athletic trainers serve vital roles in keeping all groups happily and safely active. Frani states that working with young people is great, especially when she maintains contact with them after they are out of school and they give her feedback about what she taught them that is useful to them in their lives as adults.

JOB POTENTIAL

As more states pass laws requiring athletic trainers in high schools, the teacher/athletic trainer combination may be the model for many school vacancies in the upcoming years. Initially, physical education majors who graduate with competencies in these two related fields may have to relocate to states that already have passed legislation in this area, such as Texas and North Carolina. College, university, and professional league athletic training positions are more difficult to obtain and usually require national certification (NATA), several years of experience, and advanced degrees. For those patient and willing to wait for the right position, Frani says that the jobs are available, just not plentiful.

ADVICE TO STUDENTS

Frani suggests that prospective teachers observe all levels of teaching to get a good overall perspective of the profession. Even serving as a substitute teacher provides a great opportunity for learning. Working under a well-qualified, certified athletic trainer is imperative for those interested in gaining valuable experience. She states that it is important to stay current by reading and by attending professional meetings, workshops, and seminars.

REVIEW QUESTIONS

1. What are short-term and long-term goals?
2. Why is a general, liberal arts education important?
3. What are the courses that constitute most physical education major programs?
4. How can you get certified to officiate a high school sport?
5. Why is a minor valuable?

6. What skills must an exercise testing technologist demonstrate to become certified?
7. What are two personal benefits of volunteering while in college?
8. What are two types of activities of Physical Education Majors Clubs?
9. Name and describe five leadership qualities that will enhance your career effectiveness.
10. What are the five most important questions that you should ask about your prospective career?

STUDENT ACTIVITIES

1. Talk with other students who have done volunteer work in intramurals, in athletics, or with a community group or with a business. Ask them about the positive and negative aspects of their experiences.
2. Get involved in one professionally related extracurricular activity for at least one semester. Evaluate your experiences to determine what you learned and how these could help you in the future.
3. Find out about your institution's Physical Education Majors Club and become actively involved with it.
4. Select one certification, such as in officiating, coaching, or first aid, and set short-term and long-term goals for achieving it.
5. Interview individuals in leadership positions in a career that interests you. What qualifications do they stress as most important?

REFERENCES

Academic preparation for college: what students need to know and be able to do. New York: College Entrance Examination Board, 1983.

American College of Sports Medicine. *Certification Programs.*

Blanchard, K., and Johnson, S. *The one minute manager.* New York: William Morrow and Company, Inc., 1982.

Henderson, K. A. Issues and trends in volunteerism. *Journal of Physical Education, Recreation and Dance, 56,* 30–32, January 1985.

Kennedy, C. A. Revitalize your physical education majors' club. *Journal of Physical Education, Recreation and Dance, 56,* 94–95, January 1985.

National Athletic Trainers' Association. *Certification information for athletic trainers.*

SUGGESTED READINGS

Baker, J. A. W., and King, H. A. Leading physical education doctoral programs: what characteristics do they have in common? *Journal of Physical Education, Recreation and Dance, 54,* 51–54, February 1983. Based on opinionnaires completed by fellows of the American Academy of Physical Education and directors of doctoral graduate programs in physical education, the five top-ranked doctoral programs were identified and their notable characteristics described.

Cheffers, J. T. F. Concepts for teacher education in the 80s and 90s. *Proceedings: National Association for Physical Education in Higher Education, 2,* 316–322, 1980. This author lists strategies for the future in teaching, research, planning, making students the center of the process, developing curricula, and committing oneself personally.

Dressel, P. L. Liberal education: developing the characteristics of a liberally educated person. *Liberal Education, 65,* 313–322, Fall 1979. The liberally educated person should learn to acquire and use knowledge, to possess a high-level mastery of the skills of communication, to show awareness of and respect for varying personal values and value commitments, to study, analyze, and formulate with others action-taking solutions to problems, to demonstrate awareness of and accept some responsibility for contemporary events, to seek to accumulate coherent knowledge, and to use these insights to fulfill their obligations as responsible citizens.

Fisher, R., and Ury, W. *Getting to yes: negotiating agreement without giving in.* New York: Penguin Books, 1983. This national bestseller is about how people should deal with their differences by using principled negotiation.

Hage, P. Medical care for athletes: are coaches getting the message? *The Physician and Sportsmedicine, 10,* 159–161, November 1982. Based on a survey of high school coaches, the author concludes that most are familiar with basic sports medicine information, such as treatment of strains, sprains, and heat injuries, and characteristics of pregame meals.

Standards for graduate programs in physical education. *Journal of Physical Education, Recreation and Dance, 55,* 54–62, February 1984. This article lists and interprets the standards for graduate programs in physical education as approved in 1982 by the National Association for Sport and Physical Education.

Taylor, J. L. The resident professor: a leadership role for connecting theory and practice. *Motor Skills: Theory into Practice, 4,* # 1, 51–58, 1980. The author suggests that university faculty who are willing to provide ongoing preservice programs and inservice projects in schools can provide a vital link in applying theory and research.

Wendt, J. Professional preparation: a process of discovery. *Quest, 35,* #2, 182–189, 1983. Four guidelines in professional preparation may hold the key to personal discovery and to developing "human service educators" who can achieve success, feel competent, and be aware of their potential.

Wendt, J. C., Petton, B. C., and Stevens, K. R. The university's role: assessing the professional education needs of health and physical educators and athletic coaches. *Journal of Physical Education, Recreation and Dance, 54,* 48–50, February 1983. Colleges must seek to meet the needs of teachers and coaches who return to continue their education by providing practical inservice workshops, relevant course work, and motivational tools for overcoming lack of interest in professional growth.

Wilson, P. K., and Hall, L. K. Industrial fitness, adult fitness, and cardiac rehabilitation: graduate programs specific to training exercise specialists. *Journal of Physical Education, Recreation and Dance, 55,* 40–44, March 1984. This article lists 18 colleges and universities that offer graduate programs specific to training exercise specialists and briefly describes their program emphases, entrance criteria, and degree requirements.

Seven

Teaching
Physical Skills

KEY
CONCEPTS

- Successful teachers possess communication skills, good interpersonal relationships, motivational ability, leadership abilities, and personal qualities that enhance their effectiveness.
- Teachers directly influence program quality.
- Planning, organizing, and evaluating are essential components of quality teaching in all settings.
- Developing a comprehensive unit plan helps improve the learning environment.
- Program evaluation and self-evaluation are essential for improving instruction and feedback and for meeting students' needs.

Even though you may not plan to teach in a school setting and are pursuing a non-traditional track, many of these jobs, such as a racquetball pro in a club or a corporate fitness leader, require some teaching ability. All teaching requires an understanding of how people learn skills and under what conditions they can learn them most easily and effectively. Students, patients, corporate personnel, club members, and other fitness program consumers expect to learn in their classes. Therefore, instructors in all of these settings should be prepared to meet individuals' needs and to assist them in achieving their goals. This chapter recommends ways to improve teaching skills. A discussion of teacher qualities and contributions illustrates the abilities critical to success.

TEACHER QUALITIES

Whether one is a teaching professional in a club, a public school teacher, a coach, a camp counselor, a college professor, an exercise testing technician, an instructor for a community recreation program, or an activity leader in a retirement home, several abilities can contribute to your teaching effectiveness. Employers in traditional and non-traditional settings often look for the following general characteristics:

1. Healthy life-style and appearance
2. Physical skills
3. Communication skills
4. Ability to form successful interpersonal relationships
5. Dedication and self-discipline
6. Enthusiasm
7. Intellectual ability
8. Interest and enjoyment in helping people learn
9. Motivational ability
10. Leadership ability

It is often true that what you do is far more important than what you say. Students and others, regardless of their ages and ability levels, learn more from how their teachers behave than from verbal instructions. One illustration of this is appearance. If teachers expect their students to dress appropriately for activity and then fail to set a proper example, they will have problems. As the tone-setters for the class, teachers should present themselves as positive role models.

Aligned closely with appearance is healthy behavior: how a person looks reflects whether he or she is committed to a healthy life-style. Overweight, chain-smoking individuals often impact negatively on students in a physical activity setting. This does not mean that only superbly conditioned athletes should teach; rather, since students observe how healthy teachers look, their behaviors may influence whether a similar life-style is adopted.

Two qualities are essential in the area of physical skills. First, exercise leaders should be sufficiently skilled in the activities they teach that their demonstrations are effective. Secondly, teachers need analytical abilities so they can correct improperly executed skills or movements (Logsdon, et al, 1984).

Communication skills are vital to everyone who works directly with people. Often forgotten is listening, an essential in effective communication. Let program participants assess their goals and needs; otherwise, only your input determines class content. Although written lesson plans and evaluations are important, oral communication skills are equally essential. Can you clearly explain how to execute a skill, how to do an activity, and how to correct an error? Vague generalizations are ineffective; specific instructions and feedback are needed. When you are asked to clarify a point, your response should be direct and understandable. If participants recognize a genuine concern on your part, they are more likely to be concerned. Nonverbal communication is also powerful. For example, if teachers want their students to get active as soon as they arrive at class, yet sit until it is time to start class or even arrive late, they are sending a discouraging message.

Qualities that aid interpersonal relationships include empathy, genuineness, respect, and warmth. Empathy, not to be confused with sympathy, refers to the capacity to participate in or understand another's feelings or ideas. Application of this means seeking to find out what is significant to others and basing interactions with them on these. If one person wants to lose weight, another seeks skill development, and a third desires social interaction, the teacher needs to emphasize fitness, drills, and group activities respectively, to meet all three goals. A teacher who demonstrates genuine interest does not pretend but rather is sincere, honest, and consistent. Helping participants set realistic expectations rather than saying that they can achieve the unattainable is an example, and treating all fairly and equitably is another.

Respect means showing concern for all individuals' needs and regarding

Teachers in all settings should serve as role models for healthy-life styles.

BOX 7–1

Sandy, a first-year teacher at West Junior High School, was eager to teach the seventh graders golf in their opening unit of the year. While the second-period class was progressing smoothly, fifth period was a disaster. Every instructional period the first week was interrupted by a student, Jack, who repeatedly stated that his golf pro taught the skill a different way. Initially, the students listened to Sandy and seemingly ignored Jack's comments; yet as the week progressed, a few seemed to question Sandy's knowledge and to ignore his instructions. Sandy allowed Jack to offer his ideas and added that there were often several "right" ways to execute a stroke. Instead of reacting positively to Sandy's statements, Jack became more verbal and derogatory of Sandy's instruction. Over the weekend, Sandy decided to try a different approach. Jack, who was a ranked junior golfer, was asked to demonstrate putting. Although somewhat startled, he agreed. As Jack competently showed how to putt, Sandy asked him to describe his technique. Sandy offered additional advice, making sure to keep Jack in the spotlight but to help the other students understand, too. By Sandy's praise of Jack's golfing ability and use of him as a demonstrator, the antagonistic class atmosphere between Jack and some of the other students and Sandy immediately began to disappear. Sandy and the students learned valuable lessons about being sensitive to others' feelings and about acknowledging others' abilities.

BOX 7–2

The Ridgefield Convalescent Home decided to start a recreational program for its more than 500 residents and hired Marty to initiate it. Marty, who had worked 5 years as an activity instructor in another senior citizens' facility, wanted to implement a similar program at Ridgefield. Fourteen different activities, from shuffleboard to yoga, were planned and announced to the residents. The first week's attendance at all of the activities ranged from zero to three. When questioned by the director about the program's progress, Marty expressed dismay and questioned her ability as an administrator and as a teacher. The director asked whether the residents had been asked about what activities they wanted or about preferred times. Suddenly, Marty realized that the key to a successful program at Ridgefield was to meet the needs of her clientele, not to replicate another program. Based on discussions with each of the residents during the next 3 months, Marty initiated several less strenuous programs, a few innovative activities, and some competitive programs. By the end of 1 year, 75% of the residents were involved in one or more of the recreational programs. The residents' morale was enhanced through the program, since they realized that Marty actually cared about their interests and needs.

their opinions as important and worthy of consideration. While class or program standards are important, deviation is certainly permissible and at times imperative to accommodate these needs. Respect demands that people of both sexes, all races and nationalities, and all economic groups and with various skill levels be treated equally. This does not imply that different activities and challenges cannot be structured, but it requires that fairness and consideration for all be paramount (Bain & Wendt, 1983).

The emotional trait of warmth is an extension of empathy, genuineness, and respect. Exercise leaders in all settings are challenged by poorly executed skill or movements, by apathetic participants, by chronic alibies, and by the need to keep participants motivated. A positive approach helps to overcome these problems. Encouragement and praise can promote activity and fitness. Cooperation among program members can provide for positive reinforcement. If teachers relate to all individuals fairly, courteously, and positively, others will imitate that behavior. Three examples of the importance of interpersonal relationships are illustrated in Boxes 7–1, 7–2, and 7–3.

Dedication and self-discipline indicate a commitment to a goal or a task. The committed instructor willingly gives time and effort because of the desire for learning to occur. Such devotion may even be self-sacrificing in the sense

---

BOX 7–3

The York Chemical Company began its executive fitness programs in 1982. Since that time, attendance had risen sharply as had administrative productivity. Based on these results, the Board of Directors decided to implement a fitness program for its "blue collar workers." Carol and Pete, two of the fitness leaders from the executives' program, were assigned to develop this new program for the 1,000 workers. They were given the use of the company's fitness center except for the 5 hours per day that were already scheduled. Challenges that Carol and Pete had to meet included personnel who worked in three rotating shifts throughout the year, high employee absenteeism, and a general apathy toward fitness. Carol and Pete began their efforts in recruiting program participants by talking with company managers and supervisory personnel. They asked them what types of programs employees would enjoy, when they should be scheduled, and how to motivate the employees to participate. One key to motivation was to get approval from the Board of Directors for flex-time, allowing employees to vary reporting times, leaving times, and meal and break times to allow for exercise. Another motivator was to give a 2-day vacation at Christmas to each employee with a perfect attendance record in the program for the year. A third approach that promoted involvement was to sponsor activities on weekends for employees and their families. Based on these plans, Carol and Pete promoted their programs by talking with employees during breaks and by advertising the programs through posters and bulletins. They provided exercise breaks at the work site, taught classes before, during, and after each shift, and offered employees the kinds of activities they wanted. Student interns helped make possible all of these services at no additional expense to the company. By the end of the second year, the various programs served more than 2,000 people, including families and some employees. Some people participated in more than one activity. Carol and Pete, in hiring two new staff members, stressed the essentiality of motivating employees to adhere to their activity programs because of their improved quality of life.

---

that the instructor's free time is used to help others. Yet many instructors readily respond to such requests because of the intrinsic satisfaction received. Self-discipline certainly contributes to a healthy appearance and to the development of physical skills. In fact, since self-discipline affects an individual's behavior, it may enhance all of the teacher qualities discussed.

Strong excitement or even passion describes enthusiasm. Faked enthusiasm is not genuine and bespeaks hypocrisy and insincerity. A positive teaching style, one component of enthusiastic teaching, includes the use of positive feedback for skillful movement and encourages improvement and effort. It normally leads to greater and even more intense participation, since everyone enjoys and responds to positive reinforcement. Correct tone of voice, body language, and timeliness in changing activities indicate an eagerness to get actively involved. The expectation that not only the activity but also the learning is fun contributes to students' wanting to get involved and to enjoy themselves.

Although teachers need intellectual ability and sound educational backgrounds, application of pedagogical principles overrides multiple degrees or massive research (Rink, 1985). Exercise leaders should read professional literature and attend meetings or workshops to keep abreast of the new developments in sports and activities. They should learn both how to teach skills more effectively and how to analyze movements more accurately.

Teachers' ability to motivate—to stimulate action—comes from an interest

Teachers in various activities and subjects, such as instructing for CPR certification, need effective communication skills, motivational abilities, and interest in and enjoyment of helping others.

in and enjoyment of the teaching-learning process. Watching participants develop skills, fitness, self-confidence, group interaction abilities, cohesiveness, and enthusiasm for a sport or activity is intrinsically satisfying. Good motivators are creative and ingenious. They reject the mundane for the innovative approach. For example, aerobic dance uses quite traditional movements, but when they are executed to the accompaniment of popular music, people are motivated to move.

Teachers in every situation need to be leaders. Leaders are creative, enthusiastic, responsive to others' needs, decisive, and accountable. Their success is measured by how effectively program participants learn movements, establish and achieve goals, and adhere to fitness programs. Because teachers are thrust into leadership roles, they are held accountable for the program results, and apathetic students and high absenteeism reflect negatively on the leader. Since leadership styles may differ considerably, individuals should adopt a style consistent with their own personalities.

All of these qualities enhance the experiences of both teachers and participants. They should be incorporated into every instructor's teaching in varying degrees; the outcome will be positive.

TEACHER CONTRIBUTIONS

The actual instruction, some people say, is the easy part. The stages preceding, accompanying, and climaxing in instruction are more time-consuming, yet they are essential. Planning and organizing precede instruction and continue throughout instruction, as does evaluation.

Planning encompasses organizing the learning environment (Levin, 1981). This may involve skill grouping or sequencing activities in one session for individuals with varying abilities. Planning includes considering the availability of equipment and facilities and factors such as weather and time constraints and safety considerations. Initially in planning, the teacher looks at the entire spectrum of the participants' experiences. The components of a thoroughly planned unit include:

1. Clear statements of an achievable purpose, specific objectives, and desired outcomes;
2. Safety precautions and considerations;
3. Equipment and facility needs;
4. Introduction to the sport or activity;
5. Key points of instruction for all fundamental movements;
6. Rules of the game;

The popularity of nontraditional activities in schools and in public settings has led to a demand for teachers who have developed the appropriate instructional expertise.

7. Practice drills listed along with group organization;
8. Strategies;
9. Lead-up games and game play;
10. Evaluation of skills learned.

Each class plan includes a specific objective, warm-up and conditioning activities, review of previously learned skills, key points of instruction and demonstration, practice drills, game play, and class organizational procedures.

Class presentations should be limited in time and improved in clarity to include only a brief, clear explanation of a movement skill or strategy, its relationship to previous experiences, and its importance, and a visual demonstration (*Ideas II*). Each phase of the lesson should have stated time allotments, with large amounts of time set aside for participation. Actively supervising, not just monitoring, keeps participants participating in the class, reduces safety problems or misinterpretations about the task, and allows for equitable distribution of feedback. Five characteristics result in effective use of practice time (Siedentop, 1983, p. 45):

1. Pertinent: appropriate for the abilities, interests, and experiences of participants;
2. Purposeful: participants kept on task in a safe and challenging environment;
3. Progressive: skills are correctly sequenced and lead to significant learning;
4. Paced: learning space between each activity is large enough to be challenging and small enough for success;
5. Participatory: students are active as much of the time as is possible.

Daily plans should always include more activities (drills and game situations) than will be used so that if one activity does not lead to its desired result another can be substituted. Planning also includes anticipating the unexpected, such as inclement weather, missing equipment, or unenthusiastic students.

Flexibility in organizing is necessary to adjust to changing needs and varying degrees of progress. Organizational skills are partially used in preparing the daily plan, but they also are used as each class is taught. How do you place program members for instruction and demonstration? How do you group them for activity? How do you divide them for games? How such questions

Planning for classes and for consistency within an entire program are both essential for quality instruction.

are answered determines the effectiveness of each segment of the class. Planning and organizing, therefore, interact to ensure clarity of presentations and optimal learning during activity.

One essential aspect of evaluation is providing feedback. Increasing positive feedback should be a goal of every teacher. This can be accomplished by providing feedback about the skills that are performed correctly and for appropriate behaviors. More than one half of all feedback statements should explain why it is important to do a particular aspect of the movement in the manner expected. To give effective feedback, teachers should observe each student enough times to get a good idea of the performance and then provide a sequence of feedback interactions to ensure learning. Questions can help to enhance students' involvement in the feedback process.

Teachers' self-evaluations provide information that, when factored into their behaviors, improves performances. Clarity of speech, voice projection, personal demeanor, maintenance of discipline and order, correctness and proper progression of movements taught, effectiveness of demonstrations, amount of positive feedback, and amount of enthusiasm should be examined. Improvement requires developing a professional attitude and instilling in students a desire to improve based on self-evaluation and peer evaluation.

In class, teacher activities include managing, instructing, monitoring, and interacting. The organizational details (managing), instruction, and observation of students without feedback (monitoring) should take much less time than the interacting phase. This is because positive feedback relates directly to the primary objective of teaching—helping people enjoy what they are learning and making them like the process of learning. Finally, constant evaluation, if it effects change, improves teaching.

WAYS TO ENSURE SUCCESS

Listed below is a composite of behaviors from educational and leadership sources that, if adopted, will enhance the teaching-learning process.

1. Be a good role model.
2. Diversify your teaching.
3. Enhance students' self-worth and self-confidence.
4. Interact with colleagues to learn from them.
5. Listen to your students.
6. Minimize lecturing.
7. Motivate your students to be active through a relaxed class atmosphere.

8. Praise progress.

9. Try always to do your best.

The key for personal success is the last: try always to do your best. If you genuinely want to teach and will try to develop your capabilities to the best of your ability, you should be pleased with the results.

SUMMARY

Although each of the characteristics of teachers is important, communication skills, interpersonal relationships, motivational ability, and leadership abilities may hold the key to program quality. The teacher establishes the learning environment and sets the tone for the class. Through program evaluations and self-evaluation, teachers assess their plans, the class organization and content, and individual needs to improve the quality of their students' experiences.

LOWELL W. JOHNSON

Teacher and Director of Health and Physical Education
West High School
Wausau, Wisconsin

EDUCATION

B.S., Social Services, University of Wisconsin, Eau Claire (1956)
M.A., Physical Education, University of Wisconsin, Lacrosse (1961)

JOB RESPONSIBILITIES, HOURS, AND SALARY RANGE

As head of the health and physical education program at a high school, Lowell organizes and administers the curriculum, budget, staff, facilities, schedules, and equipment. He serves as the educational leader for his staff while both teaching his classes and directing the program. Lowell's typical 7:00 A.M. to 6:00 P.M. Monday through Friday work schedule verifies his commitment to ensuring that all facets of his program are well-organized and properly conducted. The salary range for a teacher/administrator is between $20,000 and $35,000, depending on the local school district salary schedule, years of experience, and actual job responsibilities.

SPECIALIZED COURSE WORK, DEGREES, AND WORK EXPERIENCES NEEDED FOR THIS CAREER

Personnel management, budgeting, public relations, and exercise physiology are areas of particular importance as an administrator, according to Lowell. He states that being certified as an instructor in first aid, cardiopulmonary resuscitation, and Heimlich manuever and as a Water Safety Instructor is a must for a fully prepared physical educator. Lowell advocates having a double major in college to make a student more marketable on graduation. Second, he urges getting a master's degree as soon as possible, because "you can't survive on a bachelor's degree salary" and because the master's degree will also give the opportunity for advancement in the future. Jobs that will be helpful in preparing for a career in health and physical education are in summer camps, recreation programs, hospital work, and adult education programs.

SATISFYING ASPECTS OF THIS CAREER

School teachers often cite, as their primary reason for pursuing this career, a desire to serve by providing varied learning experiences so young people can grow and mature. Positively impacting on students' attitudes toward physical activity, resulting in the adoption of fitness life styles, is particularly satisfying for physical educators. Lowell enjoys meeting past students who have been out in the world and have compared what they had in high school with what others had. He appreciates his students' pride in the quality program they experienced.

JOB POTENTIAL

Declining enrollments and fewer resignations have curtailed teacher vacancies, yet most prospective teachers can find jobs if they are willing to relocate, to accept less-than-ideal instructional situations, and to teach a portion of their classes outside their major field. Obtaining a double teaching certification, such as physical education and science, math, or English, greatly enhances marketability. Most physical education teaching positions in the secondary schools carry associated coaching responsibilities in one or more sports. Job security in most schools is readily available (tenure is usually granted in 3 to 5 years for satisfactory performance). The potential for advancement into administrative positions is limited by the few positions available.

ADVICE TO STUDENTS

Lowell suggests that students involve themselves in local, state, district, and national associations now and as professionals. It is essential to hear the leaders in the profession and to keep abreast of the latest trends and developments. Teaching is not an 8:00 A.M. to 3:00 P.M. position, but a career that merits "time on task" dedication and a prioritized commitment to doing your best for your students. Lowell urges physical educators to prepare for teaching their classes as well as or better than they plan for their coaching. It is also important to realize that attitudes and programs may have a lasting impact on students.

REVIEW QUESTIONS

1. Name and describe six teacher qualities that can enhance learning.
2. Why is it important for teachers to possess communication skills?
3. List two reasons why physical education teachers need proficiency in physical skills.
4. What are four types of interpersonal relationship skills?
5. Why is positive feedback important?
6. Why is program planning essential?
7. What are four components of a unit plan?
8. Describe the five characteristics of the effective use of practice time.
9. Should a teacher spend more class time managing, instructing, monitoring, or interacting? Why?
10. What are five ways to ensure teaching success? Why are they important?

STUDENT ACTIVITIES

1. From the list of teacher qualities in this chapter, select the one that you think is most important. Be prepared to defend your choice in class.
2. Volunteer to assist instructors in activity classes at your institution for a semester to learn how they plan, organize, teach, and evaluate these classes.
3. Volunteer to assist teachers in a nontraditional setting to learn how they plan, organize, teach, and evaluate these classes.
4. Describe in one page the importance of preparing a unit plan for any physical education class.
5. Based on your experiences as a student, make your own list of ways that teachers can improve their effectiveness.

REFERENCES

Bain, L. L., and Wendt, J. C. *Transition to teaching: a guide for the beginning teacher*. Reston, Virginia: American Alliance for Health, Physical Education, Recreation and Dance, 1983.

Ideas II: a sharing of teaching practices by secondary school physical education practitioners. Reston, Virginia: American Alliance for Health, Physical Education, Recreation and Dance.

Levin, D. *The executive's illustrated primer of long-range planning.* Englewood Cliffs, New Jersey: Prentice–Hall, Inc., 1981.

Logsdon, B. J., et al. *Physical education for children: a focus on the teaching process* (2nd Ed.). Philadelphia: Lea and Febiger, 1984.

Rink, J. E. (1985). *Teaching physical education for learning.* St. Louis: Times Mirror/Mosby. This excellent textbook helps pre-service and in-service teachers understand the multi-faceted instructional process as well as how to describe, analyze, and interpret it.

Siedentop, D. *Developing teaching skills in physical education,* (2nd Ed.). Palo Alto, California: Mayfield Publishing Company, 1983.

SUGGESTED READINGS

Bain, L. L. Preparing students for the future: developing change agent skills. *Proceedings: National Association for Physical Education in Higher Education, 3,* 101–106, 1982. This paper suggests four strategies that physical educators must develop to act as change agents to improve programs more effectively in the future.

Barrett, K. R. A hypothetical model of observing as a teaching skill. *Journal of Teaching in Physical Education, 3,* 22–31, Fall, 1983. Strategies are described for developing the ability to perceive movement responses and the environment in which they occur by deciding what to observe, planning how to observe, and knowing what factors influence ability to observe.

Seidentop, D. *Developing teaching skills in physical education* (2nd Ed.). Palo Alto, California: Mayfield Publishing Company, 1983. Based on the underlying assumption that teaching skills can be systematically improved, this book describes how to become an effective teacher using preventive class management, discipline, interpersonal interaction skills, and long-term and daily lesson planning.

Templin, T. J., and Olson, J. K. (Eds.). *Teaching in physical education.* Champaign, Illinois: Human Kinetics Publishers, Inc., 1983. These proceedings from the Research on Teaching in Physical Education Symposium, held at Purdue University in 1982, include papers that describe topics such as teaching styles, research on teaching physical education, decision-making, academic learning time, student teaching, and professional preparation.

Wendt, J. C., and Bain, L. L. Prospective physical educators' perception of stressful teaching events. *Journal of Teaching in Physical Education, 2,* 49–54, Winter 1983. This exploratory study provides a profile of prospective physical educators' perceptions of stressful teaching events.

Wendt, J. C., and Bain, L. L. *Transition to teaching: a guide for the beginning teacher.* Reston, Virginia: American Alliance for Health, Physical Education, Recreation and Dance, 1983. This easy-to-read guidebook orients pre-service teachers to the experiences they can anticipate. It suggests ways to manage daily tasks and routines and explains how to function productively as a teacher, how to cope with common stresses and problems, and how to grow personally on the job.

Wildman, T. M. A perspective on the utilization of research to improve teaching. *Journal of Teaching in Physical Education, 2,* 87–98, Summer 1984. After commenting on Lawrence Locke's summary of research on teaching teachers and reviewing some other works in this field, the author suggests that there must be a utilization of the existing research to improve teaching and that teachers need to learn to inquire and to deliberate.

Unit II

HISTORY AND DEVELOPMENT OF PHYSICAL EDUCATION AND SPORT PROGRAMS

Eight

European
Heritage

KEY
CONCEPTS

- Early civilizations, including the Greeks, valued physical development to varying degrees.
- The Greek Ideal stressed the unity of the "man of action" with "the man of wisdom."
- Knightly training was the primary source of physical development valued during the Middle Ages.
- A search for knowledge and an emphasis on "a sound mind in a sound body" emerged during the Renaissance.
- Naturalism focused on teaching children when they were ready to learn and on meeting their individual needs.
- European gymnastics programs developed to train soldiers for nationalistic purposes and later influenced school curricula.
- The English popularized and spread their love of sports and games.

Throughout history, people have participated in various physical activities. In early civilizations, integral to the survival tasks of seeking food, clothing, shelter, and protection were the utilitarian skills of running, jumping, throwing, wrestling, climbing, and swimming. Before formal educational programs, tribal leaders and parents mandated that children learn and practice survival skills through imitation. Communal requirements stressed physical prowess for both aggressive and defensive reasons.

Modern programs of physical education in the United States borrowed primarily from the philosophies, activities, and developments of the Europeans from prehistoric times through the 1800s. The Greeks revered optimal physical prowess, and Greek athletics laid the foundation for many subsequent programs. Military training in many countries served utilitarian purposes and replaced aesthetic or religious ideals. After social conditions stabilized, the philosophy of naturalism stressed development of the body to educate best the whole child. Gymnastics that stressed nationalistic goals borrowed the apparatus and activities of the earlier naturalistic programs. Sports and games in England offered an alternative to these formalized gymnastics systems.

EARLY CULTURES

The Egyptians (2000 to 30 B.C.) have been recognized for their scientific, agricultural, and engineering prowess and their alphabet rather than for their educational achievements. In the absence of military and health objectives, the Egyptians were interested in physical development only if it served a vocational, recreational, or religious objective. The warrior class trained physically in hunting, charioteering, using weapons, and wrestling. For recreation, the people of all classes swam, hunted, and played ball games. Although dancing, like wrestling was used for entertainment, it was also popular for the religious and ritualistic Egyptians. Women in Egypt achieved a much higher status than did the subservient Chinese and Indian women.

The Chinese, between 2500 B.C. and 1200 A.D., adhered to an entrenched social pattern based on reverence for the aged scholar. Although in earlier eras physical training was somewhat valued, the religions of Taoism, Buddhism, and Confucianism emphasized the contemplative life. The defense-minded Chinese maintained a military class, who participated in archery, boxing, charioteering, football, and wrestling, but these activities were never popularized for everyone, although many other Chinese flew kites, played chess, practiced light exercises called Cong Fu, and hunted and fished. For the Chinese, literary studies and moral and religious training were valued most.

In India (2500 B.C. to 500 A.D.), the Hindu religion imposed an unchanging social caste system upon the people. This dogma renounced pleasure and individualism and advocated asceticism in preparation for the next life. Spiritual well-being led to healthful practices and to participation in physical exercises such as yoga, a system of meditation and regulated breathing. Buddhism sought to reform the excesses of the Indian caste system, yet it deemphasized physical activities. For various reasons, Egyptians, Chinese, and Indians engaged minimally in physical activities. Not until the Greeks did a civilization openly stress physical prowess and prescribe organized methods for its development (Howell and Howell, 1979).

Greece, regarded as the birthplace of Western civilization, provided a rich heritage that included art, drama, history, mathematics, oratory, philosophy, poetry, science, and sculpture as well as the earliest recorded athletic or sports activities. This dynamic, progressive society recognized the importance of educating the whole individual and evolved through four distinct periods. First, the Homeric era and its educational legacy encompassed prehistoric times until the first recorded Olympic victory, in 776 B.C. The totalitarian city-state of Sparta provided a second educational model. Third, democracy and individual freedom pervaded the educational framework of the early Athenian period, between 776 B.C. and the end of the Persian Wars, in 480 B.C. Later, Athenian education resulted from heightened intellectual curiosity; this fourth period lasted from 480 B.C. until 338 B.C. (Van Dalen and Bennett, 1971).

THE HOMERIC GREEKS (Before 776 B.C.)

The Homeric era was named for the Greek poet Homer, who is credited with writing the *Iliad* and the *Odyssey*, which included the earliest records of athletic competitions. Book XXIII of the *Iliad* describes the funeral games held in honor of Patroclus, Achilles' friend who had been killed in the Trojan War. The contests included a chariot race, boxing, wrestling, a footrace, a duel with spears, discus throw, archery, and javelin throw. Homeric athletics always involved individual competitions for the nobles, who sought fiercely to win.

In the *Odyssey*, Homer chronicled the wanderings and return of Odysseus from the Trojan War. Illustrative of these adventures was one episode in Book VIII in which Odysseus, taunted by the Phaeacians, responded by throwing the discus beyond the distances achieved by their athletes.

The predominant philosophy that developed during the Homeric era became known as the Greek Ideal, which stressed the unity of the "man of action" with the "man of wisdom." This all-around mental, moral, and physical excellence was called *arete*. Avoidance of development of only the body or only the mind related directly to the Greek gods. Revered as part deity and part human, the 12 major gods of the Olympic Council were worshiped as the personifications of the Greek Ideal, with superior intellectual and physical capacities, such as strength, endurance, agility, and bravery. In the funeral games held in honor of both respected soldiers and the gods, these Greek warrior-athletes competed to prove their arete, but success was valued more highly than prizes. In competing, they also sought the favor of the gods.

THE OLYMPICS (776 B.C. to 400 A.D.)

Festivals honoring the gods during the Homeric period led to the establishment of regular celebrations, which expanded dramatically in the fifth century B.C. The warrior-athletes, who were expected to perfect their skills for warfare, used these religious festivals to demonstrate their physical prowess, especially because this proved their allegiance to the Greek Ideal as personified by the gods. Some of these Panhellenic festivals also included choral and musical events and aquatic displays. Although the festivals were predominately for men, at least one, the Heraean Games, was staged for maiden women competing in a footrace.

The Olympics, unmatched in prestige among these festivals, was held every 4 years at Olympia in honor of Zeus, the chief Greek god (Spears and Swanson, 1983). It began at least by 776 B.C. (the date of the earliest existing artifact of an Olympic victory), but probably started much earlier. The sacrifices to Zeus, feasting, and athletic contests lasted 5 days in August and attained such prestige that the perennially warring city-states would guarantee safe passage to travelers en route to the games. Box 8–1 lists when each event became a part of the Olympics and provides an outline of how events were organized during the 5 days. This sequence of events reinforced the link between religious service and athletic competition.

To be eligible for the Olympics, prospective athletes had to be Greek-born and had to train for 10 months before the contests, the last month at Olympia under the guidance of the judges. While open to men from all social classes, the training requirement precluded participation by most poor citizens, who

BOX 8–1
ANCIENT OLYMPIC GAMES
Chronology
776 B.C.	Stade race
724 B.C.	Added the two stade race
720 B.C.	Added the long distance race
708 B.C.	Added pentathlon and wrestling
688 B.C.	Added boxing
680 B.C.	Added chariot race
648 B.C.	Added pancratium and horse race
632 B.C.	Added boys' events
580 B.C.	Added the race in armor
472 B.C.	Festival set as a 5-day event and the sequence of events set as follows:

First Day

Inauguration of the festival
Oath-taking ceremony
Contests for heralds and trumpeters
Contests for boys
Sacrifices, prayers, singing of hymns, and other religious
   observances

Second Day

Chariot race
Horse race
Pentathlon (discus, javelin, long jump, stade race, and wrestling)

Third Day

Main sacrifice to Zeus
Footraces

Fourth Day

Wrestling
Boxing
Pancratium
Race in armor

Fifth Day

Prize-giving ceremony
Service of thanksgiving to Zeus
Banquet

had to work. Athletes were required to take an oath of fair play. Victors received a simple wreath of olive branches to symbolize their highly respected victory. Accorded a hero's welcome when returning home, a victor revelled in triumphal processions and banquets, special privileges, and monetary rewards (Thompson, 1985, pp. 14–15). Initially, Olympia provided no luxuries for either spectators or athletes, as neither a stadium nor a site for the contests was prepared. The games were scheduled in open spaces, and the spectators sat wherever they could. Later, construction of the stadium for foot races and the hippodrome for horse and chariot races provided space for about 40,000 spectators.

The stade race, so named because it was a footrace the length of the stadium (about 200 meters), was the only event in the first Olympic Games. A two-stade race, a long race of about 4800 meters (12 laps), and a race in armor were later added to this phase of the athletic contests. Marble slabs may have provided starting blocks, and a trumpet blast served as the starting signal. In the 400-meter and 4800-meter races the athletes had to round a post at the opposite end of the stadium.

Hand-to-hand combat events included boxing, wrestling, and the pancratium. Since no weight categories existed, boxing pitted two athletes of any size against each other, until one raised a hand to admit defeat. No gloves were worn; the boxers' hands were wrapped with pieces of leather. Blows were confined to the head, often resulting in severe injuries. Wrestling, one of the most popular events because its competitors displayed agility, gracefulness, and strength, was done standing. The objective was to throw the opponent to the ground three times. The pancratium borrowed from boxing and wrestling to become an "almost anything goes" combat. Except for biting and gouging, an athlete employed any maneuver, such as tripping, breaking fingers, and strangleholds, to force an opponent's admission of defeat.

Chariots, two-wheeled vehicles pulled by four horses, were raced, as were horses, at the hippodrome, a narrow field about 500 meters long. These races were limited to the wealthy, who could afford to maintain the horses and to hire the charioteers. The victors were the owners, not the charioteers or jockeys. The chariot race consisted of 12 laps; the horse race covered 2 to 6 laps.

The winner of the pentathlon was recognized as the best all-around athlete. Although the order of events and the method of determining the victor have been lost in antiquity, the discus throw, javelin throw, long jump, stade race, and wrestling constituted the pentathlon. Like the long jump and the javelin throw, the discus throw existed only as a pentathlon event. A circular piece of stone or bronze about 1 foot in diameter and weighing 4 to 5 pounds was hurled by the athlete. In the long jump, probably similar to today's triple jump, one athlete recorded a distance of more than 55 feet. Jumpers were aided by hand-held weights, called halteres, which were swung to enhance their performances. The javelin was thrown both for distance and form

Pancratium, 550-500 B.C.

as a test of skill and strength. A leather thong was wrapped around the 8-to 10-foot javelin, giving it a rotary motion upon release, thereby increasing accuracy. The stade race and the wrestling match probably climaxed the pentathlon, although they may not have been held if an athlete had already won the first three events.

Two developments ushered in a change in attitude toward the Olympic Games and the other Panhellenic festivals. Beginning in Athens, intellectual curiosity and a search for knowledge replaced the Greek Ideal and hence lessened interest in physical development. Within the games themselves, lucrative prizes increasingly overshadowed the earlier motive of honoring the gods through displays of athletic prowess. Professional athletes who trained under coaches at the gymnasiums and who specialized in certain events became prominent in the contests. Expensive prizes led to cheating, corruption, and bribery. Although officially ended by Roman decree around 400 A.D., the Olympics had much earlier lost association with their former values.

THE SPARTANS (766 B.C. to 371 B.C.)

After the Homeric era, the people organized themselves into small governmental units known as city-states. The two dominant, though dramatically contrasting, city-states were Sparta and Athens. By the eighth century B.C., Sparta had begun its military conquests. As Sparta conquered land and took captives, a strict code of discipline, not adherence to the Greek Ideal, was imposed on its own people. The *agoge* evolved, an educational system that ensured the singular goal of serving the state. Mandating complete submission to the government, the Spartan civilization became static as everything, including education, was controlled exclusively by the government.

At birth a child was examined by a council of elders. If healthy and strong, the child was spared, but weak or sickly children were exposed to the elements to die. The mothers' roles in raising children resembled those of state nurses: they had to suppress all tender and maternalistic feelings. While sons were taught to value their roles as obedient soldiers, daughters learned about their responsibility to bear healthy children.

To prepare themselves physically for this responsibility, girls participated in state-prescribed gymnastics in addition to wrestling, swimming, and horseback riding. Dancing was also important in the education of girls and boys as a means of physical conditioning and of honoring the gods.

The boys' educational system, the agoge, was highly structured and formalized. Boys were conscripted by the state at 7 years of age and remained in military service until death. Spartan boys began their military training with running and jumping for conditioning. They progressed to swimming, hunting, wrestling, boxing, playing ball, riding horses bareback, throwing the discus and the javelin, and competing in the pancratium, a combination activity of wrestling and boxing skills. They were trained to endure hardships and pain. Discipline reigned supreme: youths who failed to develop valor, devotion to the state, and military skill were punished.

Beginning at 20 years of age, the youth engaged in intensive military maneuvers and actual warfare. These Spartan soldiers, who had been conditioned to fight until death, were unsurpassed: the Spartans demonstrated their superiority over neighboring city-states and other foes. Not only did the Spartans dominate militarily, they also won more Olympic victories than athletes from any other city-state. Spartan men, at the age of 30 years, qualified for citizenship and were expected to marry; however, their obligation to the state continued as they trained youth in the public barracks. The Spartan military machine, with its singular focus on physical prowess and disregard for intellectual development, contributed to its inability to rule its innumerable captives and lands. While they made excellent soldiers, the people were not trained to think for themselves, but rather to perform on command. Also, the Spartans were few in number because of their strict practices. Combined, these factors led to the end of their domination as a city-state in 371 B.C.

THE EARLY ATHENIANS (776 B.C. to 480 B.C.)

Athens differed sharply from Sparta. The Greek Ideal became the Athenian Ideal as this city-state sought to provide an educational system that encouraged boys to develop their physical and mental abilities. Within this framework of democracy, liberalism, and the popularization of various philosophies, physical prowess flourished as an integral part of the preparation of boys for war and as a means through which beauty and harmony could be depicted.

Girls remained at home under the care of their mothers and received little or no education. Once married, they lived secluded lives. Unlike the women in Sparta, who trained physically, the Athenian women's societal role, quite typical for that time, was very different from the men's role. Men in the lower classes, though, were as uneducated as girls.

The Athenian educational system, which valued the all-around citizen, dominated the life of upper-class boys who, under the guidance of their fathers, learned about their future responsibilities. Usually beginning at 7 years of age and lasting until 14 to 18 years of age, formal education occurred at privately owned schools. When each boy started, the length of time he attended and when he ended this phase of his education was determined solely by the father, since no governmental regulations existed. Not all boys could attend these schools, since fathers had to pay for their sons' education.

The importance attached to the all-around development ideal was evident in each boy's attendance at two schools. A music school provided instruction in arithmetic, literature, and music, while a *palaestra*, or wrestling school, trained the boys physically. Both schools were equally valued, as the unity

Greek athletes practicing.

concept prevailed. Palaestras, owned and directed by *paidotribes*, the first physical education teachers, were not elaborate athletic facilities but varied from simple rooms to separate buildings. There the boys practiced wrestling, boxing, jumping, and dancing. Some palaestras also included playing fields and a place for swimming.

At the age of 18 years, Athenian boys became eligible for citizenship. For 2 years thereafter they were subject to military service, if the state needed them, although no mandatory conscription existed. From 20 years of age throughout their lives, upper-class Athenian men did not work but spent their days at government-furnished gymnasiums. There they practiced athletics to maintain their readiness as warriors in case they were needed by the state. Intellectual discussions, governmental decisions, and social interactions were equally important occurrences at the gymnasium.

Greek dancing provided one means of honoring the gods as part of religious worship and also enhanced physical conditioning and demonstrated the symmetry and beauty adored by the Athenians. Athletics played a similar role, as festivals honoring the gods gave all Greek men the opportunity to display their physical prowess and the aesthetically pleasing male body. The importance of honoring the gods eventually led to a proliferation of festivals throughout Greece.

THE LATE ATHENIANS (480 B.C. to 338 B.C.)

The Athenian-led victory over the Persians in 480 B.C. resulted in several cultural changes. Economic expansion, self-confidence, increased leisure time, intellectual curiosity, and expansion of political franchise combined to shift the educational goals away from devotion to the state and toward a heightened pursuit of individual happiness. This rampant individualism led to a deemphasis on the physical aspects of education, because, as the dominant city-state, citizens no longer saw the need to train as soldiers. The Athenian warrior-athletes were replaced by mercenaries and professional athletes.

The gymnasiums became more like pleasure resorts than exercise areas and provided sites for philosophical discussions and the training of professional athletes. The Golden Age of Athens (443 B.C. to 429 B.C.) was so named because it was highlighted by a flowering of democracy and intellectual curiosity led by the Sophists, a class of Greek teachers of rhetoric, philosophy, and the art of successful living, and by philosophers such as Plato. Warning cries from some philosophers about the undermining of the Athenian society went largely unheeded. As a result, the Athenians were militarially unprepared and fell to the Macedonians in 338 B.C.

THE ROMAN REPUBLIC (500 B.C. to 27 B.C.)

The Roman civilization began as a small tribal community near the Tiber River during the height of the Greek civilization. By extending its rule over neighboring tribes, the Roman nobles, who were landowners, succeeded in establishing a republic around 500 B.C. Soon the common people, who had been given land for their military service, demanded and received greater voice in the government. Thus many Romans, through this democratization process, attained a higher degree of political and economic freedom.

Roman life during this era focused singularly on serving the state, even though the home provided education for youths without government involvement. Fathers and mothers taught their sons to become citizen-soldiers, including in their education a mental and physical readiness for war, respect for the law, and reverence for the gods. Accompanying their fathers to the Campus Martius or other military camps, boys learned military skills, such as archery, fencing, javelin throwing, marching, riding, running, swimming, and wrestling, through imitation, and they developed bodily strength, courage, and obedience to commands as they trained. Conscripted into the military at 17 years of age, men, were drafted for active duty, if needed, until the age of 47 years. During these years men were expected to fulfill their business and political duties as well.

Daughters were educated to assume a vital role in raising children and were expected to instill in their sons the importance of fighting for and even dying for the state. Roman women were more highly respected and socially active than Athenian women.

Religious festivals honoring the gods held as prominent a place in the Roman society as they had during Greek times, yet in these the Romans did not participate in athletic contests or dance. Rather, they offered sacrifices to their gods and then watched horse and chariot races or gladiatorial contests. These festivals provided leisure-time relief from strenuous training but served no educational purposes.

THE ROMAN EMPIRE (27 B.C. to 476 A.D.)

The economic and political freedoms accorded citizens during the Republic were rapidly undermined during the century before the Empire was established, in 27 B.C. under Augustus Caesar. The hardy peasants, who had gained land in exchange for military service, were ravaged by years of war and debts and mortgages. Powerful landowners seized this opportunity to expand their estates and to gain greater political influence. The poorer citizens who were forced off their land migrated to Rome, where they lived on handouts. Replaced by a professional army and denied political freedoms and personal dignity, the common people spent their days attending the festivals and games sponsored by corrupt, upper-class senators or the emperors. Gambling on the outcomes of these contests became a favorite pastime.

At least 200 days per year were public holidays and provided opportunities for festivals. Up to 260,000 spectators watched chariot races at the Circus Maximus, attesting to the popularity of these contests. Professional charioteers hired by the teams (the blues, the greens, the reds, and the whites) raced their low, light chariots drawn by four horses in seven-lap races around a *spina*, a distance of about 3 miles. The Colosseum became the favorite site for the gladiatorial contests, where, to the pleasure of as many as 90,000 spectators, animal fights featured elephants, bulls, tigers, lions, panthers, and bears. Condemned criminals, social undesirables, and Christians were forced to combat lions, tigers, and panthers. Massive sea battles in the Colosseum provided additional bloody, gory entertainment. Gladiators armed with shield and sword, buckle and dagger, or net and spear, fought each other for freedom or for money.

Gladiators and charioteers trained physically, but most other Romans lost interest in developing their own bodies because they were no longer expected to serve as soldiers. Instead, *thermae*, or baths, provided sites for contrast baths for both men and women, with separate hours reserved for the women. At the numerous thermae, Roman men participated in health gymnastics or ball play to overcome indolent life-styles that featured gluttonous feasts and drinking bouts. Thus the moral fabric and physical abilities of a once-strong people dissipated rapidly during an empire characterized by governmental upheavals, power struggles, and an apathetic and dependent populus. In 476 A.D., with the deposition of the last emperor by the Visigoths under Odoacer, the domination of the Roman Empire came to an ignoble end. Like that of the Athenians the demise of the Roman Empire reaffirmed that a lack of emphasis on physical development contributed to the decline of a once-powerful civilization. (See Table 8-1.)

MEDIEVAL EUROPE (500 A.D. to 1500 A.D.)

The Dark Ages, the 500 years following the fall of the Roman Empire, represented a low point physically and intellectually. The Catholic Church, in seeking a higher level of morality than displayed by most Romans, regarded the body and anything that benefitted it as sinful. The only schools that existed during this time were at the monasteries, thus restricting intellectual education to those who served the Church. Survival rather than education highlighted this era, although the monks preserved through their writings the

TABLE 8–1
COMPARISON OF ATHLETIC PROGRAMS

	Early Athens	Late Athens	Roman Republic	Roman Empire
Participants	Aristocratic citizens	Professional athletes	Citizen-soldiers	Professional gladiators and charioteers
Motivation	All-around development	Profit	Preparation for war	Profit
Training	Gymnasiums and palaestras	Gymnasiums under trainers	Military camps and fathers	Specialized schools
Events	Archery, boxing, chariot races, discus, footraces, javelin, and wrestling	Boxing, chariot races, footraces, horse races, pancratium, pentathlon, and wrestling	Archery, fencing, javelin, marching, riding, running, swimming, and wrestling	Chariot races and gladiatorial contests
Organization	Festivals	Scheduled games and festivals	Festivals	Frequent, organized festivals
Number of Stadiums or arenas	Few	Many	Few	Many
Number of Spectators	Limited	Thousands	Limited	Thousands
Professionals or amateurs	Amateurs	Professionals	Amateurs	Professionals
Awards	Some, but not most important	Lucrative benefits	Limited awards	Lucrative prizes

173

Greek philosophies until a time when they would again be studied and valued (Ziegler, 1979).

European society in the eleventh to the sixteenth centuries has been described as feudalistic. The economic, political, and social aspects of life centered around ownership of land and the military power to maintain or expand territory. The monarch, at least theoretically, owned the land. Unable to rule diverse properties successfully, the king divided the territory among nobles who, in turn, promised military service. As vassals of the king, they likewise divided their holdings among lesser vassals, with the same reciprocal protection guarantees. At the bottom of this pyramidal structure were the serfs, or peasants, who toiled in the fields. Their labors were meagerly rewarded with protection by the landowners.

These landowners, who were knights, were the only ones in the feudal society to value physical training, although the peasants engaged in various recreational pursuits. At 7 years of age, the sons of nobles left their homes to go to the manors of other knights. Under the guidance of the ladies of the castles for the next 7 years, the pages were educated through stories about *chivalry* and its code of moral and social duties of knighthood. Squires, beginning at 14 years of age, learned the arts of archery, climbing, dancing, fencing, jousting, riding, swimming, tourneying, and wrestling. As a valet for the knight, the squire served meals, cleaned armor, cared for the knight's horse, played chess or backgammon, and accompanied the knight into battle. Following 7 years of intensive training as a squire, the youth became eligible for knighthood. Once knighted, these nobles exclusively engaged in hunting and hawking and continued their training for battle.

In the isolation of the manorial system of the Middle Ages, few opportunities existed for social interaction and entertainment, so tournaments grew in popularity to fill this void. Although festive occasions, these tournaments focused on combats between knights, who divided into two teams and fought under conditions similar to war in the grand tourney, or melee. Although strict rules and blunt weapons supposedly limited the injuries, fatalities frequently occurred in the melee, leading to its demise. Another event at the tournaments was jousting, which pitted two mounted knights armed with lances in a head-on attempt to dismount each other. Since weapons were blunt and the objective was not to kill the opponent, the joust gradually became the primary event of the tournaments.

Because war served as an adventurous solution to boredom and because service to God was required of the knights, many willingly volunteered for the eight Crusades between 1096 and 1270. Instigated by the Church, these military expeditions attempted to expel the Moslems and the Turks from the Holy Land and to establish papal control in that region. However, the knights

profited from the captured spoils of war, and some took part mainly for this reason.

Interaction with people from other civilizations through the Crusades contrasted markedly with the isolated life-style of the feudalistic period, which peaked between 1250 and 1350. While the importance of the knights lessened due to the invention of gunpowder, towns were being established as trade centers. The emergence of a strong merchant class in these towns started the transition to a period of intellectual, cultural, and social reawakening.

THE RENAISSANCE AND THE REFORMATION (1450 to 1650)

A rebirth of and eagerness for learning grew out of the centuries of intellectual void of the Middle Ages. Intellectual curiosity and creativity were encouraged rather than stymied as education came to be highly valued by people of all social classes. During the Middle Ages, several allied yet diverse philosophies developed; these blossomed during the Renaissance period. They directly influenced attitudes toward physical education, although most often the mind and the body were viewed as two separate entities.

Humanistic education in Italy stressed the harmonious development of humans and embraced the Greek Ideal of unity. "A sound mind in a sound body" described this philosophy, which implemented the principles of humanism and emphasized the physical as well as the intellectual development of students. Humanists stressed the importance of a healthy body as preparation for intellectual endeavors rather than a dichotomous relationship between mind and body.

Realism, which grew out of humanism, emphasized understanding the Greek classics and stressed the importance of educating for life. The development of health through exercise and play and scientific thinking became critical educational outcomes for the realists.

Educational moralism developed during the Protestant Reformation of the 1500s and 1600s as religious fervor combined with nationalism. Although initially desirous of purifying the Catholic Church, reformers such as Martin Luther and John Calvin led this era of intense religious change. Their doctrines stressed personal salvation, moral responsibilities, and state duties. Most of these sects deemphasized physical development as a distraction to these objectives. One religious group, the Puritans, was especially vehement in its opposition to frivolous activities and tried to enforce these staunch doctrines on others in the American colonies. While humanism and realism furthered the Renaissance Ideal of "a sound mind in a sound body," moralism detracted somewhat from its educational stature.

Throughout the Renaissance, the 1700s, and most of the 1800s, education was valued for boys, especially from the upper class, who attended boarding schools or were taught privately by tutors. Seldom was this the case for girls.

THE AGE OF ENLIGHTENMENT (1700s)

The Renaissance set the stage for the Age of Enlightenment, during which two additional educational philosophies developed. John Locke wrote concerning educational disciplinarianism. He said that character, especially valued for upper-class boys, requiring "a sound mind in a sound body" developed best through moral and physical discipline. Jean-Jacques Rousseau, a French philosopher, led the rebellion against the devaluation of the individual. In *Emile*, a description of the ideal way to educate a boy, Rousseau stressed naturalism, or "everything according to nature." That is, each child possesses a unique readiness to learn in a natural developmental process that should dictate when a child is exposed to various types of knowledge. The child, free to explore nature while recreating, would thus become prepared physically for later intellectual pursuits and would, therefore, achieve optimal learning. The Age of Enlightenment provided additional insights into how to educate a child, thereby laying the foundation for European gymnastics programs.

NATURALISM (1770 to 1830)

While the French were not receptive to Rousseau's educational theories, Johann Basedow, a German teacher, was. In establishing the Philanthropinum in 1774, Basedow sought to implement naturalistic principles that focused on meeting individual needs and stressed the principle of a readiness to learn. At this school he allotted 3 hours each day to instructional and recreational activities, such as gymnastics, sports, and games, and 2 hours to manual labor. While Basedow stressed dancing, fencing, riding, and vaulting, the teacher hired to direct the program, Johann Simon, introduced Greek gymnastics, consisting of jumping, running, throwing, and wrestling. Simon utilized natural settings to provide the apparatus, such as balance beams, high-jumping poles, jumping ditches, and tree swings. Johann Du Toit, Simon's successor, added archery, skating, swimming, marching, gardening, and woodworking to Basedow's original scheme.

In 1785, Christian Salzmann patterned the program at Schnepfenthal Institute after Basedow's naturalistic lessons in games and gymnastics. Johann GutsMuths, who taught at Schnepfenthal for 50 years, was strongly influenced by Basedow's writings and provided similar activities and pieces of apparatus. GutsMuths' 3- to 4-hour daily program consisted of natural activities, such as jumping and running, Greek gymnastics, such as throwing and wrestling, military exercises, such as fencing and marching, knightly activities, such as climbing and vaulting, and manual labor, such as gardening and woodworking. GutsMuths influenced many people with two significant books: *Gymnastics for the Young* (1793), which not only described Schnepfenthal's program but also laid the theoretical foundation for modern programs; and *Games* (1796), which described the skills developed in 105 games or activities and illustrated apparatus, such as climbing masts, hanging ladders, rope ladders, and wooden horses (Gerber, 1971).

NATIONALISM (1800s)

Friedrich Jahn, a German educator and an ardent patriot, visited the Schnepfenthal Institute and borrowed many aspects of GutsMuths' program. Jahn's purpose in promoting physical development was nationalistic, rather than naturalistic, because he sought to develop fitness and strength in German youth for the eventual unification of all German people. After encouraging his students to climb trees, jump over ditches, run, and throw stones on half-holiday excursions from classes, he established, in 1811, the first *turnplatz* near Berlin. A turnplatz was an outdoor exercise area where the boys, who became known as *turners*, trained on balance beams, climbing ropes and ladders, high-jumping standards, horizontal bars, parallel bars, pole vaulting standards, broad jumping pits, vaulting horses, a figure-eight-shaped track, and a wrestling ring. Jahn also promoted nationalism through patriotic speeches and stories and group singing of patriotic songs. First boys and then, as this turner system of gymnastics expanded, males of all ages and social classes participated in the increasingly popular gymnastic exercises. Jahn explained his program, in 1816, in his book *German Gymnastics*.

The turners vigorously advocated a unified Germany, and many local turnplatz sites initially received government subsidization. After the Congress of Vienna in 1815 realigned Germany into a confederation of 38 independent states, the turners' single-minded goal of a unified nation was viewed as threatening. Finally, in 1819, government leaders succeeded in banning turner gymnastics. Not until 1840 was it again legal to participate in turner gymnastics, although underground programs thrived between 1819 and 1840. Turner gymnastics never gained widespread popularity in other nations because of their nationalistic appeal and emphasis on strength.

Adolph Spiess borrowed from his training in turner gymnastics to devise a system of German school gymnastics in the 1840s. Approval of his program in the increasing number of public schools hinged on his defense of gymnastics

German gymnastics on the parallel bars.

as a subject equal to all others, one that had progressions for various ages, for boys and girls, and for all ability levels, and one that required trained teachers and equipped indoor and outdoor facilities. Although influenced somewhat by Jahn's and GutsMuths' programs, Spiess devised a school system that stressed discipline and obedience and included diverse activities, such as marching, free exercises, and gymnastics with musical accompaniment.

Nationalism dominated Danish gymnastics in the early 1800s, too. Fitness, strength, and military competence emerged as goals of the programs developed by Franz Nachtegall. In 1799, he established a private gymnasium in Copenhagen, the first of its kind. Nachtegall's program, which borrowed extensively from the apparatus and exercises of GutsMuths, gained popularity and helped Denmark to initiate the first European school program in physical education for boys, in 1809. His *Manual of Gymnastics*, published in 1828, provided the curriculum for the schools. Teachers for the schools were initially educated alongside military men at the Military Gymnastic Institute, founded in 1804 by the king of Denmark, with Nachtegall as its director. Danish gymnastics in the military and in the schools was based totally on command-response exercises, with the rigid, mass drills resulting from the nationalistic theme.

Patriotism raged in Sweden in the later 1700s and in the 1800s, due to the loss of much of Sweden's territory to Russian foes and Napoleonic forces. This nationalistic fervor initially influenced Per Henrik Ling to study and write about the Scandinavian heritage. While pursuing this objective in Denmark for 5 years, he learned gymnastics from Franz Nachtegall and engaged in fencing, through which he improved an arthritic arm. The personal therapeutic benefits that Ling experienced resulted in his emphasis on this contribution of gymnastics throughout his career. Returning to his homeland in 1804, Ling became a fencing master and an instructor of literature and history, while also teaching gymnastics.

Ling's theory that the knowledge of Norse literature and history combined with gymnastics training could coalesce Sweden into a stronger nation influenced the king. As a result, the Royal Gymnastics Central Institute was established in Stockholm in 1814, under Ling's direction. As a training program for military men, this program allowed Swedes to stress precise execution of movements on command, mass drills, specific exercises on specially designed pieces of apparatus, and posture-correcting movements. England, Denmark, Belgium, Greece, and other countries adopted Swedish gymnastics for military training. Ling also initiated therapeutic, or medical, gymnastics to restore health through exercises. He promoted gymnastics for pedagogical (educational) and aesthetic purposes. Swedish apparatus, such as stall bars, booms, vaulting boxes, and oblique ropes, as developed by Ling, were always subordinated to the exercises and to students' needs.

When Hjalmar Ling, Per Henrik Ling's son, began teaching at the Royal Gymnastics Central Institute, he initiated the development of Swedish school gymnastics. Borrowing from his father's program the principles of progression and precise execution of movements on command, Hjalmar Ling devised the Day's Order, systematized daily exercises that progressed through the whole

Swedish school gymnastics.

body from head to toe. These lessons were appropriately graded for the age, ability, and sex of each child and used apparatus designed for children. Mass drills under a teacher's direction remained paramount.

Figure 8-1 illustrates how European philosophies and innovators influenced subsequent programs.

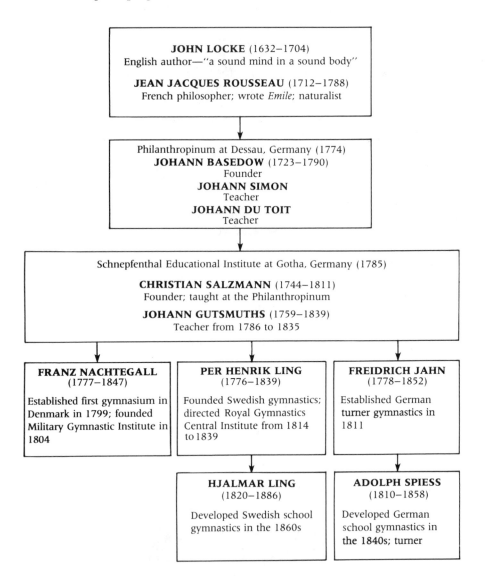

FIGURE 8-1. Origins of modern physical education.

ENGLISH SPORTS (1800s)

European gymnastics, other than to a small extent in the military, never gained popularity in England. Instead, the English legacy to both European and worldwide physical education has undoubtably been its sports and games, which were popularized by the lower classes in its industrialized society and separately by the upper classes, who flaunted their wealth and leisure time through sports and became their primary patrons. The working classes were especially attracted to pugilism (boxing), blood sports, such as cockfighting, and varieties of football (soccer). Spread through colonization, English upper-class sports, such as cricket, horse racing, tennis, golf, and rugby were introduced worldwide and gained numerous adherents.

Public schools, which correspond to today's private boys' boarding schools in America, played leading roles in the promotion of cricket, football, and rugby. Through participation in sports, boys learned moral virtues, such as cooperation, initiative, leadership, loyalty, self-discipline, and sportsmanship, for better citizenship (Mangan, 1981). Participation in a variety of sports, rather than specialization in one, playing the game rather than training in skills or fitness, and intrahouse (between the boys in various residences) competition were stressed as public school boys came to be more a product of their sports than of their scholastic efforts.

Cricket, rowing, and field hockey became the most popular sports at Oxford University and Cambridge University, where the students played despite the faculty's disfavor. The ideal of amateurs playing the game for the game's sake, rather than for remuneration, prevailed in these universities and in later years for upper-class males throughout England. This British Amateur Sport Ideal influenced sports throughout the world, especially attitudes in the United States and international attitudes about the Olympic Games.

SUMMARY

The European legacy of athletics, gymnastics, and sports laid the foundation for physical education programs in the United States. The Greeks provided a rich heritage of mind-body unity and glorified the aesthetically developed, all-around athlete. Varying dramatically from this ideal were the Spartan soldiers and the specialized, professional athletes of the later Greek era. The Romans, in the early part of the Empire, illustrated the utilitarian goal of a fit people. During the next thousand years only the knights developed their bodies, but they did so primarily for military conquest rather than for any inherent value. The Renaissance, led by philosophers and educators, reemphasized "a sound mind in a sound body," although they grappled with whether the mind and body were separate entities. Naturalism and nationalism directly influenced the development of gymnastics systems in Germany, Denmark, and Sweden. Sports and games in England added yet another alternative for the future development of programs in the United States.

JOHANN CHRISTOPH FRIEDRICH GUTSMUTHS

(1759–1839)

BACKGROUND

Johann GutsMuths taught gymnastics at the Schnepfenthal Educational Institute for 50 years. His program, based on naturalistic principles, provided the model for subsequent European and American programs, and his many writings added a philosophical framework and descriptions of his various activities. Historians have termed him the "grandfather of physical education" for his monumental contributions.

In 1786, GutsMuths ended his years as a private tutor to accept a teaching position at Schnepfenthal, where he continued the gymnastics program started by Christian André. Initially and throughout his tenure there, GutsMuths experimented with new exercises and apparatus as Christian Salzmann, the founder of Schnepfenthal, provided him with bountiful opportunities to offer activities for the students. Gymnastics were taught between 11:00 and 12:00 daily. After the noon meal and in the evening, time was set aside for recreation. Games and outdoor excursions filled Sunday afternoons under GutsMuths' guidance.

ACCOMPLISHMENTS

GutsMuths opposed the traditional European methods of education and thus eagerly practiced naturalistic principles. He stressed that health, strength, and overall physical development were essential. The influence of naturalism on the program at Schnepfenthal was readily evident. André instituted walking on the balance beam, jumping standards, pole vaulting across a ditch, vaulting, and other outdoor activities. GutsMuths introduced see-saws, rope ladders, swinging on vertical ropes, and climbing masts. In addition to activities using the above apparatus, the students engaged in leaping, jumping, running, throwing, wrestling, climbing, skipping, dancing, walking, swimming, and military exercises. GutsMuths and Salzmann's belief that manual labor was important led to instruction in woodworking and gardening. GutsMuths' program thus included influence from natural, Greek, knightly, and military exercises as well as manual labor. He divided his gymnastic exercises into three categories: for bodily improvement, for manual labor, and for social games.

CONTRIBUTIONS TO PHYSICAL EDUCATION

Although people throughout Europe visited Schnepfenthal and observed his program and teaching, GutsMuths' greatest impact resulted from his writings. His two greatest works were *Gymnastics for the Young* (1793) and *Games for Exercise and Recreation of the Body and Spirit* (1796). The first of these, 700 pages in length, was the first modern book about physical education. In exhaustive fashion, he explained exactly how and why physical education activities developed the body. Published in Denmark, England, the United States, Holland, Bavaria, France, Sweden, and Austria, *Gymnastics for the Young* went through several revisions. *Games for Exercise and Recreation of the Body and Spirit*, published in three editions, provided detailed descriptions of 105 games. GutsMuths classified these according to the function and the skills each should develop. GutsMuths also wrote *Small Manual of the Art of Swimming for Self-Teaching*, *Mechanical Avocations for Youths and Men*, *Book of Gymnastics for the Sons of the Fatherland*, and *Catechism of Gymnastics: A Manual for Teachers and Pupils*. Several of these also underwent revision.

Health and strength were the goals of GutsMuths' gymnastics program. Naturalism provided the methodology through which it could be achieved. His legacy to the programs that followed was a mammoth one, as physical educators then and later to varying degrees borrowed from his philosophy, his apparatus, or his exercises.

STUDENT ACTIVITIES

1. As a class project, reenact the ancient Olympic Games by having each student participate in one of the athletic contests. Each student will be expected to research the specifics about the assigned or selected event before "competing" against a classmate.
2. Select one activity or area of training of a page or squire during medieval times. Prepare a 10-minute oral report and demonstration of how the boys were taught and how they practiced the skill.
3. Along with several classmates, prepare a demonstration of German, Swedish, or Danish gymnastics and then lead the rest of the class in a 15-minute lesson.
4. Write a five-page paper about the early history and development of any sport that originated in England.

REVIEW QUESTIONS

1. What is the Greek Ideal, and why did it evolve?
2. How did the education of girls and boys in Sparta and in Athens differ?
3. What took place at an Athenian gymnasium during both the early and the later eras?
4. Why did the Olympic Games start, and how did they attain such a prestigious status?
5. Why were the Romans a nation of spectators?
6. How and why did the Renaissance serve as a transitional period between the Middle Ages and the Age of Enlightenment?
7. How did naturalism influence the early development of European gymnastics?
8. How did nationalism influence the development of European gymnastics?
9. What were the similarities and differences among the school gymnastics programs of Adolph Spiess in Germany, Franz Nachtegall in Denmark, and Hjalmar Ling in Sweden?
10. What outcomes were stressed to justify sports and games for boys in the public schools in England?

REFERENCES

Gerber, E. W. (1971). *Innovators and institutions in physical education*. Philadelphia: Lea & Febiger.
Howell, M. L., and Howell, R. (1979). Physical activities and sport in early societies, in *History of physical education and sport* by E. F. Zeigler. Englewood Cliffs, NJ: Prentice-Hall, Inc.
Mangan, J. A. (1981). *Athleticism in the Victorian and Edwardian public school: the emergence and consolidation of an educational ideology*. Cambridge: Cambridge University Press.
Spears, B., and Swanson, R. A. (1983). *History of sport and physical activity in the United States* (2nd ed.). Dubuque, IA: Wm. C. Brown Co.
Thompson, J. G. (August 1985). Winning—an ancient tradition. *Journal of Physical Education, Recreation and Dance 56* (6), 14–15.
Van Dalen, D. B., and Bennett, B. L. (1971). *A world history of physical education* (2nd ed.). Englewood Cliffs, NJ: Prentice-Hall, Inc.
Ziegler, E. F. (1979). *History of physical education and sport*. Englewood Cliffs, NJ: Prentice-Hall, Inc.

SUGGESTED READINGS

Baker, W. J. *Sports in the Western World*. Totowa, New Jersey: Rowman and Littlefield, 1982. The beginnings of sports in Western societies, the organized games of the Greeks, and the English popularization of sports and games provide the foundation for Americans' current passion for sports.

Broekhoff, J. Physical education, sport, and the ideals of chivalry. In *History of physical education and sport*, B. L. Bennett (Ed.) Chicago: The Athletic Institute, 1972. During the Middle Ages, *chevaliers* learned about courtly Iove, the ideals of chivalry, and, especially, the knightly arts of riding, swimming, shooting, climbing, jousting and tourneying, wrestling, fencing and fighting, courtly manners and behaviors, and playing board games.

Forbes, C. A. *Greek physical education*. New York: Century, 1929. The importance that the Greeks ascribed to the development of the body was indispensable to their culture and predominance, yet to their detriment they abandoned the gymnasium, leaving exercise to professional athletes.

Gerber, E. W. *Innovators and institutions in physical education*. Philadelphia: Lea and Febiger, 1971. Fifty outstanding leaders in European and American physical education along with 10 significant institutions are described in this comprehensive history.

Guttman, A. Recent work in European sport history. *Journal of Sport History, 10*, 35–52, Spring 1983. This article briefly analyzes the major works, including comprehensive histories, monographs, and interpretive histories, written about European sports history in the preceding decade.

Harris, H. A. *Sport in Greece and Rome*. Ithaca, New York: Cornell University Press, 1972. This classical scholar comprehensively examines Greek athletics, ball games and other pastimes, and chariot racing in both Greece and Rome and helps the reader understand the role of each in life in these early civilizations.

Kyle, D. Directions in ancient sport history. *Journal of Sport History, 10*, 7–34, Spring 1983. This essay critically examines the writings of ancient sport history and offers recommendations for greater research and analysis in this area.

Spears, B. A perspective of the history of women's sport in ancient Greece. *Journal of Sport History, 11*, 32–47, Summer 1984. Women's participation in sports in Greece between 800 B.C. and 400 A.D. was reflective of their place in society, one of insignificance when compared with the men's sports of the same period, although a few skilled women achieved notoriety at the athletic festivals.

Ueberhorst, H. *Friedrich Ludwig Jahn*. Bonn-Bad Godesberg: InterNationes, 1978. This biography of the controversial "father of gymnastics," Friedrich Ludwig Jahn, describes his achievements in promoting nationalism through turner gymnastics.

Nine

Early American Physical Education

KEY CONCEPTS

- Immigrants to the United States, especially those from England, brought with them a love for sports and games.
- Early physical education programs in the United States promoted calisthenics, light gymnastics, hygiene, and strength development.
- German gymnastics and Swedish gymnastics had many advocates and provided alternatives in the Battle of the Systems.
- Teacher training and a professional organization provided an educational foundation and a forum for the future development of physical education programs.
- Play became recognized as a right of children.
- Amateur sports in clubs and on college campuses were organized and became competitive.

Immigrants to the New World brought with them a love for sporting pastimes. Once survival was assured, time was spent bowling, racing horses, skating, wrestling, and playing various ball games. German gymnastics and Swedish gymnastics appealed to a few, but neither won full acceptance as a unified, national approach to physical education appropriate for people in the United States. Emphasizing health, strength, and bodily measurements, physical training programs in the 1800s were added to school and college curricula. Leaders established normal schools that offered course work in the theoretical and practical aspects of the emerging profession of physical education. Sports and play activities drawn from a European heritage continued to grow in popularity as college students and upper-class clubs sponsored contests and towns provided playgrounds.

PHYSICAL ACTIVITIES IN THE COLONIES

Native Americans, who inhabited what is now the United States, were different from each other and the early colonists in their styles of life and activity pursuits. Yet most participated in ritualistic dances as they sought favor from the gods of nature and the great spirit. In addition to hunting, trapping, and fishing, Native Americans played various games. Of these, *baggataway*, or lacrosse, was the most notable and lasting in popularity. Although both men and women played *shinty*, a game like field hockey and also known as double-ball, they were segregated. Entire villages often competed against other villages in various games on expansive playing areas. Injury and betting were commonplace (Welch and Lerch, 1981).

The first colonists came to the New World in the late 1500s in search of a new life, adventure, and religious freedom. During that century, the prime motivator for physical activity was survival: men hunted, fished, and grew crops while women performed domestic chores. What little time existed for relaxation was frequently spent in work-related recreation, such as barnraisings, corn-huskings, or quilting bees. Dancing and games were often a part of these gatherings.

The European, and especially the English, sporting heritage became increasingly popular in the 1700s. In spite of Puritan-initiated laws forbidding gambling, card playing, and mixed dancing, New Englanders relaxed by bowling, fishing, fowling, or playing cricket, rugby fives (a game similar to handball), or marbles.

Led by the Dutch in New York, the settlers in the middle colonies, without many of the religious prohibitions imposed on their northern neighbors, eagerly engaged in merriments such as pulling the goose (snapping off the head of a greased goose while riding horseback or while standing in a moving boat); played games, such as skittles (in which a ball or flat disc is thrown down an alley at nine skittles, or pins); and participated in outdoor amusements, such as boating, fishing, hunting, horse racing, and sleighing. These were especially pursued by those in upper-class society. Since it was prohibited by law because of its association with gambling, nine-pin bowling had a tenth pin added to it to allow bowlers, and hence gamblers, to participate legally in their favorite pastime. The Quakers of Pennsylvania favored fishing, hunting, and swimming as diversions.

Virginia, strongly influenced by the English, emerged as the leading Southern colony. Emulating the gentry across the ocean, the Southern plantation owners sought to acquire all the trappings befitting their aristocratic status, including sporting pastimes. Cockfights, bowling, card playing, and horse racing often were pursued vigorously at taverns, which were exclusively for men. Fox hunting, hawking, and watching boxing matches found many enthusiasts.

Participation in various physical activities increased throughout the 1700s, as an emerging nationalism placed emphasis on the development of health and strength. Benjamin Franklin, Noah Webster, and Thomas Jefferson were among those who supported physical activities for healthful benefits. At the same time, sports involvement continued to win new adherents because sports offered competition, freedom, and fun.

In the late 1700s, as the colonists prepared for a confrontation with the English, military days provided opportunities for marching and drilling with weapons, yet they also offered times for social interaction and game playing. This training was utilitarian in purpose and did not lead to an emphasis on physical readiness in the post-war years. This philosophy was repeated throughout the history of the United States as each war signaled a need to have trained soldiers; other than during these emergencies, there was little military emphasis on physical education programs.

·   ·   ·

Following the War of 1812, nationalism burst into popularity, setting the stage for a gradual extension of democratic rights to more people and for the provision of education for more children. Free, public education, beginning in the 1800s, consisted primarily of reading, writing, and arithmetic. These public schools initially showed little interest in physical education, although in 1853, Boston became the first city to require daily exercise for children. In contrast, an enjoyment of sports and the belief that physical activities contributed to health led to the inclusion of physical activities in the private academies and schools in the early 1800s. Prior to the Civil War few colleges provided for their students' physical development, but academies and private schools for boys and occasionally for girls (such as Mt. Holyoke Female Seminary in 1837) included physical exercises in their curricula.

INTRODUCTION OF GERMAN GYMNASTICS IN THE UNITED STATES

The most significant of the private schools was the Round Hill School, founded in 1823 in Northampton, Massachusetts. Box 9–1 lists this school's founding along with other highlights in the development of physical education in the nineteenth century. The founders of Round Hill School scheduled time each day for sports and games even before they employed Charles Beck, a German turner, to instruct the boys in the German system of gymnastics. Beck established an outdoor gymnasium, taught the first turner exercises on apparatus in this country, and translated Friedrich Jahn's treatise on gymnastics. In addition, some Harvard University students, in 1826, and Bostonians, in the 1820s, also were taught turner gymnastics by German immigrants. The interest in turner gymnastics dissipated when these Germans ceased to teach and because this system's emphasis on strength-developing work on apparatus failed to appeal to sports-minded Americans.

When a second wave of political refugees fled Germany in 1848, they, too, brought their love of gymnastics to the United States, where they established societies of turners beginning in 1848 in Cincinnati and turner festivals in 1851. These *turnfests* featured thousands of turners exhibiting their physical prowess on German apparatus. In 1866, they founded the Normal School of the North American Gymnastic Union in New York City to prepare teachers of German gymnastics. When most German immigrants migrated to the Midwest, they settled in isolated communities and maintained their national identity, including their gymnastics program. Gradually, these turner societies broadened their programs to include social functions and exercises for the entire family. Later in the 1800s they introduced the turner system into several schools, although it was modified with Adolph Spiess' school gymnastics principles. Although the influence of German gymnastics on programs in the United States was limited because of its regional nature and because of the

BOX 9–1
SIGNIFICANT EVENTS IN EARLY AMERICAN PHYSICAL EDUCATION

1823   Round Hill School established with physical education in its curriculum

1824   Hartford Seminary directed by Catharine Beecher used calisthenics as its program

1825   Charles Beck became an instructor of German gymnastics at Round Hill School

1825   New York City high schools offered gymnastics

1826   Charles Follen organized gymnastic classes for students at Harvard University

1831   John C. Warren's book, *The Importance of Physical Education,* published

1832   Catharine Beecher's course of *Calisthenics for Young Ladies* published

1837   Mount Holyoke Female Seminary opened, with calisthenics listed as part of its school program

1837   Western Female Seminary founded by Catharine Beecher

1848   Friedrich Hecker organized the first American turnverein in Cincinnati

1851   First national turnfest held in Philadelphia

1853   Boston became the first city to require daily exercise for school children

1855   Cincinnati, Ohio, first offered physical education using German gymnastics in its public schools

1856   Catharine Beecher's *A Manual of Physiology and Calisthenics for Schools and Families* published

1859   A. Molineaux Hewlitt, a black, appointed gymnasium instructor at Harvard University

1861   Normal Institute for Physical Education founded by Dio Lewis

1861   Edward Hitchcock became director of the Amherst College physical education program

1862   Dio Lewis' *New Gymnastics for Men, Women, and Children* published

1865   First women's physical education program started at Vassar College

1866   California passed the first state physical education law

1866   Normal School of the North American Gymnastic Union established

1869   First YMCA gymnasiums opened in New York City, San Francisco, and Washington, D.C.

1872   Brookline, Massachusetts, became the first community in America to vote public funds for a public playground

(continues)

(concluded)

1879   Harvard University's Hemenway Gymnasium opened under the direction of Dudley Sargent

1883   Hartvig Nissen started teaching Swedish gymnastics in Washington, D.C.

1885   Nils Posse started teaching Swedish gymnastics in Boston, Massachusetts

1885   Association for the Advancement of Physical Education founded in Brooklyn, New York

1885   YMCA Training School established in Springfield, Massachusetts

1886   Brooklyn Normal School established by William Anderson

1886   Chautauqua Summer School of Physical Education established

1887   Harvard Summer School established

1889   Boston Normal School of Gymnastics established

1889   Boston Conference on Physical Training held

1890   Posse Normal School founded

1891   Edward Hartwell became director of physical education for the Boston public school

1892   Ohio became the second state to pass a physical education law

1893   Harvard became the first college to confer an academic degree in physical education

1896   American Association for the Advancement of Physical Education began publication of *American Physical Education Review*

1897   Society of College Gymnasium Directors founded

emphasis on strength development and nationalism, during the late 1800s and early 1900s many schools and colleges incorporated exercises on German apparatus into their program. Some of these apparatus, such as the parallel bars, rings, and balance beam, remain vital parts of gymnastics today.

EARLY AMERICANS WHO INFLUENCED PHYSICAL EDUCATION PROGRAMS

Catharine Beecher, the first American to design a program of exercises for American children, tried to get daily physical activity into the public schools. As director of the Hartford Female Seminary beginning in 1824, and later, when she founded the Western Female Institute in Cincinnati in 1837, she introduced girls to calisthenics. At the latter school, she set aside 30 minutes per half day for her program of exercises, which was designed to promote health, beauty, and strength. Beecher's initial objective was to aid girls in improving their vitality so that they could better fulfill their missions in life as wives and mothers. She expanded her concepts from a *Course of Calisthenics for Young Ladies*, which she wrote in 1832 primarily for girls, to *A Manual of Physiology and Calisthenics for Schools and Families*, published in 1856. In this book, Beecher advocated the introduction of physical training in the American schools for all children. Borrowing from the therapeutic concepts of Swedish gymnastics as developed by Per Henrik Ling, Beecher, through her writings and school programs, emphasized exercises that could be executed at home without a teacher and with only diagrams from her books as guides (Gerber, 1971).

Although Beecher's efforts did not achieve their desired results, she did influence another American. Dio Lewis took Beecher's calisthenics, added light pieces of apparatus, such as bean bags, dumbbells, Indian clubs, and wands, and changed the name to light gymnastics. His promotional efforts resulted in the adoption of his system in the elementary schools in Boston. In 1861, he founded the Normal Institute for Physical Education, the first of many schools that prepared physical education teachers.

The first college physical education program was begun, in 1860, at Amherst College because the president was concerned about the health of the

Lewis' gymnastics using dumbbells.

students. As director of the Department of Hygiene and Physical Education, Edward Hitchcock, beginning in 1861 and continuing throughout his lifetime, gave health lectures, served as college physician, and supervised the required physical exercises of all students. Like most of the early physical educators, Hitchcock's primary credential for the job was a medical degree. Borrowing from Lewis' light gymnastics, Hitchcock's program, led by squad captains, included class exercises to the accompaniment of music. A portion of the 4-day-a-week classes could be used by the students to practice sports skills or to exercise on the horizontal bars, rings, ropes, and vaulting horses. Hitchcock also administered a battery of bodily or anthropometric measurements, such as height, weight, chest girth, and lung capacity, to evaluate the effects of the program on students and to compare their progress from year to year.

A second noteworthy college physical education program was developed by Dudley Sargent at Harvard University in 1879, when he was hired to direct the newly opened Hemenway Gymnasium. Since no required physical education program existed at Harvard, Sargent used an individualized approach to encourage the students to exercise. Based on numerous anthropometric measurements, Sargent prescribed a series of exercises to meet the individual student's physical needs, using chest expanders and developers, leg machines, rowing machines, and other apparatus that he had designed. While opposed

Class exercises at Amherst College.

to strict German gymnastics or light gymnastics programs, Sargent encouraged the students to participate in baseball, bowling, boxing, fencing, rowing, and running in addition to their individual conditioning programs.

INTRODUCTION OF SWEDISH GYMNASTICS IN THE UNITED STATES

The first introduction of Swedish gymnastics as a complete system was in 1883, when a Norwegian, Hartvig Nissen, opened a Swedish Health Institute in Washington, D.C. Two years later Nils Posse, a graduate of the Royal Gymnastics Central Institute in Stockholm, introduced Swedish gymnastics in Boston. Impressed by Posse's program, philanthropist Mary Hemenway volunteered to the Boston School Committee to furnish to teachers free training in Swedish gymnastics, if the schools would offer this program. This led Hemenway to finance the establishment of the Boston Normal School of Gymnastics in 1889. Hemenway's secretary, Amy Morris Homans, served as its director; Nils Posse was the first instructor. The graduates of this school taught in the Boston schools and nationally, especially in women's colleges, thus spreading Swedish gymnastics. Edward Hartwell, as Director of Physical Training for the Boston public schools beginning in 1890, was a strong supporter of Swedish gymnastics. Previously, he had directed the Johns Hopkins University gymnasium, where he experimented with many of the principles that Dudley Sargent advocated.

Between 1885 and 1900, a leading topic for discussion among physical educators was which system of gymnastics could provide a unified, national program for the United States. This raging controversy became known as the "Battle of the Systems." While there was some overlap between programs, largely the German, Swedish, and American systems developed and vied for supporters (Figure 9–1). A brief summary of the contributions of the early leaders in physical education in the United States is provided in Box 9–2.

In an attempt to introduce Swedish gymnastics to the general public and to leaders in physical training and thus to gain its acceptance as the program for American schools, Mary Hemenway, in 1889, financed the Boston Conference on Physical Training. Under the capable direction of Amy Morris Homans, this conference was highly successful and was one of the most important conferences in physical education ever held in the United States. Its significance is attributed to the exposure given to the various programs existing at that time. German gymnastics, Swedish gymnastics, Hitchcock's program, Sargent's system, and others were explained and the merits of each discussed. Sargent, after explaining his program, proposed an answer to the search for an American system. (Barrows, 1899, p. 76):

> What America most needs is the happy combination which the European nations are trying to effect: the strength-giving qualities of the German gymnasium, the active and energetic properties of the English sports, the grace and suppleness acquired from French calisthenics, and the beautiful poise and mechanical precision of the Swedish free movement, all regulated, systematized, and adapted to our peculiar needs and institutions.

Although the leaders in physical education at this conference were exposed to the various systems, no one system was found to meet completely the needs of American programs because each seemed to have its weaknesses. Still, the Boston Conference provided an opportunity for leaders to learn about the various systems and to exchange ideas for the future promotion of American physical education.

While German gymnastics in the Midwest and Swedish gymnastics in the Northeast were widely accepted, few states mandated physical education. California, in 1866, passed a law providing for twice-a-day exercises for a

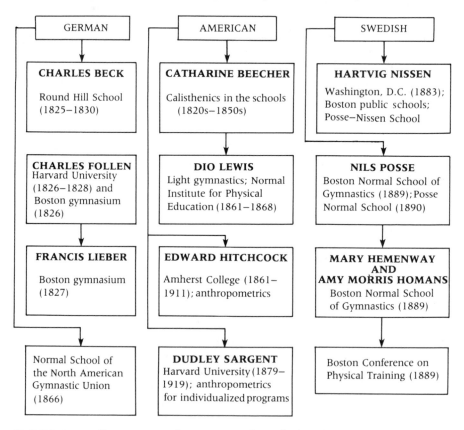

FIGURE 9–1. Influences on early American physical education programs.

BOX 9–2
EARLY LEADERS IN PHYSICAL EDUCATION IN THE UNITED STATES

Charles Follen (1796–1840)
  Established gymnasium in Boston (1826)
  Taught German gymnastics to Harvard University students (1826–
    1828)
Charles Beck (1798–1866)
  First physical education teacher in the United States (1825)
  Taught at Round Hill School (1825–1830)
Francis Lieber (1800–1872)
  Directed Boston gymnasium and opened swimming pool (1827)
Catharine Esther Beecher (1800–1878)
  Taught at the Hartford Seminary for Girls (1824)
  Started the Western Female Institute (1837)
  Promoted calisthenics in American schools for boys and girls
Dioclesian Lewis (1823–1888)
  Light gymnastics with hand-held apparatus
  Started the Normal Institute for Physical Education (1861)
Edward Hitchcock (1828–1911)
  First college professor of hygiene and physical education at Amherst
    College (1861–1911)
  First president of the Association for the Advancement of Physical
    Education (1885)
  Leader in anthropometrics
Amy Morris Homans (1848–1933)
  Director of the Boston Normal School of Gymnastics (1889–1909)
  Director of the Department of Hygiene and Physical Education at
    Wellesley College (1909–1918)
  Founded the Association of Directors of Physical Education for
    Women (1915)
Dudley Allen Sargent (1849–1924)
  Director of the Hemenway Gymnasium at Harvard University (1879–
    1919)
  Leader in anthropometrics
  Founded the Sargent Normal School (1881)
  Founded the Harvard Summer School (1887)
Edward Mussey Hartwell (1850–1922)
  Instructor (1882) and director of the gymnasium (1885–1890) at
    Johns Hopkins University
  Director of physical training for the Boston public schools (1890–
    1897)

(continues)

(concluded)

William Gilbert Anderson (1860–1947)
Initiated the meeting that led to the formation of the Association for the Advancement of Physical Education (1885)
Founded the Chautauqua Summer School of Physical Education (1886)
Founded the Brooklyn (Anderson) Normal School (1886)

Hartvig Nissen
Introduced Swedish gymnastics at the Swedish Health Institute in Washington, D.C. (1883)
Assistant director (1891–1897) and then director (1897–1900) of physical training for the Boston public schools
Taught at the Harvard Summer School and the Sargent Normal School and directed the Posse-Nissen School

Nils Posse (1862–1895)
Leader in Swedish gymnastics in the United States (1885–1895)
Graduate of the Royal Gymnastics Central Institute
First teacher at the Boston Normal School of Gymnastics (1889)
Started the Posse Normal School (1890)

Delphine Hanna (1885–1920)
Taught at Oberlin College (1885–1920)
First woman professor of physical education (1903)
Took anthropometric measurements of women
Taught Luther Gulick, Thomas Wood, Jay Nash, and Jesse Williams

minimum of 5 minutes to promote health and bodily vigor, but it was short-lived. Ohio's 1892 law was the first lasting physical education law. Louisiana, in 1894, Wisconsin, in 1897, North Dakota, in 1899, and Pennsylvania, in 1901, passed similar legislation (Lee, 1983). Most colleges included German and Swedish gymnastics in their physical education programs, but they also borrowed from Hitchcock's program and Sargent's principles and apparatus in the late 1800s.

ESTABLISHMENT OF NORMAL SCHOOLS FOR PHYSICAL EDUCATION

One method through which the various programs were promoted was the development of normal schools. The 1880s were especially noteworthy: six institutions were established to prepare physical education teachers in a specific system or in an eclectic program that borrowed from several systems. In 1881, Dudley Sargent began teaching women from Harvard Annex and other women and men who were interested in his apparatus and methodology. At the Sargent Normal School, he provided a general curriculum based on a theoretical, scientific foundation along with varied activities of a practical nature.

A unique normal school established in 1885 in Springfield, Massachusetts, was the Young Men's Christian Association (YMCA) Training School. The YMCA's goal, through its association gymnastics, was to develop the all-around man and to send him out as a physical director to the increasing number of YMCAs, both nationally and internationally. (The first YMCA gymnasiums had been opened in 1869 in New York and in San Francisco.)

In 1886, William Anderson led in the establishment of two additional institutions. While teaching in New York, he started the Brooklyn Normal School; later, when he became the director of the Yale University gymnasium, he shifted this school to New Haven, Connecticut, and renamed it the Anderson Normal School. Anderson, along with Jay Seaver, also worked with leaders in the Chautauqua movement to set up the Chautauqua Summer School of Physical Education. The curricula at both schools focused on a generalized approach with theoretical and practical course work.

Dudley Sargent, in 1887, succeeded in gaining approval to open the Harvard Summer School, which provided an opportunity for teachers already out in the field to start or continue their professional training in physical education. The diversity and breadth of the offerings, along with its outstanding faculty, made attendance at the Harvard Summer School prestigious and a certificate from it highly respected.

Swedish gymnastics was taught initially at the Boston Normal School of Gymnastics in 1889 and continued to be taught following the school's affiliation with Wellesley College in 1909. Amy Morris Homans directed both programs. Nils Posse, in 1890, established the Posse Normal School, which also promoted Swedish gymnastics.

Box 9–3 summarizes the early teacher training institutions in the United States, along with their curricula.

Beginning in the late 1800s, normal schools were replaced with teacher preparation programs. At Oberlin College, Delphine Hanna initiated a program for women students in 1885; it became a 4-year program in 1900. Only programs at Stanford University, the University of California, and the University of Nebraska preceded it.

FOUNDING OF THE NATIONAL ASSOCIATION

In the late 1800s, physical education programs were a potpourri of activities reflecting the philosophies and whims of their leaders. As a young teacher, William Anderson recognized this diversity and the fact that few opportunities existed for the exchange of curricula and philosophical ideas among individ-

BOX 9–3

EARLY PROFESSIONAL PREPARATION INSTITUTIONS IN THE U.S.

Year	Founder	Name	Program	Today
1861–1868	Dio Lewis	Normal Institute for Physical Education	Light gymnastics	—
1866–1951	Turners	Normal School of the North American Gymnastic Union	German gymnastics	Normal College of the American Gymnastic Union of Indiana University
1881–1929	Dudley Sargent	Sargent Normal School	Theoretical and practical curriculum	Boston University Sargent College of Allied Health Professions
1885–today	Young Men's Christian Association	YMCA Training School	Association gymnastics	Division of Health, Physical Education, and Recreation at Springfield College
1886–1920s	William Anderson	Chautauqua Summer School of Physical Education	Advanced theoretical and practical curriculum	—
1886–1953	William Anderson	Brooklyn (Anderson) Normal School	Theoretical and practical curriculum	Arnold College Division of the University of Bridgeport

(continues)

200

(concluded)

1887–1932 Dudley Sargent	Harvard Summer School	Advanced theoretical and practical curriculum	—
1889–1909 Mary Hemenway and Amy Morris Homans	Boston Normal School of Gymnastics	Swedish gymnastics	Department of Physical Education at Wellesley College
1890–1942 Nils Posse	Posse Normal School	Swedish gymnastics	—

uals interested in physical development. After seeking support from two recognized leaders in the field, Edward Hitchcock and Dudley Sargent, Anderson invited gymnastics teachers, ministers, journalists, school principals, college presidents, and others engaged in the promotion of physical training to meet at Adelphi Academy on November 27, 1885, to discuss their various programs and to decide whether sufficient interest existed to provide regularly a forum for professional interchange. Of the 60 people who attended, 49 responded positively, resulting in the formation of the Association for the Advancement of Physical Education, today's American Alliance for Health, Physical Education, Recreation and Dance (Box 9–4 traces its various name changes). The

---

BOX 9–4
VARIOUS NAMES OF THE NATIONAL ORGANIZATION

1885 Association for the Advancement of Physical Education
1886 American Association for the Advancement of Physical Education
1903 American Physical Education Association
1937 American Association for Health and Physical Education
1938 American Association for Health, Physical Education and Recreation
1974 American Alliance for Health, Physical Education and Recreation
1979 American Alliance for Health, Physical Education, Recreation and Dance

organization's initial objectives were "to disseminate knowledge concerning physical education, to improve the methods, and by meetings of the members to bring those interested in the subject into closer relation to each other" (Lee and Bennett, 1960, p. 27). Discussions in the early meetings focused on anthropometric measurements, the various gymnastics systems, athletics, hygiene, and military drill. To provide further for the sharing of professional expertise, the *American Physical Education Review* was first published by this association in 1896.

PROMOTION OF PLAY FOR CHILDREN

While organized school programs were being established, the play movement outside the schools was gaining support and momentum. The industrialization of the United States directly influenced this development because of the massive influx by Americans into the urban areas and immigration, resulting in overcrowded tenements. In an effort to provide suitable play space for children in this environment, sand piles were first erected in Boston in 1885. In 1888, New York passed the first state legislation that led to an organized play area for children. By 1899, the Massachusetts Emergency and Hygiene Association sponsored 21 playgrounds.

Boston constructed the Charlesbank outdoor gymnasium in 1889. Jane Addams' Hull House, a Chicago settlement house started in 1894, included a model playground. Religious leaders, school administrators, philanthropists, and social workers worked jointly or singly in the late 1800s to ensure that children were provided both places and opportunities to play. In part, these efforts demonstrated a genuine concern for the welfare of children and for society as a whole, and in part these playgrounds were used as a method of social control (Betts, 1984, pp. 141–163). Van Dalen and Bennett (1971, pp. 415–416) summarized the play movement in the late 1800s as follows:

> Philadelphia, Providence, Pittsburgh, Brooklyn, Baltimore, Milwaukee, Cleveland, Minneapolis, and Denver all opened similar playgrounds before 1900. In general, these early playgrounds showed several common characteristics. They were only for the use of preadolescent children and were maintained only during the summer vacation period. The equipment was suitable only for outdoor use. Playgrounds were located in the densely populated sections of cities. The initiative and early financial support came from philanthropic sources, although public land was sometimes used. As the beginning efforts proved worthwhile, the municipal governments began to furnish financial aid. In a number of instances, policemen were either assigned or volunteered for playground duty, because such supervision was effective in preventing juvenile delinquency associated with street play. The growing

recognition of the right of children to play was one aspect of a nascent social philosophy that led to the passage of child labor laws.

DEVELOPMENT OF AMATEUR SPORTS

Americans' love for sports began with the founding of the United States but really blossomed after the Civil War, as baseball became the national sport of men of all ages and for amateurs as well as professionals. Races between cyclists, horses, runners, and yachts, with associated gambling, were especially attractive to the upper class. Normally these races, as well as sports such as cricket, golf, and tennis, were staged by or played by members of elite social clubs. In 1879, the New York City Athletic Club led in the formation of today's Amateur Athletic Union (AAU). This organization sought to promote amateur sports while checking the evils of professional sports. In 1853, Scottish immigrants, through their Caledonian games, began to promote native sports, such as hammerthrowing, putting stones, and tossing the caber. The Czechoslovakian Sokols also promoted physical activities through mass displays in national festivals, such as that first held in 1879 in New York City.

Two sports were developed in the YMCA and received their early promotion through this association. In 1891, at the YMCA Training School, James Naismith developed the rules for and initiated the first game of basketball. The game was designed as an indoor sport to fill the void between football and baseball seasons. Five years later, William Morgan, at a YMCA in Holyoke, Massachusetts, originated volleyball as a less vigorous indoor game for businessmen. Both sports met a need and found more of their early adherents in the YMCAs than in the private clubs and colleges.

COLLEGIATE SPORTS FOR MEN

Sports on college campuses initially were organized as extracurricular activities because administrators and faculty viewed them as extraneous to the mission of higher education. The first intercollegiate event, in 1852, matched Harvard and Yale in rowing. The two early favorites in collegiate sports were baseball, which first matched Amherst against Williams in 1859, and football, which actually began as rugby in a game between Princeton and Rutgers in 1869. For these three sports and track, students founded organizations to standardize rules for competitions.

College faculties paid little attention to sports until problems began to infringe on students' academic work. Missed classes, decreased academic per-

Virginia vs. North Carolina, college baseball in 1895. (Courtesy of North Carolina Collection, UNC Library at Chapel Hill)

formance, injuries, property damage on campus and in nearby towns during victory celebrations, lack of academic eligibility of team members, playing against professional teams, commercialization, and a general overemphasis on athletics compelled faculties to take action. In 1882, a group of Harvard University faculty members recommended that a tripartite committee of three faculty members, three students, and three alumni should control athletics. Representatives of nine eastern colleges met in 1883 as the Intercollegiate Athletic Conference and proposed that colleges should not compete against professional teams, no professional athletes should coach college teams, students should be permitted only 4 years of participation in athletics, contests should take place only on campuses, and faculties should control athletics. Because only three colleges ratified them, these regulations failed to take effect. In 1895, The Intercollegiate Conference of Faculty Representatives, made up of one faculty member from each of seven midwestern institutions, adopted rules that required enrollment of all players as students, enrollment of transfer students for 6 months at the institution prior to participation on a team, and maintenance of academic performance standards by athletes for eligibility to play. These few efforts did not control the overwhelming growth of student-initiated and student-administered intercollegiate athletics in the late 1800s (Lucas and Smith, 1978).

COLLEGIATE SPORTS FOR WOMEN

In the late 1800s, archery, croquet, and tennis were among the first sports to attract women as participants because they did not require immodest clothing and were non-vigorous. Societal and supposed physical restrictions prohibited women from engaging in aggressive and more competitive sports. Bicycling introduced a radical change in attire with the bloomer costume, or divided skirt, which allowed freedom from the appropriate attire of the day that included voluminous skirts and petticoats and tightly laced corsets. Bloomers and middy blouses became the accepted costume for gymnastics and other physical activities, with students at the Sargent Normal School among the first to wear them.

Miss Senda Berenson, in long dress, with Smith College students in Northampton, Mass. where women played the first public basketball game on March 22, 1893. (Courtesy of Basketball Hall of Fame)

Typical bloomer-type uniforms worn by women who first played basketball at the turn of the century. (Courtesy of Basketball Hall of Fame)

Women eagerly adopted basketball and adapted and modified its rules to make the game less strenuous and not as rough. In 1896, the first intercollegiate contest between women, from the University of California and Stanford University, occurred. Field days for track events became popular in the women's colleges in the 1890s, while upper-class women began to compete nationally in archery (1879), tennis (1887), and golf (1896).

SUMMARY

Early physical education in the United States underwent a transition from recreational sports and games to organized school and college programs that emphasized one system of gymnastics or a combination of exercises from the various systems. A Battle of the Systems raged as Swedish and German gymnastics had their advocates, but neither found national acceptance. Health and strength were favored outcomes, but even these did not seem fully to satisfy Americans' needs. Prior to 1900, teachers of physical education had completed programs in normal schools, and a fledgling national association existed, but still a unified, national program had not emerged. With the popularization of children's play and of sports in the late 1800s in amateur clubs and on college campuses, the stage was set for the development in the 1900s of an American program based primarily on playing sports and games.

DUDLEY ALLEN SARGENT

(1849–1924)

EDUCATION
B.A. Bowdoin College (1875)
M.D. Yale Medical School (1878)

BACKGROUND

Dudley Sargent, one of the most influential leaders in physical education in the United States, contributed significantly in the areas of individualized programs, measurements of the dimensions and the capacities of the body, and teacher training. He also accepted leadership positions in professional organizations, wrote numerous papers, and made scholarly presentations.

After an early career as a professional acrobat, Sargent obtained a bachelor's degree from Bowdoin College and a medical degree from Yale Medical School. While a student at these institutions for 9 years, he worked as Director of Gymnastics (at Bowdoin) and Director of the Gymnasium (at Yale). In 1879, he began his 40-year tenure at Harvard University after being named Director of the Hemenway Gymnasium and Assistant Professor of Physical Training.

ACCOMPLISHMENTS

Sargent immediately implemented an individualized program that focused on meeting the needs of the Harvard students who were physically underdeveloped. Sargent took a series of anthropometric measurements and, based on this thorough examination, prescribed an individual exercise program for each student. Measurements of each student's progress were taken periodically and followed by changes in the prescribed program. Sargent opposed the heavy, German apparatus as well as Dio Lewis' light apparatus and instead designed or improved devices adaptable to students' various abilities. In addition to chest weights and pulleys, he provided chest expanders and developers, leg machines, inclined planes, and hydraulic rowing machines—about 80 developing machines in all.

Athletes' abilities were also measured through various tests. Rather than opposing athletics, as some detractors have accused, Sargent encouraged students to engage in boxing, rowing, fencing, bowling, running, and baseball. Sargent's anthropometric measurement procedures and charts for athletes and all other students were widely used and contributed to physical education's entry into the scientific world.

Also a pioneer in the realm of teacher training, Sargent in 1881 opened the Sanatory Gymnasium to students at Harvard Annex and to women and men who wanted to become teachers of physical education. Although it was coeducational between 1904 and 1914, few men enrolled. The high female enrollment made it the largest normal school in the United States as its more than 3,000 graduates spread the Sargent system throughout the country. The eclectric curriculum at the school consisted of theory courses emphasizing the sciences and practical exercises as varied as free movements, light gymnastics using dumbbells and Indian clubs, marching, sports, and heavy gymnastics.

CONTRIBUTIONS TO PHYSICAL EDUCATION

The Harvard Summer School of Physical Education, established by Sargent in 1887, became the most significant source of professional physical education in the United States during physical education's early years. During a time when teachers had minimal or no training in physical education, Harvard Summer School met these teachers' needs in an exemplary manner. An eminent faculty, often the recognized authorities in their subjects or activities, provided both theoretical and practical instruction, resulting in school administrators' regarding highly a certificate from Harvard Summer School. Most of the students were teachers, but physicians, army officers, and other professionals attended, too. During its 46 summers, more than 5,000 students attended.

REVIEW QUESTIONS

1. What types of physical activities were used as recreation by the colonists in the 1700s? How did these differ by region of the country?
2. Why did German gymnastics not gain wide acceptance in the United States in the 1820s and in the 1850s to 1880s?
3. What constituted the program of hygiene and physical education at Amherst College?

4. What were the basic principles of Dudley Sargent's program for Harvard University students?
5. Why was the Boston Conference on Physical Training in 1889 significant?
6. Why were normal schools for physical education established, especially in the 1880s?
7. Why was the Harvard Summer School significant?
8. Why was the Association for the Advancement of Physical Education founded?
9. What early occurrences or developments started the playground movement?
10. Why did the faculty get involved in men's intercollegiate athletics?

STUDENT ACTIVITIES

1. As a class, reenact the Boston Conference on Physical Training (1889) by having each student report on one of the following "systems:" Swedish, German, Amherst College's, Harvard University's, military drill, or sports and games. Alternatively, a student may challenge the effectiveness or appropriateness of any one "system."
2. Read about the founding of the first professional organization in physical education (today's American Alliance for Health, Physical Education, Recreation and Dance) and report your findings orally to the class or in a three-page paper.
3. By examining histories of your state or region, find the most popular sport or recreational activity for one of the following groups:
   a) Indian males
   b) Indian females
   c) Indian children
   d) Early settlers (males)
   e) Early settlers (females)
   f) Children of early settlers
   g) Upper-class males in the 1800s
   h) Upper-class females in the 1800s
   i) Upper-class children in the 1800s
   j) Middle-class males in the 1800s
   k) Middle-class females in the 1800s
   l) Middle-class children in the 1800s
   m) Lower-class males in the 1800s
   n) Lower-class females in the 1800s
   o) Lower-class children in the 1800s

4. Find out the name(s) and the starting date(s) of the oldest "normal" school(s) for physical education for males and for females in your state.

REFERENCES

Barrows, I. C. *Physical training.* Boston: George H. Ellis Press, 1899 (*sic*).

Betts, J. R. (1984). The technological revolution and the rise of sports. In Riess, S. A. (Ed.). *The American sporting experience: a historical anthology of sports in America.* West Point, N.Y.: Leisure Press, 141–163.

Gerber, E. W. (1971). *Innovators and institutions in physical education.* Philadelphia: Lea & Febiger.

Lee, M. (1983). *A history of physical education and sports in the U.S.A.* New York: John Wiley and Sons.

Lee, M., and Bennett, B. L. This is our heritage. *Journal of Health, Physical Education and Recreation,* April 1960, *31,* 27.

Lucas, J. A., and Smith, R. A. (1978). *Saga of American sport.* Philadelphia: Lea and Febiger.

Van Dalen, D. B., & Bennett, B. L. (1971). *A world history of physical education.* Englewood Cliffs, N.J.: Prentice–Hall.

Welch, P. D., and Lerch, H. A. (1981). *History of American physical education and sport.* Springfield, Ill. Charles C Thomas, Publisher.

SUGGESTED READINGS

Bennett, B. L. Dudley Allen Sargent: the man and his philosophy. *Journal of Physical Education, Recreation and Dance, 55,* 61–64, November/December 1984. Harvard University students benefitted from Dudley Sargent's individualized exercise prescriptions for 40 years, while prospective teachers learned this and other systems at the Sargent Normal School and the Harvard Summer School.

Cavallo, D. *Muscles and morals: organized playgrounds and urban reform, 1880–1920.* Philadelphia: University of Pennsylvania Press, 1981. This history reveals the cultural and political implications of the urban social reformers' efforts as they sought to transfer control of children's play from the children and their families to the state between 1880 and 1920.

Eyler, M. H. What the profession was once like: nineteenth century physical education. *The Academy Papers, 15,* 14–20, April 1981. Drawing extensively from research written about this century, the author traces the significant themes and developments as physical education emerges as a unified field.

Howell, R. (Ed.). *Her story in sport: a historical anthology of women in sports.* West Point, New York: Leisure Press, 1982. Forty-two signed articles about outstanding innovators, successful programs and teams, and major developmental trends describe the beginning, emerging, and equality seeking of women in sports.

Lee, M., and Bennett, B. Alliance centennial: 100 years of health, physical education, recreation and dance. *Journal of Physical Education, Recreation and Dance, 56,* 17–66, April 1985. This article reprints the "This Is Our Heritage" historical series, 15-year thematic sections that highlight significant occurrences related to the activities of today's American Alliance for Health, Physical Education, Recreation and Dance, and chronicles the profession's major developments between 1960 and 1985.

Leigh, M. H. Edward Hitchcock, Jr.: dean of the profession. *Journal of Physical Education, Recreation and Dance, 53,* 19–21, October 1982. Edward Hitchcock established the first college physical education at Amherst College in 1861 and served as a distinguished leader of the profession for the next 50 years.

Lucas, J. A., and Smith, R. A. *Saga of American sport.* Philadelphia: Lea and Febiger, 1978. Throughout this exhaustive examination of colonial to twentieth century sport in America, the authors show that sports have reflected the dominant social themes in existence during each period.

Pekara, J. Luther Halsey Gulick. *Journal of Physical Education, Recreation and Dance, 54,* 69–70, 73, October 1983. Gulick, a dynamic and innovative leader in physical education, served the YMCA, the New York City schools, the Playground Association of America, and the Camp Fire Girls during his illustrious career.

Spears, B. Amy Morris Homans: a heritage of excellence. *Journal of Physical Education, Recreation and Dance, 54,* 15, February 1983. Amy Morris Homans personified excellence in her leadership of the Boston Normal School of Gymnastics and of Wellesley College's Department of Hygiene and Physical Education; at the same time she demanded that her students attain and demonstrate the highest professional standards.

Spears, B., and Swanson, R. A. *History of sport and physical activity in the United States* (2nd Ed.). Dubuque, Iowa: Wm. C. Brown Company, Publishers, 1983. This study of various sports and physical activity in the United States uses a chronological approach of six eras, each with a focus on pastimes, amateur sports, professional sports, and Olympic sports.

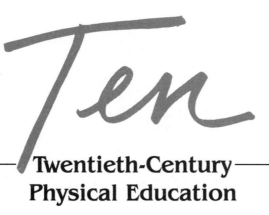

C H A P T E R

Ten

Twentieth-Century Physical Education

KEY
CONCEPTS

■ The new physical education, following the Battle of the Systems, emphasized complete education.

■ The national association and many outstanding leaders increasingly published journals and books, and shared philosophies and programs at conferences.

■ Men's intercollegiate sports expanded from intramural origins into commercialized businesses.

■ Women's intercollegiate sports featured mass participation until the late 1960s, when competition became a primary goal.

■ The children's play movement expanded first into a recreational emphasis for all and then into a mania for fitness.

■ Today's new physical education results from program changes and includes a great variety of activities.

213

The controversy concerning which system of gymnastics would best meet the needs of students in the United States continued into the early years of the twentieth century. Beginning in the 1920s, the "new physical education" offered an alternative based on educational outcomes. Physical education curricula then evolved to emphasize sport, recreational, lifetime activities and fitness. Since the turn of the century, the popularity of athletics at all levels and for both sexes has expanded tremendously. The new physical education of the 1980s seeks to meet the fitness and lifetime sports needs of students as well as the diverse clientele professionals serve in other environs.

THE NEW PHYSICAL EDUCATION

The Battle of the Systems had not resulted in the adoption of one gymnastics program by the end of the nineteenth century. The formal nature of the alternatives had failed to appeal to a broad base of physical educators and their students, who were seeking activities that offered competition, fun, and more freedom of expression. Five men succeeded in filling this curricular need, while leading the effort to achieve public acceptance of sports-based physical education programs as vital to the complete development of children. Four of them, Luther Gulick, Thomas D. Wood, Jay B. Nash, and Jesse Williams, shared a common introduction to physical education at Oberlin College under Delphine Hanna; Thomas Wood directly influenced the fifth of the new physical educators, Clark Hetherington.

LEADERS IN THE NEW PHYSICAL EDUCATION

Luther Gulick became an instructor at the YMCA Training School in 1887 and, 2 years later, was named superintendent. While at the YMCA Training School, he emphasized sports in the physical directors' curriculum and started the YMCA's Athletic League to promote amateur sports. Stressing unity in developing the body, mind, and spirit, he designed the YMCA triangle (Figure 10–1), emblematic of the all-around man. He then moved to New York and

The YMCA symbol of an inverted, equilateral triangle, designed by Luther Gulick, represents the importance of the spirit supported by the body and the mind. Gulick based the meaning of the triangle on Deuteronomy 6:5:"And thou shalt love the Lord thy God with all thine heart, and with all thy soul, and with all thy might."

FIGURE 10–1. YMCA emblem.

taught before accepting the position of Director of Physical Training for the New York City public schools (Jable, 1979). Although Gulick supported gymnastics as the basis of school curricula, he founded the Public School Athletic League to provide after-school play opportunities for boys, especially in track and field activities.

Another Gulick legacy focused on play. In 1906, he helped establish the Playground Association of America and served as its first president. Through his advocacy of the provision of playgrounds and public recreation in this country, his initiation of the Campfire Girls in 1913, and his leadership in the camping movement, Gulick promoted play.

Thomas D. Wood, speaking in the 1890s, forecasted the outcome of the Battle of the Systems when he proposed that physical training had merit only if it contributed to the complete education of the individual (Wood, 1983). No system was accepted; rather physical education curricula increasingly stressed activities that met overall educational objectives. At the same time, G. Stanley Hall's developmental theories and John Dewey's social education concepts encouraged physical educators to design experiences to meet students' needs.

Wood developed his first undergraduate teacher training curriculum in physical education at Stanford University beginning in 1891. Ten years later, he joined the faculty of Teachers College of Columbia University, where he led in the establishment of the first master's (1910) and doctor's (1925) degree programs in physical education. He was instrumental in the development of health education as a separate field of study while at Teachers College. *The New Physical Education*, which he co-authored with Rosalind Cassady in 1927, provided the philosophical foundation for the refocusing of school programs from gymnastics to sports, games, dance, aquatics, and natural activities.

At Stanford University, Wood taught and greatly influenced Clark Hetherington. This is evident from Hetherington's use of the term "new physical education" and in his advocacy of organic, psychomotor, character, and intellectual development as descriptive of physical education's objectives. G. Stanley Hall, a second mentor for Hetherington, emphasized developmentalism, which paralleled Hetherington's philosophy that play was a child's chief business in life. At the University of Missouri, the University of Wisconsin, New York University, and Stanford University, Hetherington helped establish undergraduate physical education programs. At New York University he led in the development of graduate degree programs.

One of the first graduates from New York University's Ph.D. program in physical education was Jay B. Nash. Nash had served as the California Assistant Supervisor of Physical Education under Hetherington before joining the faculty at New York University in 1926 as Hetherington's replacement. Nash stressed that recreational skills should be learned early in life and could then supplement satisfactions from work. Fearing an overemphasis on spectating in the United States, Nash stated that school programs should teach carry-over, or lifetime, sports to encourage people to adopt active lifestyles; that is, people should be educated for leisure.

Influenced by Wood's concept of complete education and John Dewey's social education theories, Jesse Feiring Williams emphasized that the development of physical skills in the schools could be justified only if such activities helped to educate the total child. According to Williams' theories, educating a child to live in a democratic society through social and intellectual interactions within physical education justified its inclusion in the schools. Through his 41 books and the students he influenced in the highly regarded graduate physical education program at Teachers College of Columbia University, Williams became one of the most influential leaders in physical education, especially between 1930 and 1960.

Figure 10–2 summarizes the influence of these five new physical educators on each other. It is also interesting that they signaled a change in the professional training of physical educators. Whereas Gulick, Wood, and Williams held medical degrees, Nash earned a Ph.D.

LEADERS IN THE PROFESSION

While the new physical education emerged during the early part of the twentieth century, programs such as Hitchcock's, Sargent's, and Hanna's continued, and others developed as numerous colleges and universities instituted teacher preparation programs in physical education in the early 1900s. Several of the normal schools affiliated or merged with colleges as the public schools began to require that teachers obtain college degrees rather than certifications. During this time, physical education benefitted from the contributions of many outstanding leaders and progressed gradually into a recognized field.

Jessie Bancroft, after serving 10 years as Director of Physical Training in the Brooklyn public schools, assumed the position of Assistant Director of

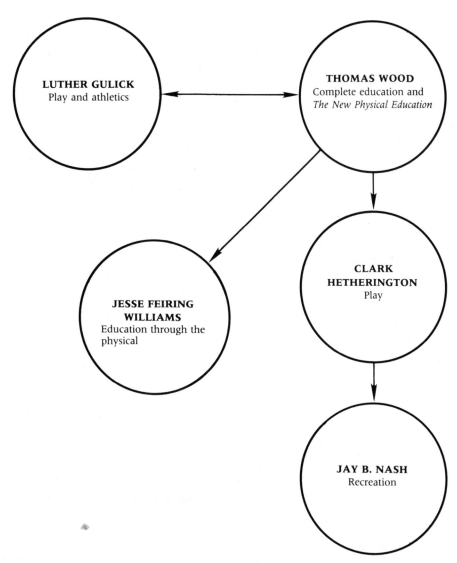

FIGURE 10–2. New physical educators.

Physical Training in the New York City Schools, in 1903, under Luther Gulick. During her 25-year tenure in this position, her curricular emphasis changed from strictly advocating gymnastics to promoting sports and games. To this, Bancroft added the importance of adjusting the difficulty of the games to the needs of children. She wrote *Games for the Playground, Home, Schools, and*

Gymnasium to explain her beliefs, which paralleled the evolving nature of elementary physical education programs.

When Luther Gulick started a Girls' Branch of the Public School Athletic League in 1905, he selected Elizabeth Burchenal to direct it. Burchenal, who founded the American Folk-Dance Society and served as president from 1916 to 1929, shared a love for folk dancing with Gulick as well as a belief in the appropriateness of this activity for girls as an after-school program. Burchenal also led in the development of standards for girls' and women's participation in sports through the Committee on Women's Athletics within the American Physical Education Association.

A graduate of and teacher at the Boston Normal School of Gymnastics (1892 to 1906), Ethel Perrin left the strict advocacy of Swedish gymnastics and changed her educational philosophy. The program she began, in 1909, as Supervisor of Physical Culture in the Detroit public schools emphasized co-educational play, informal classes, appropriate costumes in which girls could move freely, and interschool sports for boys and girls. During the next 14 years, she expanded the number of physical educators from 6 to 365, as Detroit led the nation in the provision of specially trained physical educators at all levels of instruction. As an advocate of sports participation for girls, she became a leader in the Women's Division of the National Amateur Athletic Federation in the 1920s.

Although Canadian by birth, R. Tait McKenzie left his mark on physical education in the United States. After serving as a physician and a physical educator in Canada, he continued contributions in both areas after accepting a position at the University of Pennsylvania in 1904. By avocation, McKenzie was an artist. Significant among his many works was his sculpture *The Joy of Effort*, which received the King's Medal at the Fine Arts Competition at the 1912 Stockholm Olympics (Lee, 1983).

Mabel Lee, in 1931, became the first woman president of the American Physical Education Association. In addition, she provided leadership to the National Association of Physical Education for College Women, the American Academy of Physical Education, and the National Section on Women's Athletics as well as teaching at the University of Nebraska (1924 to 1952) during her long and distinguished career.

Charles McCloy, in dramatic contrast to the educational objectives emphasized by Williams, stressed organic and psychomotor development as the most important objectives for physical education. During his more than 20 years with the YMCA and especially in his tenure at State University of Iowa, McCloy stated that the uniqueness of physical education depended on the development of skills. He encouraged teachers to promote sports skills and to measure progress through standardized tests.

While McCloy defended physical education's specific contributions to phys-

R. Tait McKenzie's *The Joy of Effort* won the King's Medal at the 1912 Stockholm Olympic Games. (Courtesy of The University of Tennessee Press)

ical well-being, Jesse Williams claimed that physical education merited inclusion in the schools because it helped attain social, emotional, and intellectual goals and thus better prepared students to live in a democratic society. Williams rigorously defended his philosophy of "education through the physical" while McCloy was equally firm in his belief of "education of the physical." By adamantly stating their contrasting philosophies, Williams and McCloy may have added credibility to the mind/body dichotomy that has plagued physical education since the Greeks, as focusing on one aspect of the person often resulted in a deemphasis on the whole person. Even in the 1980s, many educators, parents, and legislators, all of whom influence programs, still separate children's curricula into academic and physical entities. However, research is verifying increasingly that through movement, many content areas, such as math, science, and reading, can be enhanced.

A student of McCloy, Eleanor Metheny, who taught at the University of Southern California from 1942 to 1971, was recognized as an insightful author and an inspirational speaker. She advocated ideas about the meaning of human movement that revolutionized the conceptual base of physical education. The many contributions of these leaders are summarized in Box 10-1.

INTRAMURALS

Most college athletic teams and some physical education programs in the late 1800s and early 1900s evolved out of intraclass competitions organized by male students. As athletics and physical education developed their own separate programs, a need still existed for recreational activities for the student body. In 1913, the University of Michigan and Ohio State University appointed the first intramural directors. At Michigan, beginning in 1919, Elmer Mitchell led in the development of sports opportunities for students who were not varsity athletes but who wanted more competition than was available in physical education classes. Originally in the colleges and after the mid-1920s in the schools, intramurals offered league and class, or homeroom, competition in individual and team sports. In the 1940s, the introduction of corecreational activities became popular. The greatest expansion in these com-

Coeducational leisuretime activities, such as volleyball, are offered by recreation departments, YMCAs and YWCAs, corporate recreation programs, and school intramural programs.

BOX 10–1

TWENTIETH CENTURY LEADERS IN PHYSICAL EDUCATION IN THE UNITED STATES

Luther Halsey Gulick (1865–1918)
   Instructor (1887–1900) and Superintendent (1889–1900) of the Department of Physical Training at the YMCA Training School
   Director of Physical Training for the New York City public schools (1903–1908)
   Established the Public School Athletic League in New York City (1903)
   Helped establish the Playground Association of America (1906)
Thomas Denison Wood (1864–1951)
   Taught at Stanford University (1891–1901)
   Taught at Teachers College of Columbia University (1901–1932)
   Formulated the philosophical cornerstone for the "new physical education"
   First professor of health education at Teachers College of Columbia University
Clark Wilson Hetherington (1870–1942)
   Director of Physical Training and Athletics at the University of Missouri (1900–1910)
   Established a Demonstration Play School at the University of California, Berkeley (1913–1917)
   Taught at the University of Wisconsin (1913–1918)
   State Supervisor of Physical Education for California (1918–1921)
   Taught at New York University (1923–1929)
   Taught at Stanford University (1929–1938)
Jay Bryan Nash (1886–1965)
   Taught at New York University (1926–1953)
   Influenced by Clark Hetherington and extended his theories as well as those of Luther Gulick and Thomas Wood
   Promoted recreation and carry-over sports
Jesse Feiring Williams (1886–1966)
   Taught at Teachers College of Columbia University (1911–1916 and 1919–1941)
   Stressed educational values, social education, and education through the physical
   Dominate influence in physical education (1930–1960)
Jessie Hubbell Bancroft (1867–1952)
   Director of Physical Training in the Brooklyn Schools (1893–1903)
   Assistant Director of Physical Training in the New York City Schools (1903–1928)
   Founder and first president of the American Posture League (1914–1922)

(continues)

(concluded)

Elizabeth Burchenal (1876–1959)
Founder and first president of the American Folk-Dance Society (1916–1929)
Executive Secretary of the Girls' Branch of the Public School Athletic League (1906–1916)
First chairperson of the Committee on Women's Athletics of the American Physical Education Association (1917)

Ethel Perrin (1871–1962)
Supervisor of Physical Culture in the Detroit public schools (1909–1923)
Executive Committee of the Women's Division of the National Amateur Athletic Federation (1923–1932)
Assistant/Associate Director of Health Education for the American Child Health Association (1923–1936)

Robert Tait McKenzie (1867–1938)
Taught (1891–1904) and served as Medical Director of Physical Education (1896–1904) at University Medical College (Canada)
Professor on Medical Faculty and Director of Physical Education (1904–1931) and Professor of Physical Therapy (1907–1931) at the University of Pennsylvania
Sculptor of hundreds of athletic events in aesthetic harmony of bodily proportion and expression

Mabel Lee (1886–   )
Director of physical education for women at the University of Nebraska (1924–1952)
First woman president of the American Physical Education Association (1931–1932)
Outstanding professional leader, proponent of wholesome sport for women, and author

Charles Harold McCloy (1886–1959)
Worked for the YMCA in the United States and internationally (1908–1930)
Research professor in physical education at the State University of Iowa (1930–1954)
Stressed the development of skills and organic vigor as the primary objectives of physical education and education of the physical

Eleanor Metheny (1908–1982)
Taught at Wellesley College and at the Harvard Fatigue Laboratory (1940–1942)
Taught at the University of Southern California (1942–1971)
Leader in the study of meaningful movement experiences

bined male–female events occurred in the 1970s. Today, many intramural programs operate as campus recreation programs, having greatly expanded the scope of their activities. To competitive leagues and corecreational events have been added club sports, extramural competitions, faculty–staff programs, instructional clinics, special events and tournaments, and provision for free play. Over the years, many of these intramural–recreational sports programs have moved from receiving funds first from athletics departments and then from physical education departments to being supported by student fees. At the school level, where intramural activities vary from traditional competitions to unusual contests and events such as Superstars and Ultimate Frisbee, and where these events are squeezed into times throughout the day, physical educators normally provide the expertise while school budgets provide the equipment. Intramural programs in business, industry, and the military also have become popular.

LEADERSHIP FROM THE NATIONAL ASSOCIATION

In the early 1900s, the American Physical Education Association (APEA) was dominated by Easterners who attempted to build a strong profession through the exchange of ideas and shared projects. James McCurdy, who served as editor of the APEA's *American Physical Education Review* for 23 years, was one outstanding leader during the early years.

In the 1900s, dancing and athletics were frequently added to school and college programs, challenging the former supremacy of gymnastics. Besides these two, frequently discussed topics at the annual meetings of the APEA included school hygiene, the value of gymnastics, skill and fitness testing, and standards for teacher preparation and graduate education. There was a proliferation of professional preparation in physical education between 1920 and 1927: 70 new college programs were begun.

Following the combination of the Midwest Society with the national APEA in 1930, Elmer Mitchell assumed the editorship of the *Journal of Health and Physical Education* and the *Research Quarterly* and served in this capacity for 13 years. The Department of School Health and Physical Education of the National Education Association merged with the APEA in 1937, to become the American Association for Health and Physical Education (recreation was added to its name in 1938). The national organization was subsequently composed of six geographical districts.

After World War II, the AAHPER sponsored numerous conferences focusing on facilities, undergraduate professional preparation, graduate professional preparation, fitness, and other interest areas. In conjunction with the President's Council on Youth Fitness, it promoted fitness for children nationally through such programs as Operation Fitness. In 1974, it was restructured into an alliance composed of seven (now, six) associations (see Chapter 4) to allow greater autonomy in providing leadership and programs for its diverse interest areas.

In 1985, the Alliance's centennial celebration focused on recalling its service and leadership to health, physical education, recreation, dance, and sports. The April 1985 issue of the *Journal of Physical Education, Recreation and Dance* traced 100 years of the profession by highlighting special events and notable leaders. The message conveyed in this publication and through the centennial convention was that the Alliance, through its membership, had enriched programs for many diverse populations.

TEACHER PREPARATION

A perennial concern of the AAHPER and its preceding organizations has been the lack of professional preparation standards for teachers. Each normal school, as it developed, was free to pursue its own course of study, with little interest in what was being taught at the others. When 4-year degree programs were developed in colleges and universities, each institution had the latitude to design and implement its own curriculum. Since, in the early 1900s, there were no accreditation procedures or standards, great program diversity resulted. The Department of School Health and Physical Education of the National Education Association, in the 1930s, established a committee to evaluate teacher education curricula and to establish standards. In 1948, the National Conference on Undergraduate Professional Preparation in Health Education, Physical Education, and Recreation recommended standards and programs in teacher preparation. The AAHPER voted, in 1960, to accept the National Council for Accreditation of Teacher Education (NCATE) as the official accrediting agency in its fields of study. This led to state departments of instruction certifying only teachers who graduated from NCATE-approved institutions. In the 1970s, many state departments began to require that certain competencies be met in professional course work before future teachers would be certified. Each of these developments enhanced the quality of the graduates of teacher education programs.

In the 1980s, many people have expressed concern about the lack of standards for or credentials of individuals engaged in various sports and fitness programs. For example, there is no national certification for aerobic dance instructors. Seemingly anyone with a leotard and coordinated tights and leg warmers who can enthusiastically motivate people to exercise to the resounding beat of the latest hit tunes can teach. Knowledge about human anatomy, exercise physiology, first aid, cardiopulmonary resuscitation, psychology, and teaching progressions is not a prerequisite. This has led to repeated injuries, some serious, high dropout rates, and a general lack of accountability on the part of the instructors and the sponsoring groups. The American College of Sports Medicine, with its new certification programs for fitness instructors and leaders, has begun to fill the gap in this area, but still such training is optional rather than mandatory. Unless a sport (e.g., scuba diving or skiing) regulates its own instructors' training, anyone is free to teach it (e.g., weight training, karate, or racquetball) outside the schools.

AMATEUR AND COLLEGIATE SPORTS

The popularization of sports in the twentieth century has been phenomenal. In addition to becoming the nucleus of physical eduation programs, sports are organized for competition both inside and outside the schools.

COLLEGIATE SPORTS FOR MEN

Problems in collegiate sports focused on football in the early 1900s, primarily because of the injuries and deaths that occurred with shocking regularity (Guttmann, 1978). While President Theodore Roosevelt expressed concern, college presidents threatened to ban intercollegiate football. As a direct result of football injuries and deaths, today's National Collegiate Athletic Association (NCAA) was formed in 1906. Although composed of a small group of faculty representatives with power only to recommend, the NCAA attempted to control the roughness and brutality of football by revising its rules. Gradually, football overcame these problems and emerged as the major collegiate sport. Baseball in colleges, though rivalled by the major leagues, retained a degree of popularity secondary to the pros and to football while intercollegiate competitions in boxing, golf, tennis, track and field, and wrestling began but never seriously challenged the supremacy of college football (Falla, 1981). Basketball emerged as the second leading collegiate sport, but not until the 1950s. The NCAA continued as the sole voice of and controlling organization for college athletes until 1938, when the National Junior College Athletic Association (NJCAA) was founded to provide competitive opportunities for students in two-year institutions, and 1952, when the National Association of Intercollegiate Athletics (NAIA) began to sponsor championships for the small colleges. Box 10–2 lists these and other major sports organizations for men and for women.

Collegiate athletics for men in the 1980s are very different than they were in the 1940s. Under faculty control by representative vote, the NCAA remained primarily an advisory organization during its first 40 years. The control rested with the institution, where most frequently athletic councils composed of alumni, faculty, and students exercised authority over athletics. Institutions that held membership in conferences agreed to follow additional regulations and guidelines. Other than standardizing the rules and providing championships, the NCAA had not been granted power by the institutions to legislate or to mandate rules. Beginning with the national acceptance of athletic grants-in-aid in 1951, the role of the NCAA changed dramatically during the next decade, because institutions were willing to relinquish some

---

BOX 10–2
SPORT GOVERNANCE ORGANIZATIONS

Sport Governance Organizations for Boys and Men

1888   Amateur Athletic Union (AAU)
         *1879—National Association of Amateur Athletes of America
1910   National Collegiate Athletic Association (NCAA)
         *1906—Intercollegiate Athletic Association of the United
             States
1922   National Federation of State High School Athletic Associations
             (NFSHSAA)
1938   National Junior College Athletic Association (NJCAA)
1952   National Association of Intercollegiate Athletics (NAIA)
         *1940—National Association of Intercollegiate Basketball

Sport Governance Organizations for Girls and Women

1974   National Association for Girls and Women in Sports (NAGWS)
         *1917—Committee on Women's Athletics
         *1927—Women's Athletic Section
         *1932—National Section on Women's Athletics
         *1953—National Section on Girls and Women in Sports
         *1958—Division of Girls and Women in Sports
1971   Association for Intercollegiate Athletics for Women (AIAW)
         *1966—Commission on Intercollegiate Athletics for Women

First championships offered for girls and women:
1916   Amateur Athletic Union
1976   National Junior College Athletic Association
1980   National Association of Intercollegiate Athletics
1981   National Collegiate Athletic Association

* Earlier name of the same organization.

College football in the 1930s. (Courtesy of North Carolina Collection, UNC Library at Chapel Hill)

of their autonomy to the NCAA to ensure that other institutions would comply with the regulations governing grants-in-aid and recruiting. A second development, beginning with the first negotiation of television contracts in 1952, provided the NCAA with enforcement leverage and thrust it into the dominant position in intercollegiate athletics (Baker, 1982). The NCAA could penalize an institution economically by disallowing television appearances, at least until 1984, when its television negotiations on behalf of its football playing members were ruled unconstitutional, thus allowing the teams and conferences to arrange their own appearances. By the 1980s, the NCAA had emerged as the most powerful amateur sports organization in the United States and possibly the world.

COLLEGIATE SPORTS FOR WOMEN

Sports for women were strictly controlled by women physical educators, who consistently followed societal expectations during the early 1900s. Caution about a potential overemphasis on competition or on unladylike behavior led to modified rules in several sports. Mass participation in class exercises, field days, play days, and sports days, rather than competitive athletics, became the norm. Physical education, especially for its healthful benefits, was stressed for girls in schools and for women who attended colleges in the early

1900s. Outfitted in middy blouses and bloomers, the traditional gymnasium costume of the day, these women exercised in mass drills, engaged in therapeutic Swedish gymnastics, and enjoyed sports such as archery, basketball, field hockey, rowing, and tennis. Field days were normally conducted once or twice a year on campus, and all students were urged to participate. Play days, beginning in the 1920s, provided for social interaction as women students met and formed teams composed of representatives from several institutions. These teams played one or more sports before reassembling for a picnic or other social event. Evolved from these play days were sports days, on which college teams competed, frequently in only one sport, but still with the emphasis on social interaction and fun (Gerber, 1982, pp. 432–459).

In 1917, a Committee on Women's Athletics was established by the American Physical Education Association (today's AAHPER) to establish standards and policies that advocated mass participation while vigorously opposing varsity competition. The Women's Division of the National Amateur Athletic Federation, between 1923 and 1942, also opposed highly competitive sports, including those in the Olympic Games, as inappropriate for women.

In the 1960s, a gradual change in societal attitudes regarding women in sports paralleled a liberalized philosophy displayed by women leaders in physical education. As long as the welfare of the athletes was guaranteed and high standards were maintained, competitions were permitted and even encouraged, especially beginning in 1969, when the Commission on Intercollegiate Athletics for Women began the sponsorship of national tournaments. Two years later, the Association for Intercollegiate Athletics for Women (AIWA), an institutional membership organization, assumed this responsibility. During the next 11 years, the AIAW provided championships and established standards and policies governing women's intercollegiate athletics. With equal opportunity mandated by Title IX of the 1972 Education Amendments Act, colleges and schools financed increased sports competitions for girls and women. In 1976, the NJCAA and, in 1980, the NAIA began offering championships for college women; these smaller institutions benefitted financially from having one membership fee, one governance structure and set of rules, and similar sport schedules for all athletes. Although the NCAA paid teams' and athletes' expenses in national championships beginning in 1981, the AIAW could not afford to provide these. Thus many institutions elected to compete in the NCAA events, resulting in the demise of the AIAW in 1982.

AMATEUR SPORTS

The amateur sports scene in the United States outside the colleges remained largely under the direction of the AAU through the 1970s, since this organization sponsored a great diversity of sports competitions for people of all ages. Basketball, boxing, swimming, and track and field especially attracted thousands of participants. Because championships in these sports were offered by NCAA institutions, these two organizations frequently clashed. Repeatedly, when the time arrived for the selection of Olympic teams, controversies raged. In 1922, the National Amateur Athletic Federation was formed to mediate in this dispute, with few positive results. The conflicts inevitably affected the athletes as these two associations refused to sanction events, to certify records, or to permit their athletes to participate in the other's events. The Amateur Sports Act, passed in 1978, resolved some of these problems by requiring that every Olympic sport have its own (single-sport) governing body and by establishing guidelines governing the selection of these organizations.

The AAU has led the United States' involvement in the Olympic Games following their reestablishment in 1896. Founded by Frenchman Pierre de Coubertin, the modern Olympic Games have sought to generate friendship among athletes of the world and to promote fitness and sports. Heavily influenced by the British Amateur Sport Ideal, de Coubertin advocated that only athletes who competed for the love of sport (hence amateurs) were welcome. As in the Greek Olympic Games, only men were eligible. From a small beginning (311 competitors from 13 countries) in Athens, the Olympic Games have grown in both numbers and popularity, as evidenced by the media attention focused on the 1984 Los Angeles Games and by the membership of more than 150 national Olympic committees in the Olympic movement. While de Coubertin stated that the most important thing was not to win but to take part, success in the Olympics has been highly prestigious both for the athletes and for their countries' promotion of their sociopolitical systems. These intense competitions for elite athletes contrast dramatically with the advocacy of play and fitness for all.

PLAY TO RECREATION TO FITNESS

PLAY

The playground movement continued apace in the early 1900s (Betts, 1974), as the Playground Association of America (PAA), founded in 1906 by Luther Gulick and Henry Curtis, provided the necessary leadership. Gulick served as its first president and was instrumental in the publication of its monthly magazine, *The Playground*. The provision of adequate playgrounds throughout the country was also enhanced by the support of President Theodore Roosevelt. Clark Hetherington supervised the writing, in 1910, of *The Normal Course in Play*, the book used to prepare recreation leaders. Joseph Lee, as president of the PAA, helped expand the play concept to include the value of play and recreation for all ages, leading to the reorganization of the

PAA in 1911 and its new name, the Playground and Recreation Association of America (PRAA).

RECREATION

In 1930, the PRAA became the National Recreation Association, verifying the importance of the worthy use of leisure time by people of all ages. The depression years suddenly gave people large amounts of leisure time, but, for many, limited financial resources. The federal government helped resolve this problem in two ways. Federal agencies, such as the Works Progress Administration, provided jobs by funding construction of camping sites, golf courses, gymnasiums, playing fields, and swimming pools, and once completed, these were opened for recreational use by everyone. Especially popular sports during the 1930s were bowling and softball.

War production brought the United States out of the Depression. At the same time, sports competitions and recreational programs were initiated to revive the spirits and bodies of soldiers and the workers back home. While the armed services used sports for training and conditioning soldiers, industries began to provide sports teams and competitive opportunities for its employees, realizing that this positively affected productivity and morale. Industrial recreation continued to expand even after the war crisis ended.

Outdoor education emerged as the recreational thrust of the 1950s. As the country became more mechanized and technological, the appeal of camping, hiking, and similar back-to-nature activities provided people with the chance to get away from it all. Some schools and colleges began to offer backpacking, rock climbing, spelunking, winter survival, ropes courses, and orienteering, which have maintained their popularity in programs in the 1980s.

Jay B. Nash, as early as the 1930s, promoted carry-over, or lifetime, sports within the curriculum. By the 1960s, this philosophy gained numerous supporters and affected programs. Led by the Lifetime Sports Foundation with joint sponsorship by the American Association for Health, Physical Education and Recreation, archery, badminton, bowling, golf, and tennis were introduced into many schools. Slowly, programs expanded from offering only team sports to the inclusion of these and other lifetime sports.

FITNESS

A mania for fitness began in the 1970s, with joggers leading the boom. In 1970, the lonely runner was suddenly joined by thousands of marathoners and road racers of all ages and both genders, while tennis became everyone's game and swimming became the most popular activity. The pervasiveness of this fitness mania could be verified by observing the sport paraphernalia that enthusiasts used and wore, along with the popularity of sporting attire for everyone. This fitness phenomenon continued into the 1980s as aerobic dance, racquetball, and weight training became favorite activities outside and sometimes inside the schools. The people most involved in getting and keeping in shape came from the middle and upper classes, rather than being equally drawn from all economic levels. Also, many school-aged children in the 1980s, rather than becoming fitness advocates, have preferred to watch television, play video games, or become sports spectators.

FITNESS FOR CHILDREN

In 1953, the results of the Kraus-Weber Minimal Muscular Fitness Test were published (Kraus and Hirschland, 1953). The results showed that European children (only 9% failed) were more fit than children in the United States (57.8% failed). President Dwight Eisenhower demonstrated his desire to rectify the situation by calling a White House Conference. This resulted in the establishment, in 1956, of the President's Council on Youth Fitness, the first time not during a war when fitness became a national issue and compulsion. Since the six-item Kraus-Weber Test measured primarily flexibility and abdominal strength, and thus received the criticism that it inaccurately assessed fitness, the physical education profession developed the AAHPER Youth Fitness Test. To the dismay of professionals, the 1958 results of this eight-item test battery showed that children in the United States had a low level of fitness. Between 1958 and the second national administration of this test in 1965, teachers promoted fitness through daily physical education classes, periodic testing, and an increased consciousness of the importance of fitness. These efforts were rewarded with improvement by all age groups in all skills, except for 17-year-old girls in the softball throw. Unfortunately, these vigorous efforts lapsed, so few improvements in the fitness levels resulted in the 1974 test administration.

In response to widespread criticism that the AAHPER Youth Fitness Test failed to measure the major components of fitness, in 1981 the AAHPERD introduced the Health Related Lifetime Physical Fitness Test. Its items measured strength with sit-ups, flexibility using a sit-and-reach, cardiovascular endurance in a 1.5 mile or 12-minute run, and body composition by taking skinfold measurements. While more accurately measuring the recognized components of fitness, the test norms only confirmed the lack of fitness of school-aged children.

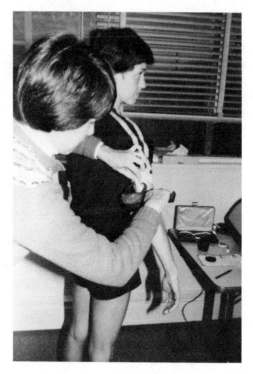

Body composition, measured as a part of the AAHPERD Health-Related Physical Fitness Test and many other physical assessment tests, is an excellent indicator of overall physical fitness. (Courtesy of Diane Victorson)

THE NEW PHYSICAL EDUCATION OF THE 1980s

Today's physical education programs reflect the many transitions through which the profession has moved. For example, in many high schools curricula focus is on traditional team sports—volleyball in the fall, basketball in the winter, and softball in the spring. Some schools have expanded their curricula to include archery, badminton, dance, golf, gymnastics, soccer, tennis, track and field, and weight training, although seldom are all of these taught in one school because limitations in budgets, equipment, facilities, and the number and certification of teachers. In many states the time allotted to physical education has been shortened so that health education can be taught.

Movement education, using problem solving and guided discovery, began in the United States in the 1950s, as a methodology based on exploration of the body's potential. Rather than emphasizing sports and games initially, movement education stressed learning basic movement skills, such as running, jumping, and throwing, and manipulative skills with balls, ropes, and other objects. Movement education broadened both the scope and the objectives of physical education by emphasizing that children explore movement and that they progress at individual rates. Children developed better motor skills as movement education grew into a combination of the process and the product and emerged as a vital ingredient in the new physical education of the 1980s.

IMPACT OF TITLE IX

Title IX, passed in 1972, requires that all students have equal opportunity in school programs, including physical education. Although this law mandates co-educational classes for all age levels, except in contact sports, many schools frequently maintain single-sex classes in violation of the law. Those schools that have complied now provide girls and boys with the same curricular instruction and opportunities for participation. Although some students have resisted this transition because of traditional stereotypical attitudes, most have acknowledged the right of all students to equal treatment.

FITNESS EMPHASIS

Most physical educators agree that the foundation for later school programs and for lifetime fitness begins in the elementary grades and that failure to provide instruction in movement during the developmental years means that children have been neglected physically. Children need to learn to enjoy and understand movement and to develop locomotor, perceptual-motor, manipulative, and fundamental sports skills.

The fitness mania, of course, is another influence on physical education today. The recognition by adults that physical activity can improve and help maintain health will affect school programs in one of two ways. On the one hand, parents may reflect on the poor or nonexistent programs they experienced and judge the expenditure of funds for physical education unnecessary, especially since their children can join them in community-based activities. Problems with this approach are readily evident. First, schools provide physical education for all students, while community, fee-based programs exclude those in the lower income levels. Second, many nonschool programs have no standards for the instructors and no accountability for the content, and often do not match children's developmental needs. On the other hand, parents may decide that fitness is essential for the quality of life they desire for their children and insist that schools meet this need. Inherent in this decision is their willingness to fund teachers, equipment, and facilities and to hold schools accountable for helping students become fit as well as for teaching about developing healthy life-styles.

CHALLENGES FOR SCHOOL PROGRAMS

The new physical education faces numerous trials and struggles for acceptance. As a part of education as a whole, it has been ridiculed, derided, and called inept. Everyone seems to conclude that education is facing a crisis; as a result, every facet of education is being reviewed, analyzed, and questioned regarding its relevance and contributions.

School physical education seems especially targeted for cutbacks in budget and personnel and faces a loss of prestige. Either because of poorly taught programs or a lack of understanding about the role that physical education plays in a child's education, many administrators view it as a low priority in scheduling, or as a frill. Another challenge is how to get Americans to break out of the spectator role. Just as in ancient Rome, persons of all ages seem to prefer watching the Super Bowl, a college basketball game, or even a made-for-television sporting event to getting active themselves. We should learn from the Romans not to become compulsive spectators.

Problems that plague many junior and senior high school programs include poor student discipline, lack of interest, failure to participate, lack of administrative support, infrequent division of classes based on skill levels, and crowded teaching situations. On the positive side, many teachers are providing a variety of activities and challenges to interested students, fitness is stressed, administrative and financial support is evident, and students are leaving physical education classes turned on to an active life-style.

New professionals in physical education join a field with a tremendously challenging future. Within the schools, they will confront the issues and have the chance to implement positive changes. The excellent programs that exist must serve as models so that the poor ones are eliminated and replaced. Nonschool opportunities to help people improve the quality of their lives in meaningful ways are expanding both in number and diversity. The new physical education has an exciting future, if you are willing to make it happen.

SUMMARY

Built on the gymnastics programs of the 1900s, recent curricula in physical education provide a blend of dance, fitness, health, intramurals, recreation, and sports. The new physical education, beginning in the 1920s, led in this transition and advocated that physical education contribute to the complete education of its students. Box 10-3 highlights many of these significant occurrences. The AAHPER, along with numerous other organizations, has promoted changing sports-based into fitness-oriented activities in play, recreation, and athletics for all ages. In the 1980s, physical education faces the dilemma of meeting the needs of less-than-fit school-aged children while at the same time responding to the enthusiastic demand for fitness by the thousands who want to improve the quality of their lives.

BOX 10–3
SIGNIFICANT EVENTS IN TWENTIETH CENTURY PHYSICAL EDUCATION

1900   Grammar School Athletic League of Philadelphia created
1903   Public School Athletic League formed in New York by Luther Gulick (Girls' Branch began in 1905)
1906   Playground Association of America founded
1909   Publication of Jesse Bancroft's *Games for School, Home, Playground, and Gymnasium,* Clark Hetherington's *The Normal Course in Play,* and R. Tait McKenzie's *Exercise in Education and Medicine*
1910   Teachers College of Columbia University offered the first master's degree with a specialization in physical education
1910   The National Society for the study of Education published the *Ninth Year Book,* calling for sports to be substituted for gymnastics in the schools
1913   First departments of intramural sports started at the University of Michigan and the Ohio State University
1916   New York became the first state to appoint a director of physical education, Thomas A. Storey
1919   Fred Leonard published *Pioneers of Modern Physical Training*
1919   Eastern District of the APEA founded
1924   National Association of Physical Education of College Women started
1924   James H. McCurdy's *Physiology of Exercise* and Elmer Mitchell's *Intramural Athletics* became the first books published for both subjects
1925   Teachers College of Columbia University conferred the first Ph.D. with a specialization in physical education
1926   American Academy of Physical Education founded
1928   Southern District of the APEA founded
1930   First publication of the *Journal of Health and Physical Education* and the *Research Quarterly*
1931   Mabel Lee elected first woman president of the American Physical Education Association

(continues)

(concluded)

1931 Northwest District of the APEA founded
1934 Central District and Midwest District of the APEA established from the former Middle West District
1935 Southwest District of the APEA founded
1937 American Physical Education Association merged with the Department of School Health and Physical Education of the National Education Association to form the American Association for Health and Physical Education
1938 The AAHPER established a national headquarters at the National Education Association in Washington, D.C.
1947 The AAHPER published *A Guide on Planning Facilities for Athletics, Recreation, Physical and Health Education*
1948 National Conference on Undergraduate Professional Preparation in Health Education, Physical Education, and Recreation held
1950 National Conference of Graduate Study in Health Education, Physical Education, and Recreation held
1953 Results of the Kraus-Weber Minimal Muscular Fitness Test published
1954 American College of Sports Medicine founded
1955 AAHPER began an Outdoor Education Project
1955 *Physical Education for High School Students* published by AAHPER
1956 President's Council on Youth Fitness established
1956 AAHPER Fitness Conference held
1958 Administration of the AAHPER Youth Fitness Test began
1959 The International Council on Health, Physical Education, and Recreation established
1961 National Conference on Interpretation of Physical Education held
1965 Lifetime Sports Foundation established
1971 Association for Intercollegiate Athletics for Women established
1972 Title IX of the Education Amendments Act passed
1972 National Conference on Professional Preparation of the Elementary Specialist held
1974 National association restructured into the American Alliance for Health, Physical Education and Recreation comprised of seven associations
1974 Association for Fitness in Business founded
1975 Education of All Handicapped Children Act passed
1978 National Association for Physical Education in Higher Education began as a merger of the college men's and women's organizations
1978 Amateur Sports Act passed

(continues)

JESSE FEIRING WILLIAMS

(1886–1966)

EDUCATION

A.B. Oberlin College (1909)
M.D. Columbia University (1915)

BACKGROUND

Jesse Feiring Williams has been called the dominant physical educator between 1930 and 1960. Espousing objectives in harmony with those of education, he emphasized that the development of the individual was physical education's raison d'être and that physical education was obligated to equip students to live in and to contribute to society. Through his voluminous writings and the students he taught, his philosophical influence spread throughout the country.

Williams obtained his bachelor's degree at Oberlin College and while still an undergraduate served as Director of Athletics and a coach and a tutor at Oberlin Academy. For the majority of his career (1911–1913 and 1919–1941), he taught at Teachers College of Columbia University; after 1923, he also served as head of the department. Numerous students at Teachers College, one of the foremost institutions for graduate study in physical education in the United States, were influenced directly by Williams' philosophy. The most significant of his 41 books was *The Principles of*

Physical Education, which was published in eight editions between 1927 and 1965. In addition, Williams authored numerous articles published in the *Journal of Health and Physical Education, Journal of Higher Education, School and Society, Teachers College Record*, and other professional journals.

ACCOMPLISHMENTS

Throughout his writings, Williams emphasized that the role of education, and hence physical education, should be to prepare children to live in a democratic society. He stressed that physical education merited its inclusion in the educational realm because it provided opportunities for equality of learning opportunity, for developing personal worth, and individual responsibility and for realizing self-fulfillment. The development of social values, such as a sense of belonging, working together as a member of a group, and group responsibility, reinforced Williams' belief that physical education should help individuals adjust to and serve society.

Programmatically, Williams opposed formalized gymnastics because they thwarted, rather than enhanced, the learning of moral and social values. In contrast, sports and games provided the mechanism through which values such as initiative and self-discipline were learned. In his advocacy of this change in curricular content, he paralleled the ideas of Thomas Wood, who also taught at Teachers College.

Williams reiterated constantly that humans were unified beings. To overemphasize physical development distorted harmony and acknowledged a mind-body dualism. He insisted that physical education must concern itself with developing proper emotional responses, personal relationships, group behavior, mental learning, and other related outcomes. To achieve these objectives, he advocated that more time be devoted to class discussions, even at the expense of activity.

CONTRIBUTIONS TO PHYSICAL EDUCATION

Heavily influenced by the social and educational theories of John Dewey, Williams' philosophy answered an especially timely concern. Namely, he stated that the objectives of education and physical education were inextricably interwoven. Education's mission must rest on inculcating students with society's values, and physical education provided a vital laboratory for learning these lessons. So forceful were his writings that he convinced the profession that it should afford opportunities for individuals and groups to learn mentally and socially as well as physically.

REVIEW QUESTIONS

1. How are the philosophies of the new physical educators of the 1920s and the 1980s similar and how are they different?
2. What did Charles McCloy advocate as physical education's primary objective? Why?

3. Why were intramural programs begun? Why did they flourish in the colleges?
4. What are several programs for which the American Alliance for Health, Physical Education, Recreation and Dance has provided leadership?
5. Why were standards for teacher preparation in physical education developed?
6. How are the National Collegiate Athletic Association's influence and power different today from its earlier years?
7. Why were the sports opportunities provided for girls and women from the 1920s to the late 1960s different from those provided for boys and men?
8. What recreational developments have highlighted each decade since the 1930s? How popular has each been?
9. What have been the major developments in the promotion of youth fitness since the 1950s?
10. How do the characteristics of the new physical education of the 1920s compare with those of the new physical education of the 1980s?

STUDENT ACTIVITIES

1. Interview someone in the sports information office, athletic department, library, or news bureau who can help you learn about the earliest intercollegiate men's and women's sports at your institution. Based on this and information that you can obtain from other sources, write a two-page summary about each of these two categories.
2. Write a five-page comparison of the philosophies and major contributions of the five "new physical educators."
3. Learn about the test items of the AAHPERD Youth Fitness Test and the AAHPERD Health-Related Physical Fitness Test and assist in the administration of each to students.
4. Ask one of your professors who he or she thinks has been the most important physical educator of the twentieth century. Based on your reading, summarize this person's career and contributions in a two-minute class presentation.

REFERENCES

Baker, W. J. (1982). *Sports in the western world*. Totowa, N.J.: Rowman and Littlefield.
Betts, J. R. (1974). *America's sporting heritage: 1850–1950*. Reading, Mass.: Addison-Wesley Publishing Company.

Falla, J. (1981). *NCAA: the voice of college sports.* Mission, Kans.: National Collegiate Athletic Association.

Gerber, E. U. (1982). The controlled development of collegiate sport for women, 1923–1936. In Howell, R. (Ed.). *Her story in sport: A historical anthology of women in sports.* West Point, N.Y.: Leisure Press, 432–459.

Guttmann, W. A. (1978). *From ritual to record: the nature of modern sports.* N.Y.: Columbia University Press.

Jable, J. T. (1979). The Public Schools athletic league of New York City: Organized athletics for city school children, 1903–1914. In *Sport in American education: history and perspective*, W. M. Ladd, and A. Lumpkin, Washington, D.C.: American Alliance for Health, Physical Education, Recreation and Dance.

Kraus, H., and Hirschland, R. P. (December 1953). Muscular Fitness and health. *Journal of Health, Physical Education and Recreation, 24*, 17–19.

Lee, M. (1983). *A history of physical education and sports in the U.S.A.* N.Y.: John Wiley and Sons.

Wood, T. D. (1893). Some unsolved problems in physical education. *National Education Association Proceedings, 32*, 621.

SUGGESTED READINGS

Adelman, M. L. Academicians and American athletics: a decade of progress. *Journal of Sport History, 10*, 80–106, Spring 1983. The past decade of scholarship on the history of American sports is described along with suggestions for continued research.

Bandy, S. Clark Wilson Hetherington: a pioneering spirit in physical education. *Journal of Physical Education, Recreation and Dance, 56*, 20–22, January 1985. Throughout his many years of service at Missouri, Wisconsin, New York University, and Stanford and in other professional positions, Clark Hetherington stressed achieving education objectives and reinforced his advocacy of play.

Davenport, J. Thomas Denison Wood: physical educator and father of health education. *Journal of Physical Education, Recreation and Dance, 55*, 63–65, 68, October 1984. Stressing educational outcomes, Thomas Wood, at Stanford and Teachers College, Columbia University, initiated bachelor's degree programs in professional physical education. At the latter institution he also started master's and doctor's degree programs in physical education and an undergraduate health education program.

English, E. B. Charles H. McCloy: The research professor of physical education. *Journal of Physical Education, Recreation and Dance, 54*, 16–18, April 1983. Charles McCloy led in producing a scientific body of knowledge for physical education, especially in the area of strength tests, cardiovascular measures, classification indices, anthropometric scores, and character/social traits.

Gerber, E. The controlled development of collegiate sport for women, 1923–1936. *Journal of Sport History, 2*, 1–28, Spring 1975. During the 1920s and 1930s, women physical educators through their professional organizations curtailed intercollegiate competition for women in schools and colleges as play days minimized competition while providing physical activity and skill development for all women.

Gerber, E. W. The ideas and influence of McCloy, Nash, and Williams. In *The History of Physical Education and Sport*, B. L. Bennett, Ed. Chicago: The Athletic Institute, 1972. These three leaders of the profession displayed diverse philosophies of physical education and emphasized quite different objectives and program concepts, yet the period of 1930 to 1960 showed physical education to be an amalgamation of Jesse Williams' social goals, Jay Nash's lifetime activities, and Charles McCloy's advocacy of physical development.

Kozar, A. R. Tait McKenzie: A man of noble achievement. *Journal of Physical Education, Recreation and Dance, 55,* 27–31, September 1984. Canadian R. Tait McKenzie successfully contributed throughout his life to significant advancements in the fields of physical education, medicine, and art.

Rader, B. G. *American sports: from the age of folk games to the age of the spectators.* Englewood Cliffs, New Jersey: Prentice–Hall, Inc., 1983. After briefly discussing the 2½ centuries of folk games, Rader describes the age of the player, the national pastime of baseball, sports for the masses, and upper-classes, youth sports, and the era of the spectator, highlighted by analyses of the popularity of team and individual sports, ebbs and flows in college and professional sports, and minorities seeking equal opportunities in sports.

Riess, S. A. (Ed.), *The American sporting experience: A historical anthology of sport in America.* West Point, New York: Leisure Press, 1984. Colonial sport, antebellum sports, the rise in popularity of sports, the Golden Age of Sport, and sports in contemporary America are topical headings for the 24 signed articles in this anthology.

Slusher, H. S., and Lockart, A. S. *Contemporary readings in physical education* (3rd Ed.). Dubuque, Iowa: Wm. C. Brown Company Publishers, 1975. This anthology includes 55 significant writings from physical educators from 1930 to 1975.

Unit III

ISSUES, TRENDS, AND THE FUTURE OF PHYSICAL EDUCATION

Eleven

The Changing Nature of Physical Education

KEY CONCEPTS

- Movement education and various movement experiences underscore today's physical education programs.
- Federal legislation mandates equal opportunity for both genders and for special populations.
- Teacher certification and program accreditation help ensure quality teacher education programs.
- National guidelines seek to promote quality school physical education programs.
- An expansion of research by specialists in physical education and technological advances contribute to an expanding knowledge base.

Physical education constantly experiences changes along with society as a whole, although traditionally physical education has focused primarily on teaching sports and games to school children. There have been programmatic changes to guarantee that there are opportunities for all persons to meet their unique needs while engaged in progressively challenging experiences. Certification requirements, national guidelines, competency standards, statewide curricula, and program accreditation are among the efforts to improve the quality of education for students. Research, technology, and the scholarly pursuit of knowledge also furnish stimuli in this process of change.

MOVEMENT EDUCATION—THE "WHAT" OF PHYSICAL EDUCATION

Physical education involves learning about movement and moving. The nucleus of the field is often defined as the art and science of human movement, because physical educators study about and engage in various sports and activities. As we examine the changing nature of physical education, let us first examine one aspect of movement.

Rudolf Laban, a dancer and a movement analyst, originated many of the theories and concepts that underscored the training of movement educators in England beginning in the 1940s. He was one of the first individuals to emphasize that people need to understand both the how and the why of movement. Using the concepts of spatial awareness and body awareness, movement qualities of flow, force, space, and time, and relationships to others or to objects, the Laban Art of Movement Center taught people to explore their bodies' potential by learning through movement experiences. Participants learned about their own space—relative to body size, movement task, and equipment—thereby gaining insights into their own capabilities and becoming more skilled individually and collectively. Laban's students learned to phrase challenges so that children would experiment with how their bodies moved individually and in relation to equipment and other children. As they grew and developed, they gained a greater understanding about how space and time affected movement skills. Learning to strike a ball is one example

246

of the use of these movement qualities: the flow or the action of the arms while swinging a bat toward a ball; the force or the amount of wrist rotation or weight transfer that imparts power on contact; the space or the relationship of the batter to other players, to the plate, or to self; timing or judging when to swing based on the speed and trajectory of the ball.

As popularized in elementary schools in the United States beginning in the 1960s, movement education stresses the following concepts. First, the lessons are both activity-centered and student-centered; each child largely determines specific movement patterns within teacher-set parameters, and the emphasis is on experimenting through moving, not on following instructions. Second, children are encouraged to analyze and to explore a space, their bodies, and various uses for the pieces of equipment, with the focus on self-directed or individualized learning rather than group drills and class goals. Third, problem-solving and guided discovery are incorporated using challenges that students may respond to in many ways. Thus the teacher guides students through movement experiences by imaginatively and creatively involving both their minds and their bodies. Fourth, the children, independently and at their own rate of development, think about the challenges and then move in response. Since many solutions are possible and no group goals exist, each child is evaluated individually. Fifth, informality in class structure allows children to create freely and to learn at their own levels of achievement.

Movement education encourages students to explore their physical skills and to develop them further. (Courtesy of Gid Alston)

Movement education is both a methodology for learning movement patterns and sports skills and a portion of a comprehensive physical education curriculum. Key concepts are that children start at their own levels of achievement, progress based on their own abilities from these levels into new movement experiences, and achieve success and self-confidence, leading to greater exploration of movement challenges.

Teaching the pleasure of movement may be the greatest challenge facing physical educators today. Toddlers, senior citizens, and everyone in between must become cognizant of the fact that moving is essential to living, or at least impacts the quality of life. No longer can physical education focus mainly on teaching sports and games to school-aged students. We must recognize the need to teach everyone the joy of moving (Logsdon, 1984). Since most Americans are physically unfit, it is our task to change the status quo.

We must overcome apathy and lethargy. Physical educators in all settings must ensure that their students, clients, and personnel learn motor skills and develop fitness to the extent that their participation will continue after they achieve their goals and enjoy success. Ways to promote these outcomes include emphasizing cooperative rather than competitive behavior, establishing realistic individual goals, and rewarding improvement and participation. Enthusiastic exercise leaders need to provide organized, progressive, and participatory programs that offer a variety of activities. It is hoped that this will help motivate people to want to move.

FEDERAL LEGISLATION

Although early leaders of this country, such as Benjamin Franklin and Thomas Jefferson, were promotors of physical education, not until recent years has the federal government become involved. Legislation that directly influences physical education includes mandates for equal opportunity for both genders and for the disabled.

CO-EDUCATIONAL PHYSICAL EDUCATION

Title IX of the 1972 Education Amendments Act requires equal opportunity in all educational programs and states as its basic principle that "no person in the United States shall, on the basis of sex, be excluded from participation in, be denied the benefits of, or be subjected to discrimination under any education program or activity receiving federal financial assistance." Specific to physical education, this means it is illegal to discriminate against either gender in curriculum content, equipment and facility usage, teacher quality, or other program areas.

An increasingly popular school elective in physical education for both girls and boys is weight training.

Although this is the law, some schools and colleges resist change, thereby defying Title IX, because of teachers' refusal to instruct students of the opposite gender or because the administration does not insist on compliance. Many institutions use joint class rolls as a smokescreen but offer single-gender instruction and activity. As attitudes and behaviors gradually change, some teachers will instruct mixed classes but refuse to allow girls and boys to compete with and against each other (Wendt and Carley, 1983).

In spite of these stumbling blocks, Title IX has led to substantial changes. Elementary school children today largely accept as the norm classes composed of both girls and boys. As girls and boys participate with and against each other during the developmental years, the differences in their levels of performance may lessen. Teachers must assess abilities and evaluate performances to ensure fair standards and groupings. Table 11–1 lists comparisons between running and swimming performances for elite men and women athletes in the Olympics. Olympic performances of women are almost equal today to those of men in the late 1960s and early 1970s. Women at this level, and maybe at all levels, may be reducing the gender gap in sports performances. Increasingly, students in the secondary schools accept combined classes, learning respect for the capabilities of those of the opposite gender. Gradually acceptance and appreciation of women and girls actively participating in sports will lead to recreation and fitness programs that will welcome all who seek to enjoy activity and to develop physical capability.

TABLE 11-1
COMPARISON OF OLYMPIC PERFORMANCES

	1960	1964	1968	1972	1976	1980	1984
Men's events: swimming and track							
100-m freestyle	55.2	53.4	52.2	51.22	49.99	50.40	49.80
200-m freestyle	—	—	1:55.2	1:52.78	1:50.29	1:49.81	1:47.44
400-m freestyle	4:18.3	4:12.2	4:09.0	4:00.26	3:51.93	3:51.31	3:51.23
100-m dash	10.2	10.0	9.95	10.14	10.06	10.25	9.99
200-m dash	20.5	20.3	19.8	20.0	20.23	20.19	19.80
400-m dash	44.9	45.1	43.8	44.66	44.26	44.6	44.27
800-m dash	1:46.3	1:45.1	1:44.3	1:45.9	1:43.5	1:45.4	1:43.0
Women's events: swimming and track							
100-m freestyle	1:01.2	59.2	1:00.0	58.59	55.65	54.79	55.92
200-m freestyle	—	—	2:10.5	2:03.56	1:59.26	1:58.33	1:59.23
400-m freestyle	4:50.6	4:43.3	4:31.8	4:19.44	4:09.89	4:08.76	4:07.10
100-m dash	11.0	11.4	11.0	11.07	11.08	11.06	10.97
200-m dash	24.0	23.0	22.5	22.4	22.37	22.03	21.81
400-m dash	—	52.0	52.0	51.08	49.29	48.88	48.83
800-m dash	2:04.3	2:01.1	2:00.9	1:58.55	1:54.94	1:53.42	1:57.6

ADAPTED PROGRAMS FOR THE DISABLED

Historically, physically disabled students have no. been given opportunities to participate in activity classes or were assigned to so-called "corrective" or "remedial" classes, with a resulting social stigma. The development of adapted programs takes a more individualized approach. *Adapted physical education is for exceptional students who are so different in mental, physical, emotional, or behavioral characteristics that, in the interest of the quality of educational opportunity, special provisions must be made for their proper education.* Since not all schools made such provisions for students' special needs, the federal government became involved.

Section 504 of the Rehabilitation Act of 1973 specifies that "no otherwise qualified handicapped person shall, on the basis of handicap, be excluded from participation in, be denied the benefits of, or otherwise be subjected to discrimination under any program which receives or benefits from Federal financial assistance." Thus every student is guaranteed access to the entire school program, including physical education. The Education Amendment Act of 1974 mandates that each child must be placed in the least restrictive environment, or the setting in which his or her optimal learning and development can occur.

The Education of All Handicapped Children Act of 1975 (Public Law 94-

Through individualized programs and instruction and specialized equipment, such as a chair lift in a pool, more disabled persons are enjoying the pleasures of physical activity often denied them in the past.

142) specifically refers to physical education in its guidelines. Generally it requires that physical education, specially designed if necessary, must be provided for every disabled child in the public schools within regular physical education classes, unless the student has unusual restrictions. These unusual restrictions are met through the development of an individualized education program (IEP), a written plan for a disabled child that has been designed by a representative of the public agency (school) who is qualified to provide or to supervise special education, the child's teacher, one or both of the child's parents, the child (when appropriate), and other individuals selected at the discretion of the parent or school. One problem in the development of these IEPs has been the frequent failure to involve physical educators, even though Public Law 94-142 specifies that the children's physical needs must be met.

Each IEP must contain:

1. A statement of the child's present levels of educational performance;
2. A statement of annual goals, including short-term instructional objectives;

BOX 11–1
INDIVIDUALIZED EDUCATION PROGRAM

Student: Sarah Miller   Age: 9   Grade: 3
School: Eastwood Elementary   Height: 4'2" Weight: 62
Placement: Mainstreamed   Date of Annual Review:
                               August 1986

Present Level of Performance: Sarah is mildly mentally retarded and lacks balance and eye–hand coordination skills. She prefers sedentary to vigorous activity. She can toss and catch a rubber ball thrown from 12 feet, 3 times out of 10. She can do two bent-knee sit-ups and comes within 6 inches of touching her toes with her legs straight.

Annual Goals: 1. Increase abdominal strength
              2. Increase flexibility
              3. Increase eye–hand coordination
              4. Increase balance

Sample Performance Objectives	Sample Activities	Evaluation Measure	Completion Date
1. Perform 10 bent-knee sit-ups without stopping	1. Teacher-assisted sit-ups daily; leg lifts held for 1 to 10 seconds	1. Observation	1. August 1986
2. Touch toes with fingers without bending knees and hold for 2 seconds	2. Lower and upper leg stretches; teacher-assisted toe touches	2. Observation	2. August 1986
3. Toss and catch a 20-inch rubber ball, at 20 feet, 6 times out of 10	3. Self-toss, wall toss, and partner toss from 10, 15, and 20 feet	3. Observation	3. August 1986

(continues)

(concluded)

4. Walk 6 feet on a 4-inch balance beam placed 6 inches off the floor	4. Walk on a 4-inch line on the floor; teacher assistance while on balance beam	4. Observation	4. August 1986

Date: _____   Teacher: _____

3. A statement of the specific special education and related services to be provided to the child, and the extent to which the child will be able to participate in regular educational programs;

4. Projected dates for initiation of the services and anticipated duration of the services;

5. Appropriate objective criteria and evaluation procedures and schedules for determining, on at least an annual basis, whether the short-term instructional objectives are being achieved.

Box 11–1 provides a sample IEP.

Mainstreaming, the integration of exceptional students into the regular school program, is the recommended way to meet the requirements of Public Law 94-142 if a child's needs can be best met in this environment. Helping nondisabled students overcome prejudices and enhancing understanding among all students are two positive outcomes of mainstreaming, because socialization and coping skills learned through interactions would be impossible in an isolated setting. Disabled students may learn from the other students, but they may also negatively affect the academic environment of other students by increasing class sizes or by making the teacher's job more difficult. Rather than automatically mainstreaming all disabled children, the trend today is to place each child in the setting where optimal learning can occur. The least restrictive environment varies from child to child. Whether mentally retarded, learning disabled, emotionally disturbed, or physically handicapped, all disabled children can benefit from having individualized programs that are appropriate for their developmental levels.

LEGAL LIABILITY

The rights of all participants in physical education programs are protected. Due to the predisposition of many to seek redress for grievances concerning mistreatment and because of the movement inherent in physical education classes and in activity settings everywhere, teachers, leaders, supervisors, and administrators must both understand and comply with their responsibilities. Each of us must not be negligent, failing to do something that leads to injury or unreasonable risk of harm to those we instruct or supervise; nor can we act in a way that results in injury or harm. Not to be found guilty of negligence, we must act reasonably by recognizing potentially hazardous conditions or situations and by protecting our students and clients from them.

The following guidelines are important precautions to which each of us should strictly adhere:

1. Always supervise in person all activity, even free play and warm-up routines.
2. In activities involving greater risk, such as a new, more difficult skill or a demanding activity, maintain specific supervision.
3. Evaluate skills and abilities of participants and increase specific supervision as warranted by the situation.
4. Make sure that participants' fitness levels are appropriate to the demands of the activity.
5. Instruct participants thoroughly in proper techniques for skill execution and appropriate safety precautions.
6. Ensure the safety of all equipment and facilities on a regular basis.
7. Maintain up-to-date first-aid training and develop a plan about what to do and what not to do if an injury occurs.

Closely following each of these suggestions will help you meet your obligation to those you instruct. Also, physical educators in all settings should purchase liability insurance.

STATE CONTROL

CHANGES IN CERTIFICATION REQUIREMENTS

State control of education has resulted the establishment of certification standards for public school teachers. Most states' departments of education (or the equivalent) specify the number of college or university hours or credits that must be completed before a person can teach. This includes specific courses in the theory and application of instructional methodologies and in educational psychology and sociology, and also includes a period of supervised student teaching. Physical education programs include disciplinary content, specialized methodology of teaching, and application of knowledge to students. Chapter 6 discusses sample curricula that meet certification requirements.

More and more states are requiring that students in all disciplines, including physical education, take the National Teachers' Examination (NTE) to ensure that they possess both the general and the specialized knowledge necessary to teach. The NTE provides a consistent measure of teachers' knowledge. Many states have reciprocity agreements with other states, so that certification in one is equivalent to certification in the other. Certification in a nonreciprocating state requires the teacher's completion of one or more courses.

Only a few states have state requirements for coaching certification. The majority either hire only teachers as coaches or have the freedom to use anyone. Some certification programs for fitness leaders, sports instructors, and aerobic dance teachers are becoming available, although currently remain outside any state control.

COMPETENCY-BASED TEACHER EDUCATION

The conceptual basis of competency-based teacher education (CBTE) is that every teacher must possess certain competencies to be successful, and since the institution teaches and evaluates these, then its graduates qualify for certification. Box 11–2 illustrates such competencies. In practical terms, CBTE requires attainment of disciplinary competencies such as knowledge of the

---

BOX 11–2
COMPETENCIES REQUIRED OF PHYSICAL EDUCATION TEACHERS

1. Understand the scientific and philosophical bases of physical education.
2. Develop a comprehensive knowledge about analyzing movement.
3. Develop a wide range of motor skills, especially these related to the area of teaching.
4. Study the teaching–learning processes specifically related to the area of physical education.
5. Become knowledgeable about planning, organizing, administering, supervising, evaluating, and interpreting various aspects of a balanced physical education program.
6. Participate in extensive laboratory experiences that provide opportunities for direct association with students.

oxygen transport system, the learning curve, feedback, and motor skill acquisition, and the demonstration of minimal skills. The institution is responsible for ensuring that all specified competencies are evaluated.

Information concerning any of these aspects of state control in education can be obtained from the individual state departments of education. Although not under the jurisdiction of state or federal governments, accreditation standards help ensure optimal quality education for teachers, too.

ACCREDITATION STANDARDS AND EVALUATIONS

The process of accreditation emphasizes quality assurance. Based on established criteria or standards, accreditation in teacher education makes institutions accountable for program content. The National Council for Accreditation of Teacher Education (NCATE) is a nongovernmental agency with six regional associations. Although compliance is voluntary, most schools require that prospective teachers graduate from NCATE-accredited programs. Degrees from these institutions are especially important if a teacher seeks an out-of-state position.

Two phases basic to accreditation are the institutional self-study and the peer evaluation. Nationally established standards and an institution's stated purposes and goals provide the measuring devices for the self-study. After a comprehensive examination of each institution's governance, curricula, faculty, students, physical resources, self-evaluation, program review, and long-range planning, the accreditation committee documents the degree of adherence to the standards. Next, a visiting team of evaluators conducts an objective study to determine the accuracy of the report. Its judgments are submitted in writing to the accrediting agency, which decides to grant or to deny accreditation for a 7-year period. The accreditation may be extended to 10 years if a mini-team evaluation in the fifth year of the cycle again positively evaluates the program quality (Christensen, 1980). The importance of accreditation for quality assurance and the desire of the teaching profession to govern itself have resulted in the establishment of separate commissions for accrediting secondary schools and elementary schools as well.

DEVELOPMENT OF GUIDELINES FOR SCHOOL PROGRAMS

In recent years, three groups within the National Association for Sport and Physical Education (NASPE) of the American Alliance for Health, Physical Education, Recreation and Dance have issued guidelines for elementary, middle, and secondary school programs.

The Council on Physical Education for Children (1981) named six components that contribute to a quality instructional program. The Council recommended that each child develop motor skills and efficient movement patterns, achieve a high level of fitness, learn to express and to communicate through movement, gain self-understanding, interact socially, and gain psychomotor, cognitive, and affective outcomes. The Council also advocates that elementary school children participate in an instructional program of physical education for a minimum of 150 minutes per week, exclusive of the time allotted for free and/or supervised play.

A Committee on Middle Schools, appointed in the 1970s to study the status of programs in the newly emerging middle schools, recommends that programs for these grades should ensure that students progress individually with increasing self-direction in motor skills, knowledge, and social interactions (*Guidelines*, 1979). Interest and ability grouping rather than sex role discrimination and stereotyping are viewed as essential in this transitional period, for both social and emotional growth. The guidelines also recommend the provision of at least 250 minutes of physical education per week, distributed over 3 or more days.

Guidelines for the learning experiences, published by the Secondary School Physical Education Council (1979), include sharpening skills in varied activities but especially in at least three lifetime ones, understanding the value of and maintaining an optimal level of fitness, and demonstrating positive social behavior and interpersonal relationships in activity. The standard for meeting these objectives is a daily period of directed physical education equal to other subjects in length and class size.

INCLUSION OF *BASIC STUFF*

In addition to the above-mentioned guidelines, the NASPE itself is also working to improve school programs. One of its approaches has been the publication of *Basic Stuff* (nine books broken into two series) that seeks to incorporate these concepts into school programs (1981).

Physical education teachers, once away from their institutions of higher education, find it difficult, if not impossible, to keep abreast of the constantly expanding body of knowledge in this field. To help remedy this situation, in 1981, NASPE, through a group of school and university teachers, identified the common core information that should pervade any physical education course of study. Series I of *Basic Stuff* focuses on exercise physiology, kinesiology, motor learning, psychosocial development, humanities (art, history, and philosophy), and motor development concepts. These six books, designed for teachers, present the content knowledge that should be taught to children aged 2½ to 18 years. Not only is the latest information presented, but the books also describe how to teach and how to apply the concepts to meet children's needs. Series II books, emphasizing three age groups—early childhood, childhood, and adolescence—detail learning activities that utilize the concepts presented in the other six books. Health, appearance, achievement, socialization skills, aesthetic appreciations, and coping with the environment are discussed. The illustrations in Boxes 11–3 and 11–4, taken from *Basic Stuff*, show how these concepts can be incorporated into a class lesson.

BOX 11–3

Humanities

Sportsmanship in competitive athletics requires being and discovering a worthy opponent.

Why Is It Important?

1. Opponents need to be relatively equal for a genuine contest.
2. Opponents must demonstrate respect for their competitors.
3. Athletes often credit their opponent's performance as a motivating factor for personal excellence.

How Do I Get It?

Learning Experiences
1. As a teaching strategy when assigning groups for competitive activities, conscientiously choose students of similar competency. Do the opposite when grouping students in cooperative activities. Be sure students are aware of the goal differences in these assignments as well as the differences in skill ability.
2. Prior to a class period of cooperative activities and competitive activities, have students discuss examples of cooperative effort necessary for success. In competitive activities, discuss and agree on the rules, conduct, and attitudes appropriate to the activity. Such discussions in cooperative activities could involve maximizing the enjoyment by avoiding conflict and replaying points if there is a question of fairness or suggesting techniques to opponents to improve skill and strategies. In competitive activities, discuss such things as cheating, which diminish the contest in some way.
3. In cooperative and competitive activities, provide all students with experience and understanding of the official's responsibility. Discuss pre- and post-activity time, the difficulties associated with monitoring an activity for fairness and safety concerns, and the inappropriate behavior of contestants and spectators.

From AAHPERD.

BOX 11–4
AEROBIC CONDITIONING

Training to improve aerobic endurance capacity involves four basic elements: mode; intensity; duration; frequency of exercise. A training program which does not contain all four to an adequate degree is not likely to be effective.

The *mode of exercise* may be any form of large muscle activity which is continuously carried out (or with many repetitions). Running, swimming, cycling, cross country, and downhill skiing are all proper modes of exercise. Games like soccer, basketball, racquetball, or tennis also involve continuous, large muscle activity. These games are also appropriate modes provided the elements of intensity, duration, and frequency are also present.

Intensity is how hard a person exercises. The simplest way to measure the intensity of exercise is for the person to monitor his or her heart rate (HR) during or immediately after exercise. The HR response to exercise relates to the person's individual capabilities.

Although everyone is different, HR during exercise should be between 150 and 185 beats/min. for ages 12–25. This is the target HR zone. For persons starting with lower than average aerobic endurance such as those who have difficulty running more than a short distance, an exercising HR as low as 130 may still do some good while the HR may need to be raised to 190–195 to gain maximal benefit for the athlete.

A person's maximum HR slowly declines with age. Therefore the target HR zone mentioned above should slowly drop as well. Data on a desirable training intensity for children under age 12 is very limited but a reasonable estimate for the target HR zone is 160–190 beats/min. for the 6–12 year old. By 30 the target zone should drop slightly from the recommended level for ages 12–25. Similar progressive drops are recommended for healthy persons of increasing age.

Duration is the amount of time a person exercises. The *minimum* length of time required for an improvement in aerobic endurance approximates 10 to 15 minutes per day. An alternative form of training called *interval training* can also be used to improve exercise duration. In this case the individual trains for 3–5 minute intervals with rest periods of similar length between each training bout. Whether using continuous or interval training methods the more work done the greater the improvement in aerobic endurance. Thus endurance athletes often spend several hours each day in training. However for the nonathletic individual who is interested in developing and maintaining an adequate level of aerobic endurance, 15–60 minutes per day is considered adequate.

Frequency refers to how often a person exercises. The recommended minimum frequency is 3 days per week with 4, 5, or 6 days per week providing progressively smaller additional benefit.

(continues)

(concluded)

It must be remembered that as with any form of training aerobic endurance training must be progressive. Unless progression occurs the training benefit derived from specific exercise levels will slowly plateau and eventually only contribute to maintaining existing fitness.

To summarize, if the mode of exercise involves large, continuous muscular activity at an intensity to bring the HR into the appropriate zone and if that exercise is done at least 10 to 15 minutes per day and 3 days per week the aerobic endurance capacity of most persons is likely to improve. Such training is not likely to cause an improvement if one or more of these basic elements (intensity, duration, frequency, and mode) is not present to an adequate degree.

From AAHPERD.

The widespread dissemination of the *Basic Stuff* books demonstrates a genuine effort on the part of teachers not only to keep current with changes in physical education's core content, but also to learn how to incorporate best this knowledge into worthwhile experiences for their students. Many colleges have also included *Basic Stuff* in their teacher education curricula so that future teachers will be able to use these concepts effectively. The conceptual knowledge in the *Basic Stuff* books reflects the pervasiveness of the disciplinary orientation in physical education today.

GENERALISTS REPLACED BY SPECIALISTS

The quality and quantity of knowledge concerning physical education continue to increase, largely due to expanded research efforts. This rapid growth of information has led to increasing specialization by physical educators. Recently, more and more students select some area of particular interest to them, such as sport administration or sport journalism, for their major, rather than pursuing a general degree.

Another example of this trend toward specialized studies is the changing nature of master's and doctor's degree programs. Graduate students with a career goal of becoming exercise physiologists or sport psychologists study a specific core of information rather than concentrating on the broad field of physical education. The need for these specialists is readily evident in nontraditional settings, such as corporate fitness programs and amateur and professional sports programs. In colleges and universities, commitment to a specialization often leads to scholarly productivity, while the pressure to publish in this setting only intensifies an identification with a specialty.

PROLIFERATION OF RESEARCH

Within the past decade, the quantity of scholarly publications and presentations has been overwhelming. Responding to university mandate, specialists dedicated to the expansion of knowledge in their areas are eagerly researching and reporting their findings. For many, the surging tide of scholarly research is becoming the primary justification for physical education's existence within institutions of higher education. Physical educators in nontraditional settings, such as corporate fitness centers, recreation programs, and sports and health clubs, are conducting research on their clientele and programs and sharing their findings.

Another growing area of research in physical education focuses on pedagogy. Studies in this disciplinary area include observations of teaching, analyses of time-on-task and academic learning time, and expectancy effects (how a teacher expects a student to respond or to perform). Although a relatively new area, the research in this specialization has the potential to affect dramatically the quality of physical education classes in all settings.

Technology contributes to the proliferation of research. With computer literacy as a basic skill, researchers today can produce analyses and reports much more rapidly and efficiently. Biomechanical, physiological, and psychological research are especially enhanced by advances in equipment, design, and programming. Data collection and analyses enhance program prescriptions for the corporate executive or the rehabilitating athlete. What is truly phenomenal is that the burgeoning of technology in physical education is still in its infancy.

A frequently mentioned criticism of researchers in physical education is their failure to apply their findings. Technology can help to alleviate at least part of this problem by focusing on practical as well as theoretical studies, by disseminating new information more widely, and by focusing on specific situations in need of change rather than on generalities. Physical educators who could benefit from the findings also have a responsibility to work with researchers to apply new information in a timely fashion. Versatile equipment, data processing, and assistance with thorough and accurate experimental design in studies are but a few of the contributions that technology can make to closing the research-to-practice gap.

Data analysis using computers enhances the quality of increasing numbers of physical education research projects.

SUMMARY

One fact remains certain—physical education will continue to change in the years ahead. The study of movement education reaffirms the importance of understanding what we are about and encourages everyone to get active. Federal legislation regarding equality of educational opportunity will remain in effect, as will laws to protect the rights of activity participants. Tougher standards for state certification and accreditation seem inevitable as accountability requirements increase. A virtual knowledge explosion, accompanied by expanded research activities and technological advances, will have widespread implications for the future of physical education. For example, physical education majors' curricula will include revised teacher education tracks that are based more on research and its application. Majors' programs will continue to broaden by offering specialized studies to prepare students for nontraditional physical education careers. Standards for all physical educators will be higher to ensure quality programs for the various populations served. Essential for all programs are the dissemination of the latest research findings and the practical utilization of this information.

DeDe OWENS

Director of Recreation Therapy
Woodrow Wilson Rehabilitation Center
Fisherville, Virginia

EDUCATION

B.S., Physical Education, Winthrop College (1968)
M.S., Physical Education, University of North Carolina at
Greensboro (1970)
Ed.D., Physical Education with an emphasis in Adapted Physical
Education, University of Virginia (1980)

JOB RESPONSIBILITIES, HOURS, AND SALARY RANGE

Professionals in recreation therapy depend on knowledge, expertise, and experience
from the fields of recreation, adapted physical education, and therapy. DeDe uses this
background in her responsibilities in program development and supervision and research implementation relative to recreation therapy. She also is in charge of the public
relations aspect of this program. Typical hours for this career are 8:00 A.M. to
5:00 P.M. Monday through Friday, plus some nights and weekends. Salaries in this
career range from $17,000 to $21,000.

SPECIALIZED COURSE WORK, DEGREES, AND WORK EXPERIENCES NEEDED

Courses in supervision, counseling, special education, and therapeutic recreation are
especially valuable in preparation for this career. General knowledge in an undergraduate physical education program provides a good foundation for specialized study
in adapted physical education at the graduate level. Recreation courses focusing on
services for special populations, program planning, group dynamics and leadership,
and administration would also provide a strong background for this career. DeDe
recommends volunteering for a variety of roles relating to recreation and physical
education for special populations, such as a hospital aide, a worker at the Wheelchair
Games, and a worker in camps for disabled persons.

SATISFYING ASPECTS OF THIS CAREER

Many recreation therapists and recreation specialists select this broad career pathway
because of the opportunities to serve people. DeDe prefers the "people" orientation
in this career and the intrinsic satisfaction of helping others enjoy physical activity.

Professionals in recreation can choose to work with most age groups, skill levels, and physical activities in various settings, allowing great latitude in job mobility and providing numerous options for career advancement.

JOB POTENTIAL

Although a financially limiting field, there are numerous jobs, such as in retirement homes and in hospitals, for those committed to recreation therapy and humanitarianism. Specialized recreation therapy clinics in health clubs, corporate fitness programs, and community recreation programs may also become more available in the near future.

ADVICE TO STUDENTS

As leisure time increases in the next century and the values of lifetime physical activity are emphasized even more, specialists who are genuinely interested in serving people's recreational needs will be in demand. Students can prepare for these careers by gaining experience through internships, field work, and part-time jobs. Specific to recreation therapy, DeDe suggests seeking practical experiences with individuals who have a variety of disabling conditions and developing strong communication skills and supervisory abilities. She states that a combined course work preparation in physical education and recreation is important in a rehabilitation setting as well as in other recreation careers because it can lead to greater marketability.

REVIEW QUESTIONS

1. What are five characteristics of a movement education program?
2. What does Title IX require?
3. What does Public Law 94-142 require?
4. What are the benefits of mainstreaming?
5. What is the difference between general and specific supervision?
6. What are two ways that states certify teachers?
7. How does accreditation affect school programs?
8. What is *Basic Stuff*, and what is its importance?
9. What is the difference between a generalist approach and a specialized approach to physical education?
10. In what ways does a research explosion within physical education exist today?

STUDENT ACTIVITIES

1. Find out whether the state in which you are attending college certifies teachers upon completion of specified hours and credits or on a competency-based approach.
2. Secure a copy of your own elementary, middle school, or secondary school guidelines or objectives for physical education and compare them with the national guidelines discussed in this chapter.
3. Select one of the federal laws discussed in this chapter. Research any changes in the interpretation and application of it within the past 5 years.
4. Read one article in any professional journal or popular magazine that describes how an expanded knowledge base in physical education has positively affected nonschool programs. Summarize this impact in two or three sentences.
5. Read articles about negligent behavior by people in physical education–related careers. What action did they take or fail to take? What was the outcome of the litigation if there was litigation?

REFERENCES

Basic stuff, Series I (Exercise physiology, Kinesiology, Motor learning, Psycho-social aspects of physical education, Humanities in physical education, and Motor development) and Series II (Early childhood, Childhood, and Adolescence). Reston, Va.: American Alliance for Health, Physical Education, Recreation and Dance, 1981.

Christensen, D. Accreditation in teacher education: a brief overview. *Journal of Physical Education and Recreation, 51,* 42–44, 83, 1980.

Essentials of a quality elementary school physical education program. Reston, Va.: Council on Physical Education for Children of the American Alliance for Health, Physical Education, Recreation and Dance, 1981.

Guidelines for middle school physical education. Reston, Va.: American Alliance for Health, Physical Education, Recreation and Dance.

Guidelines for secondary school physical education. Reston, Va.: American Alliance for Health, Physical Education, Recreation and Dance, 1979.

Logsdon, B. J., et al. (1984). *Physical education for children: a focus on the teaching process* (2nd Ed). Philadelphia: Lea and Febiger.

Wendt, J. C., and Carley, J. M. Resistance to Title IX in physical education—legal, institutional, and individual. *Journal of Physical Education, Recreation and Dance, 54,* 59–62, 1983.

SUGGESTED READINGS

American alliance for health, physical education, recreation and dance, Detroit, Michigan, April 11, 1980. Including: A history of the influence of English movement education on physical education in American elementary schools. Including: Riley, M., The fifties; Logsdon, B. J.,

The sixties; Barrett, K. R., The seventies. These papers trace the influence of the theories and concepts of movement education on physical education programs in the United States in the decades of the 1950s, 1960s, and 1970s.

Bain, L. L. *Basic stuff* series. *Journal of Physical Education and Recreation, 52,* 33–46, February 1981. This group of articles by several authors describes the books of the *Basic stuff* series and suggests strategies for applying concepts in the curriculum.

Barlow, D. A., and Bayalis, P. Computer facilitated learning. *Journal of Physical Education, Recreation and Dance, 54,* 27–29, November/December 1983. Biomechanical analyses, fitness concepts, and racquetball strategies and three programs of computer-assisted learning currently operational at the University of Delaware.

Brassie, P. S. Can accreditation promote integrity without destroying creativity? *Journal of Physical Education and Recreation, 51,* 38, March 1980. Accreditation, which measures the quality of professional preparation programs, in the 1980s focuses on the attraction of qualified students in a time of declining enrollments, innovations in curriculum and instruction to meet students' needs, and adequate financial support for technological advances in the discipline in the 1980s.

Cushing, D. Physical education: integrating the handicapped. *The Physician and Sportsmedicine, 8,* 121–125, January 1980. Disabled students, depending on their needs, may benefit from either individualized programs, being mainstreamed in regular physical education classes, or a combination, but involvement of a physician is critical to implementing successfully any of these programs.

Darst, P. W., and Steeves, D. A competency-based approach to secondary student teaching in physical education. *Research Quarterly for Exercise and Sport, 51,* 274–285, (2) 1980. Based on observations of seven secondary school physical education student teachers, it was found that an intervention strategy of a competency-based learning module, feedback, and goals had large effects on teachers' use of feedback.

Griffin, P. Coed physical education: problems and promise. *Journal of Physical Education, Recreation and Dance, 55,* 36–37, August 1984. Title IX's mandate against sex-segregated classes has been less than enthusiastically accepted by many because of a lack of teacher commitment, curricula that overemphasize competitive team sports and game play rather than instruction, and permissiveness of intimidating behaviors and inequitable participation patterns and student groupings.

Henderson, D. H. Physical education teachers: how do I sue thee? Oh, let me count the ways!" *Journal of Physical Education, Recreation and Dance, 56,* 44–48, February 1985. Inadequate supervision, inadequate or improper instruction, improper conditioning or training, failure to enforce safety rules and regulations, improper treatment of students' injuries, use of inadequate or defective equipment, failure to prohibit physical education activities in unsuitable and/or unsafe areas, use of unqualified persons to supervise classes, and inadequate preparation of physical education teachers are examples of negligent behavior that result in lawsuits.

Mawson, L. M. Insurance against the nation's risk: extended professional preparation for physical education. *Proceedings: National Association for Physical Education in Higher Education, 5,* 138–145, 1984. Several national reports on the status of education in the United States in the early 1980s echo the desire of many physical educators to expand the time that undergraduates have to gain specialized knowledges in their field as they adapt to a world of advanced technology and communication.

Wendt, J. C., and Carley, J. M. Resistance to Title IX in physical education: legal, institutional, and individual. *Journal of Physical Education, Recreation and Dance, 54,* 59–62, September 1983. Although threatened with loss of federal funding for failure to comply, many institutions and individuals defy Title IX's requirement of equal opportunity in educational programs.

C H A P T E R

Twelve

Issues
in Physical Education

KEY
CONCEPTS

- Physical educators are accountable for programming and professional competence.
- Factors contributing to career burnout must be recognized and eliminated to ensure productivity, aid in job security, and allow the receipt of merit pay.
- Activity adherence is a major goal for all physical education programs, and required versus elected programs is a philosophical issue.
- Public relations and influencing political decision-making are essential if physical education programs are to continue.

Accountability—accepting responsibility for what occurs—is involved in almost every type of work. Regardless of their career choices, most individuals are expected to serve or to produce at a quality level even when faced with financial cutbacks, limited facilities and equipment, and salaries that may not keep pace with the inflationary cost of living. This chapter examines the impact of the demand for accountability on a diverse number of physical education careers. Related to this are issues such as the competency or qualifications of physical educators in traditional and nontraditional careers, merit pay, career burnout, and job security, which negatively affect accountability. Required versus elected programs and adherence to activity will also influence the future of physical education. Also addressed is influencing political decision-making, which may become essential for program survival.

COMPETENCE AS A PHYSICAL EDUCATOR

The course work required to major in physical education and the minimal quality control directed toward it was discussed in Chapter 6. Yet despite improvements in teacher preparation programs and nontraditional majors, such as athletic training, exercise science, or sport management, some unqualified individuals still graduate with teacher certification or pursue careers in physical education. Most colleges and universities must admit their undergraduates into majors' programs, even if some of the students lack minimal competencies, making it difficult for them to develop the skills and abilities necessary to become productive physical educators. Selective admissions, which require that prospective majors demonstrate specified physical skills and mental abilities, have already been implemented by some institutions, as have strict exit criteria, which require additional and more extensive physical and mental competencies. Both may one day be mandated by the National Council for Accreditation of Teacher Education, the American Alliance for Health, Physical Education, Recreation and Dance, and specialized groups, such as the American College of Sports Medicine.

A decline in the demand for teachers and salaries that have not kept pace with those in nonschool careers are just two factors that negatively affect teachers' performances (Annarino, 1981). While some teachers have sought higher-paying jobs in other fields, other teachers interested in career changes are reluctant to leave their secure positions for fear of not being able to return if they wish. Fewer jobs also mean that the typical yearly infusion of enthusiastic and often innovative teachers into the schools occurs less often than in earlier years. Repeated claims that the schools are failing to educate children properly have also adversely affected teacher morale. Thus, lower public esteem, depressed salaries, and limited teacher mobility contribute to a too-pervasive attitude of complacency.

Many of the former physical education teachers who opted for nontraditional careers faced competition for jobs for two reasons. First, many of the people who initially got involved in fitness, recreation, sports club instruction and management, clothing and equipment sales, and other nontraditional physical education careers were ill-prepared for their responsibilities. Yet this has resulted in somewhat of an acceptance of people in these careers with diverse backgrounds, rather than preparation in physical education. Although success stories abound about learning while doing, many of these jobs now list prerequisite skills and knowledge for employment.

Second many former teachers are somewhat limited in their backgrounds because they focused on learning how to teach rather than on a broader perspective of physical education. By contrast, today's majors in physical education may opt for any of several nontraditional tracks that will better prepare them for a variety of nonschool careers. The selection of the area to emphasize as an undergraduate is important and should be made only after considering one's interests and aspirations, since these will greatly increase the potential for quality performance.

Students entering their careers must understand the necessity of maintaining and enhancing their credentials. Since retention of what is learned is less than 10%, learning must be ongoing. Teachers can attend workshops, professional conferences, and in-service programs to keep abreast of the latest research in the field. Those in nontraditional careers should also attend seminars and read about the latest developments in their fields. All of these activities not only relate to personal job performance, and hence accountability, but they also lead directly to career advancement.

MERIT PAY

Directly associated with competency in the work place is the concept of merit pay, whereby the employee is paid based on quality of performance rather than years of service and a general salary scale. While not a new issue, merit pay is a volatile one for the many states and school districts that are considering it. Proponents emphasize that merit pay rewards teachers for superior service and ability, thus encouraging effective teaching and professional productivity. Opponents stress the difficulty of fairly evaluating quality teaching, administering a merit pay system, and dealing equitably with all teachers interpersonally as well as financially. For any merit pay plan to work, each school district and state, with teacher involvement, should examine all the possibilities and devise the plan that best meets its local and state needs. For example, California, Florida, and Tennessee combine merit pay with differential staffing (i.e., rewarding teachers for fulfilling responsibilities in addition to teaching).

Merit pay has long been in use outside of education as a mechanism for retaining and advancing quality performers, and by nonreward often eliminating those who do not contribute. Freelance sports journalists or sports photographers readily accept the merit pay concept: they are paid for their work that is published. Periodic evaluations or assessments based on job performance criteria are essential if an equitable merit pay program is to be implemented in any setting. Monetary reward, while certainly not the only motivator, is important to most people. Failure to be rewarded adequately may also contribute to career burnout.

Instead of merit-based pay, some states have adopted the career ladder approach. Outstanding teachers enjoy career advancement into more challenging and intrinsically rewarding jobs rather than receiving large monetary rewards. These may include coordinator positions, such as program head or lead teacher, or administrative roles, such as principal and district supervisor.

CAREER BURNOUT

One increasingly evident drawback to accountability is burnout. Austin (1981, p. 35) explained why many teachers burn out:

> Constant stress coupled with a lack of independence, a sense of low professional achievement, and a poor attitude or behavior, along with a feeling of isolation from fellow teachers, and long work hours may all produce burnout. . . . A lack of professional mobility, less turnover on teaching staffs, fewer new teachers recharging faculty batteries, low public opinion about education, and the spending limitations by school districts which curtail programs and threaten the job security of some teachers all contribute to the problem.

Other contributing factors include the repetitiveness of teaching, the lack of resources and administrative support, and coaching duties added to a full day of teaching. Box 12–1 lists signs and symptoms of burnout. Persons in physical

---

BOX 12–1
SIGNS AND SYMPTOMS OF BURNOUT

1. Constant tension from too little or too much stimulation
2. Less enjoyment of work and even leisure activities
3. Bodily changes, such as fatigue, high blood pressure, insomnia, digestive disorders, or increased heart rate
4. Overeating or undereating
5. Excessive drinking or abuse of drugs
6. Frustration with job-related factors, such as task repetitiveness, lack of recognition, overwork, and impossibility of advancement
7. Anxiety and depression

---

education careers other than teaching may also find their jobs unrewarding intrinsically and extrinsically, frustrating due to a lack of change or too much innovation too fast, unchallenging or too routine, confining in hours and work required, or lacking in potential for advancement.

Often burnout occurs as a result of a combination of these factors. For example, a beginning physical education teacher often is hired both to teach a full load of classes and to coach one to three sports. Lesson plans, grades, reports, and associated teaching duties combine with year-round planning, practices, competitions, and administration of the teams fill most days and nights. One of three patterns usually then develops: (1) a tenured teacher decides that the small coaching supplement is not worth the time demands, so he or she resigns from these duties; (2) the teacher concentrates on either teaching or coaching (most often coaching), putting little effort into repetitive and unrewarding duties; (3) the teacher resigns or is almost totally apathetic about both jobs.

Since anxiety, frustration, and stress are often causes as well as consequences of burnout, combatting them becomes essential to career survival. Job satisfaction necessitates taking a positive approach toward work responsibilities. Financial reward, job challenge, observation of and work with others, promotion, variety in responsibilities, and in-service development all may contribute to job satisfaction. Also vital is receiving positive feedback: if people are constantly bombarded by negative comments, they cannot continue to function effectively. Recognition and praise for completion of responsibilities often lead to positive changes and an enhanced self-motivation.

When individuals are given the opportunity to take part in the planning process, a greater allegiance to the resultant programs or goals is readily ev-

Excessive work demands may lead to job-related stress and eventually to burnout.

ident. Finally, physical educators should interact with others both on the job and by attending seminars, workshops, and conferences. At least once a year, everyone needs to rejuvenate commitment to and enthusiasm for job responsibilities (Rosenthal, 1983, pp. 125–135).

Work-related stress probably cannot be avoided, yet each of us should understand what causes stress and how to eliminate as much as we can and how to counteract the rest. Physical educators have a definite advantage in the latter case, because they know that exercise reduces stress. We need to attain and maintain a personal level of fitness that not only positively affects our productivity and quality of life but also allows us to serve as role models for others.

JOB SECURITY

Job security is a concern for many physical educators, especially those in schools and colleges. Competent completion of job responsibilities in most cases results in continued employment, but this is not always guaranteed.

Many nontraditional physical education careers do not offer a secure future because they depend on public demand and payment for the services rendered. By contrast, teaching jobs have traditionally offered security in the form of tenure after the successful completion of 3 to 7 years of service to a school district. Tenure guarantees academic freedom and safeguards against political pressure, while providing a buffer to job uncertainty for professionals. However, after receiving tenure some persons may stagnate as ineffective teachers, making it impossible to hire those who are more competent.

Many colleges and universities that have faculties who are well over 70% tenured face similar difficulties in having few vacancies for young, ambitious holders of Ph.D.s. Again, some of those who are tenured may be less productive scholars than those seeking positions. Once hired, these young academicians often find that quality teaching is not as readily rewarded as is scholarly productivity, so they respond accordingly. The tenure issue in both schools and colleges will gradually be resolved through faculty retirements, tougher standards for receiving tenure, and an increase in the number of physical educators pursing nontraditional careers.

REQUIRED VERSUS ELECTIVE PROGRAMS

A question facing school and college faculty and administrators is whether children in the United States should have physical education in kindergarten through the twelfth grade or none at all. The rationale for including physical education in schools includes the importance of learning motor skills, fundamental sports skills, and lifetime sports; developing fitness; gaining knowledge about sports rules and strategies; enhancing social and emotional skills; and learning how the body responds to exercise. Advocates of required programs also emphasize that physical education is for every student and should be treated the same as other subjects. It has the added potential of being able to affect students' quality of life immediately as well as later.

Probably the two leading justifications for elective programs are potential financial savings and the belief that physical education is a nonessential. Facilities and equipment make physical education more expensive than most other subjects. Those who believe that physical education is not cost-effective often point to community programs or interscholastic athletics and say that schools could eliminate physical education classes without denying students opportunities to be active. Also, many claim that recess for elementary students is equal to organized physical education. While certainly some school programs are nonacademic, that is, a "roll out the ball," noninstructional period, others provide excellent learning experiences for students.

Basic instruction or activity programs on most college campuses have undergone significant changes within the past 25 years. Changing attitudes toward graduation requirements have precipitated some of these; another causal factor has been budget limitations. In 1961, Oxendine (pp. 37–38) reported that 84% of the surveyed colleges and universities required at least 1 year of physical education. By 1977 this number had dropped to 57% (Oxendine, 1978). The trend, although a gradual one, was seemingly away from mandatory programs. The 1977 study also showed that 94% of the colleges and universities offered physical education activity courses for their students.

Critics of the elective approach fear that enrollments will decline sharply unless there is a requirement. Although in some cases enrollments drop temporarily, this usually reverses itself. Elective programs must appeal to students' interests through such offerings as personal fitness classes and lifetime sports.

Colleges that retain their requirements advocate that students need encouragement to be active and that this is especially important for the poorly

Lifetime sports are popular offerings in college physical education programs.

skilled or those who have had poor physical education experiences in the past. Without a requirement, they say, those who need physical education the most will not elect to enroll.

Due to financial cutbacks, some institutions have eliminated their requirements regardless of the faculties' philosophies. One alternative to departmental support is to make programs entirely self-supporting: students elect any activity courses available, but they pay a fee for the instruction, facility usage, and equipment rental. Instructors' salaries come from these fees rather than from state appropriations. On some campuses, the pay-as-you-play approach applies only to some nontraditional and off-campus offerings, with other courses free to students.

While the required versus elective question may have started as a philosophical issue, today its resolution is also a financial one. Both schools and colleges may have to adopt the pay-as-you-play concept. This, of course, would mean that only those who are genuinely interested in a particular activity or sport and who can afford it can participate. If enthusiasm for developing fitness and maintaining healthy life-styles affects school-aged children as it increasingly characterizes many college students, then the popularity of physical education elective programs may be ensured.

ACTIVITY PROGRAM ADHERENCE

Related to the issue of required versus elective physical education is the challenge of how to get individuals who have begun exercise programs to continue them. Adherence is a pervasive concern of everyone who prescribes exercises and activities. Whether the corporation or the individual is paying for the fitness or wellness prescription, the desire is for positive outcomes that are lasting. Box 12–2 lists 13 factors recommended at the Aerobics Center, a nationally recognized research and exercise prescription institution, that contribute to activity adherence. Most adult exercise programs emphasize similar strategies to enhance permanent and positive life-style changes. Most importantly, all people need appropriately designed programs that they understand, important goals that are feasible and monitored, and positive experiences that will encourage them to participate.

The Aerobics Center, just one example of many excellent programs, illustrates the essentiality of providing a sound, scientific basis to those involved in fitness programs. Its physicians, exercise physiologists, and other physical educators prescribe exercises for chief executive officers as well as for school children. Under the direction of the founder, Kenneth Cooper, the Aerobics Center conducts research and consults extensively in the area of fitness.

BOX 12-2

THE AEROBICS CENTER—PROGRAM ADHERENCE FACTORS

1. *Administrative support* is present and is communicated to participants. Top management is involved with policy designed to operate the program. Top management provides leadership, often by first getting participants involved in their own program.
2. A *long term* commitment is based upon the realization that results take time. Faith and the realization that an investment in human resources is necessary over a period of time.
3. *Programs are convenient;* schedules and facility use are arranged to be convenient for participants.
4. A *goal orientation* directs participants' effort(s). Reasonable goals are individualized to maintain commitment.
5. Programs are *safe* and *progressive* to avoid injury and to maintain enthusiasm.
6. Adequate *supervision* ensures safe and effective programs, providing the "human" element in programming.
7. Programs are *personalized,* especially for sedentary adults, to take individual preferences and needs into account.
8. *Education* is associated with the activity in which persons participate.
9. *Motivation* is not left to chance, but is planned systematically.
10. Both formal (such as a reporting system) and informal measurement and evaluation are employed to ensure *feedback.*
11. *Social involvement* is emphasized through spouse, family, and peer programming.
12. Programming is *fun;* all program elements have a positive emphasis.
13. Using skilled *role models* as leaders makes use of identification and modeling—critical motivational tools.

From AAHPERD.

Physical activity can provide bountiful opportunities for people of various ages to socialize while getting exercise.

PUBLIC RELATIONS

Physical educators must recognize the necessity of convincing people of the essentiality of physical education at all times, but especially when facing program elimination and financial cutbacks. Florida and other states have either saved programs or gotten increased program requirements and additional teachers' positions specifically through the use of public relations strategies. Physical Education Public Information (PEPI), a part of the National Association for Sport and Physical Education, provides news releases and other promotional materials to assist states, associations, and individuals in their efforts.

In 1983, the American Alliance for Health, Physical Education, Recreation and Dance published *Shaping the Body Politic: Legislative Training for the Physical Educator*, which focuses on the relationships of state legislatures to policies about public education. It stresses that to play the political game, one must understand the regulations and traditions that govern the passage of legislation. Lobbying techniques recommended include implementing a legislative action plan, writing letters, making phone calls and personal visits, issuing press releases, writing editorials, and holding news conferences (Seiter, 1983).

What does this mean to you personally? Physical education programs at

JUMP ROPE FOR HEART

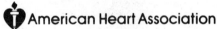

American Heart Association

One public relations and fund-raising project of the American Alliance for Health, Physical Education, Recreation and Dance in conjunction with the American Heart Association has involved school children who have skipped for fitness and fun. (Courtesy of the American Alliance for Health, Physical Education, Recreation and Dance)

all levels face financial cutbacks. In some cases this is a small loss of funding; in others entire programs may be eliminated. Frequently, this occurs because physical education is considered a frill, because its purposes are misunderstood, or because legislators have not been informed about its positive outcomes. Regardless of the reason, it is vital that physical educators take immediate action. Unless we can convince legislators at the state level and members of local school boards that physical education is essential to each child's well-being, monies will be cut even more severely. Through public relations, we need to educate parents (voters) and legislators that physical activity enhances each child's health and leads to a happier, more productive life. Daily physical education classes, taught by competent, qualified specialists, can achieve this goal. Box 12–3 contains three statements that clearly support skill development and fitness for children in comprehensive physical education programs. Messages such as these need to be shared with decision-makers to ensure continuation of school programs.

BOX 12-3
NATIONAL ORGANIZATIONS SUPPORT PHYSICAL EDUCATION*

A Statement of the USOC Sports Medicine Council

A comprehensive physical education program motivates and guides the individual to gain the skills, concepts, and interests necessary to sustain a lifestyle that contributes to personal health, muscular endurance, cardiopulmonary fitness, physical agility, and a sound concept to self. This is best accomplished through associated applications to a diversity of sports under qualified educational leadership and medical supervision.

From such efforts will emerge the satisfying pursuit of sport appropriate to the person's relative talent, interest, opportunity, and commitment, including but not limited to future Olympians. The USOC thereby encourages public and corporate support of comprehensive physical education programs and the national organizations dedicated to quality guidance of that support.

March 1983

A Statement from the Special Advisors to the President's Council on Physical Fitness and Sports

Physical Education—An Essential School Subject for the Nation's Work Force

WHEREAS, the lack of physical fitness among the Nation's work force results in an alarming waste of human and financial resources; and

WHEREAS, substantial evidence supports the belief that serious, chronic health problems, such as cardio-vascular and low back disabilities, begin in childhood and adolescence; and

WHEREAS, studies have shown that a relationship exists between quality physical education of children/youth and the physical activity habits of adults;

THEREFORE, be it resolved that the Special Advisors to the President's Council on Physical Fitness and Sports strongly urge all school districts to require daily physical education for all children and youth for grades K-12. In addition, the Special Advisors recommended that schools emphasize the following areas in physical education:

1. Identification of the physically underdeveloped pupil and provision for appropriate, progressive, developmental physical activities to correct this condition.
2. The attainment of an optimal level of physical fitness by all pupils.

February 1982

(continues)

(concluded)

A Statement from the American Association of Fitness Directors in Business and Industry

> WHEREAS, the lack of minimal physical fitness among the nation's work force results in extensive waste of human and financial resources, and
>
> WHEREAS, empirical evidence now supports the belief that serious chronic health problems such as heart disease and low back disabilities begin in early childhood and adolescence; and
>
> WHEREAS, research has shown that a strong relationship exists between quality physical education programs and the physical activity habits of adults:
>
> THEREFORE BE IT RESOLVED that the Board of Directors of the American Association of Fitness Directors in Business and Industry strongly urges all school districts to require daily physical education for all children in grades K–12. In addition, the Board of Directors recommends that educational institutions emphasize the following areas in physical education.
>
> 1. Identify physically underdeveloped pupils and provide for appropriate, progressive, developmental, physical activities to aid in correcting these situations.
> 2. Encourage the attainment of specific physical fitness goals at all primary and secondary levels.
> 3. Encourage the satisfactory completion by all students by grade 12 of a course in preventive health maintenance through lifestyle modification.
>
> September 1978

From AAHPERD.

SUMMARY

Accountability is inextricably linked with all of the issues discussed in this chapter. Physical educators in all careers must fulfill their job responsibilities competently to maintain employment, to receive rewards, and to ensure financial support. Individuals must overcome limitations associated with their jobs, yet they should expect to receive appropriate levels of recognition, such as merit pay, and job security, such as through tenure. Professional involvement and interchange among colleagues are but two of the ways to combat job stress and career burnout. Colleges and schools seem to favor elected programs that offer a diversity of courses to meet students' needs, although many have retained some requirement. It is hoped that students and exercise participants of all ages will increasingly enjoy activities, reach their goals, and adhere to their appropriately designed programs. Public relations efforts on the part of physical educators in all settings may bolster exercise adherence while encouraging greater funding for physical education in the schools.

PATRICIA ANN HIELSCHER

President
P.H. Enterprises of Apex, Inc.
Apex, North Carolina

EDUCATION

B.S., Physical Education, University of North Carolina at Greensboro (1966)
M.S., Physical Education, University of North Carolina at Greensboro (1970)

JOB RESPONSIBILITIES, HOURS, AND SALARY RANGE

Developing your own sports business permits absolute freedom to design it in any way. Based on her interests and expertise, Pat's business offers three related yet different services and products. She conducts volleyball camps and clinics, markets and sells volleyball uniforms and equipment, and sells T-shirts featuring women athletes. Ordering, billing, selling, and stocking her product lines are vital parts of her responsibilities. Generally Pat works from 9:00 A.M. to 5:00 P.M. and some evenings, typical hours for this career. The time worked determines the salary or income, so the range for a private sporting goods and services business is between $15,000 and $30,000.

SPECIALIZED COURSE WORK, DEGREES, AND WORK EXPERIENCES NEEDED FOR THIS CAREER

Pat recommends that students interested in forming their own sports products and service businesses take physical education courses with a coaching emphasis, psychology, and business courses, such as marketing and accounting. Although no degree is absolutely necessary, based on her experiences, a bachelor's degree in physical education and in coaching combined with a business minor would be ideal. Pat has found her background in coaching, including administrative duties such as managing a team, ordering equipment, and fund raising, and her master's degree in physical education most helpful. Coaching, personal contacts with people in athletics, general background in sales, and some work in business are important experiences to help prepare for this career.

SATISFYING ASPECTS OF THIS CAREER

The popularity of sports and leisure activities provides a bountiful market for services and products that anyone may wish to furnish as a career. Satisfaction comes from helping others select the equipment, shoes, and clothing that will enhance their pleasure in participating, while teaching skills in a sport can motivate people to start or to continue participating in a sport. Pat designed her business so she could enjoy a continued association with female athletes and coaches and could maintain involvement with the promotion of women's sports.

JOB POTENTIAL

There are many jobs for men and women in athletic sales and services throughout the country, especially in urban areas. These include running one's own businesses as well as jobs working for others. For Pat specifically, as owner of her own business, there is no security except that which comes from her belief in herself. While working for others may lead to greater job security, self-employment guarantees maximal freedom to design a custom-made career. Pat adds that her business is successful because 90% is with people she knows, her products are good quality and priced fairly, and she maintains a pleasant, trusting relationship with her customers.

ADVICE TO STUDENTS

First, Pat suggests talking with people in this career and considering their advice. Second, she advocates working for someone else before starting a business, to get vital training and experience, especially in marketing, sales, and accounting. Third, she recommends getting experience in athletics as a player, coach, and official to learn the needs and preferences of future customers as well as to learn to communicate with them. Last, she cautions not to become discouraged by people who say that women's sports or a particular sport cannot provide a viable career.

REVIEW QUESTIONS

1. What is accountability?
2. What are three ways to enhance performance of any job related to physical education?

3. What are two advantages and two disadvantages of merit pay?
4. What are five contributing factors to career burnout?
5. What are three ways to improve job satisfaction?
6. What are two reasons why required activity programs are defended and two reasons why elected activity programs are supported?
7. Why and how must physical educators become actively involved in public relations?
8. What are five factors that can enhance activity adherence?
9. What is the greatest risk associated with tenure in schools and colleges?
10. What strategies should physical educators use to get financial support for physical education from legislators?

STUDENT ACTIVITIES

1. Write a one-page paper about your personal accountability in a job you have held in a physical education–related field, such as lifeguard, official, camp counselor, or salesperson. (If you have not had any of these experiences, talk with those who have and report their impressions.)
2. Give two real world examples of what you consider to be career burnout. What changes would you have recommended that might have prevented these situations from occurring?
3. Write a press release for a newspaper or a letter to a legislator explaining and justifying why physical education should be required or elected in grades K–6, 7–9, or 10–12, or in college.
4. Make a list of the skills and abilities that you think physical education majors should possess when they graduate.
5. Talk with five of your friends about any individual exercise program that they formerly participated in or in which they are currently involved. Summarize the factors that led to their quitting or adhering to their programs.

REFERENCES

Annarino, A. A. Accountability: an instructional model for secondary physical education. *Journal of Physical Education and Recreation*, March 1981, *52*, 55–56.

Austin, D. A. The teacher burnout issue. *Journal of Physical Education, Recreation and Dance*, November/December 1981, *52*, 35.

Oxendine, J. B. The service program in 1960–61. *Journal of Health, Physical Education and Recreation*, September 1961, *31*, 37–38.

Oxendine, J. B. The general instructional program in physical education at four year colleges and universities, 1977. *Journal of Physical Education and Recreation*, January 1978, *49*, 21–22.

Rosenthal, D., et al. (1983). The relationship between work environment attributes and burnout. *Journal of Leisure Research 15* (2), 125–135.

Seiter, M. M. *Shaping the body politic: legislative training for the physical educator*. Reston, VA.: American Alliance for Health, Physical Education, Recreation and Dance, 1983.

SUGGESTED READINGS

Annarino, A. A. Accountability: an instructional model for secondary physical education. *Journal of Physical Education and Recreation, 52*, 55–56, March 1981. A mastery learning model designed to ensure achievement for students in secondary physical education is founded on the concepts of individual learning time and rates of progress, broader and more indepth learning opportunities both within and outside classes, maximal use of instructional resources and personnel, and personal and active involvement of all students.

Austin, D. A. Economic impact on physical education. *Journal of Physical Education, Recreation and Dance, 55*, 35–36, May/June 1984. Erosion of federal financial support for education necessitates an activist strategy for support programs in physical education on both the state and grassroots levels.

Cushing, D. The new physical education: cooperation on the move. *The Physician and Sportsmedicine, 8*, 153–156, March 1980. The humanistic, cooperative, and movement-oriented 1980s approach to physical education is compared with the traditional, competitive, skill-oriented programs of the past.

Davis, F. W. Job satisfaction and stress. *Journal of Physical Education, Recreation and Dance, 52*, 37–38, November/December 1981. High intergroup morale, career commitment, and encouragement of leader behavior are among the predictors of job satisfaction, whereas negative feedback from various groups is the prime source of stress.

Gettman, L. R., Pollock, M. L., and Ward, A. Adherence to unsupervised exercise. *The Physician and Sportsmedicine, 11*, 56–60, 62–63, 66, October 1983. Supervised exercise participants dropped out of their walking and jogging programs at a higher rate (45%) than unsupervised participants (35%). Those in both groups who adhered to their programs increased significantly in measures of cardiovascular fitness.

Golding, L. A. Partnerships for the fit. *Journal of Physical Education, Recreation and Dance, 55*, 51–53, November/December 1984. While colleges and universities have traditionally prepared school physical educators, the YMCA has been a partner in both the training and the employing of fitness leaders.

LaPoint, J. D. Taking a new look at the physical activity program on the college and university level: current status. *Journal of Physical Education, Recreation and Dance, 53*, 49, 51, May 1982. Although many colleges and universities have dropped their requirements, enrollments in basic activity classes are increasing due to enhanced student awareness of the healthful benefits of regular physical activity.

Ostro, H. Of teaching, coaching and merit pay. *Scholastic Coach, 53*, 4, 6, 8, 10, 12, February 1984. Physical education, instead of reacting to controversies about the quality or enthusiasm of its prospective teachers, must respond by requiring stronger academic abilities and by lobbying to see that they are rewarded, through such avenues as merit pay.

Rolloff, B. D. Public relations: objectives for physical education. *Journal of Physical Education, Recreation and Dance, 56*, 69–71, March 1985. The author recommends 15 steps for effective public relations, including enlisting the assistance of various people by informing them of the values and demonstrated outcomes of physical education and the importance of their financial support to ensure the continuation of quality physical education programs.

Tenoschok, M., and Sanders, S. Planning an effective public relations program. *Journal of Physical Education, Recreation and Dance, 55,* 48–49, January 1984. Educating the parents, other teachers, and administrators about physical education programs that are innovative, enjoyable, and beneficial to students can best occur through phone calls, newsletters, newspaper articles, public service announcements, demonstrations, and special awards systems.

Thirteen

Issues
in Sports

KEY
CONCEPTS

■ Girls and women are increasingly involved in sports and have been aided by Title IX in these advances.

■ Minorities, senior citizens, and disabled individuals, while enjoying greater activity, still struggle for equality in sports.

■ Rather than emphasize winning and other misplaced values, the benefits and program goals of community youth sports and interscholastic athletics must be reinforced.

■ As many intercollegiate athletic programs are besieged with problems associated with big-time sports, colleges and universities must strive to ensure the attainment of educational values.

■ The United States Olympic Training Center was established in an effort to address some of the organizational and financial issues confronting the Olympic Games movement in this country.

Competitive sports, although sometimes a part of and related to school physical education, when highly organized take on new dimensions and face unique problems. Girls and women, blacks, senior citizens, and disabled persons, while being treated more equitably in sports today, still face discriminatory practices and biases. Public and private youth sports organizations, interscholastic programs, and elite competitions at the collegiate and international levels share some common problems, although each must confront unique challenges. Several controversial issues and some proposed solutions are offered in this chapter. Some insight into sports, ethics, and human values shows the importance placed on sport in the United States.

GIRLS AND WOMEN IN SPORTS

Even though the Greeks excluded women from the ancient Olympic Games, and the founder of the modern Olympic Games viewed their role as cheering spectators, there is a gradual acceptance of girls and women as sports participants. Traditionally, both physiological and societal factors contribute to the inequality that many girls and women experience when they initially seek to compete in sports. Some researchers contend that, in general, males aged 10 to 70 years have advantages in sports that emphasize speed, strength, and power, but this does not justify the past virtual exclusion of females from sports. These researchers rely on evidence that females are not as strong, shorter, and lighter, have lower maximum oxygen uptakes, and, due to size, have smaller lung capacities, vital capacities, and cardiac outputs. Actually, the physical potential of girls and women is not yet known, since girls and women must first have equal opportunities in sports to achieve maximally. Contrary to the writings of the early 1900s, women do not become sterile but instead benefit physically from strenuous training and competition.

Societal attitudes change slowly: sports have traditionally been viewed in the United States as masculine—for males only. Familial and environmental influences affix a gender identification to sports. For example, boys are usually given balls and outdoor toys, while girls usually receive dolls or quiet and passive toys. Early in life, girls learn that if they participate in sports they risk being called a tomboy or being viewed as less feminine or less attractive. Peer group pressure results in a role conflict, making choosing sports more difficult, so some girls just opt out. The more determined ones may compensate by always emphasizing a feminine appearance, by downplaying their athletic involvement (and their successes), and by selecting a sport that is viewed as more acceptable, such as golf, gymnastics, swimming, or tennis. The other alternative is to participate actively in sport, regardless of the consequences. Although few chose this route in the past, this is gradually changing.

Television commercials that portray women as sports enthusiasts still have sexist overtones and innuendos. Newspapers and periodicals that include sports stories on women (even if on the sports pages, rather than the society news) seldom use them as lead stories and never cover them as extensively as they do males' sports. Because women have lower salaries, they have less discretionary income to spend for sporting equipment and fitness club memberships. Women enjoy less leisure time for recreational activities because of work, family, and housework obligations. There is not equal access to facilities and programs.

Girls and women in sports at the youth, school, collegiate, and international levels are enjoying expanded opportunities to play and to compete. City recreation programs and private clubs are trying to attract more women, and the fitness boom stimulates greater acceptance of women who not only look and dress fit but *are* fit. Myths will die slowly, and prejudicial attitudes are even more resistant to change. As girls' and women's sports performances improve and as each generation of parents senses that equity is just, this issue in sports will come closer to resolution.

TITLE IX

While not legislating equality, Title IX does mandate equal opportunity in educational programs, including athletics. After much discussion and many raging controversies about its impact in this area, the Final Policy Interpretations in December 1979 specified three major areas of compliance:

1. Financial Assistance (Scholarships) Based on Athletic Ability—available on a substantially proportional basis to the number of male and female participants in an institution's athletic program;
2. Program Areas—male and female athletes should receive equivalent treatment, benefits, and opportunities in equipment and supplies, games and practice times, travel and per diem, coaching and academic tutoring, assignment and compensation of coaches and tutors, locker rooms, practice and competitive facilities, medical and training facilities, housing and dining facilities, publicity, recruitment, and support services;
3. Meeting the Interests and Abilities of Male and Female Students—males and females must be equally accommodated.

What exactly is the impact of each of these on girls and women in interscholastic and intercollegiate sports?

The first policy relates only to athletic assistance (scholarships or grants-in-aid) in those institutions that award them. It requires that these monies be distributed to athletes on the basis of numbers. For example, if there are 100 female athletes and 200 male athletes, the men overall may receive twice as much money. Therefore, unequal spending in this area is legal if the distribution is made proportional to the number of participating female and male athletes.

The program areas in the second policy represent a comprehensive overview of all those components that affect athletic benefits and opportunities. In the assessment of equivalent treatment and services, comparisons should include availability, quality, quantity, and other relevant factors.

To comply with the third policy, institutions must first measure the interests and abilities of the group whose athletic opportunities have traditionally been limited. The institution may then be required either to sponsor a separate team for this previously excluded group or to allow them to try out for the existing team, unless the team is playing a contact sport. Inherent in the selection of sport by an institution are that coed teams are not required and that an institution is not required to offer the same sports teams for both women and men, unless interests and abilities warrant this. The provision of equal competitive opportunity requires that the number of teams be proportional (not necessarily equal) to the institution's enrollment to meet the inadequately represented gender's interests and abilities, and that teams for both women and men compete at comparable levels.

Prior to these policy interpretations, the extent of program adjustments varied dramatically. Although Title IX had been enacted in 1972, not until 1975 were its regulations explained, and secondary schools and colleges were given until 1978 to comply. The attitudes of school and college administrators, athletic directors, and coaches led to enhanced opportunities and financial support in some institutions; others chose to ignore the law. Participation in interscholastic athletics for women increased from 7% in 1970 to 35.7% in 1982 (or from around 300,000 to nearly 2,000,000), while during the same period intercollegiate athletics for women rose from 15.6% to 30%. Between 1972 and 1980, college women benefitted from an increase from 2% to 16.4% of their institutions' athletic budgets ("In Money, Numbers," 1984). These percentages, however, are averages that include many institutions that have chosen not to comply either partially or fully because of prejudicial gender biases, limited budgets and facilities, lack of coaches, or resistance to change. Since no school or college has ever lost federal funding due to noncompliance, this situation probably will continue.

At the same time, women in other settings have benefitted from substantial changes. In some cases, women receive approximately one third of their college's athletic budgets for extensive travel schedules, recruiting, coaches' salaries, medical treatment, publicity, and athletic scholarships. Some college administrators say that such dramatic improvements occurred because of a moral obligation to treat all students equitably rather than because of Title IX's threat. This may be true for a few major public institutions, but the timing of the changes indicates that Title IX was largely responsible for these greater sport opportunities for women. The continuation of these programs, however, may depend on societal and institutional attitudes and pressures: in February 1984, the Supreme Court, in *Grove City College v. Bell*, ruled that Title IX was applicable only to educational programs that are direct recipients of federal funding. Since most athletic programs do not receive these direct monies, they are exempt from the aforementioned regulations. In addition, the failure of the passage of the national Equal Rights Act of 1984 indicates that pressure for equal opportunity will not come from legislation. Thus, administrators are free to reduce teams and budgets for women or to continue to make progress.

The reality is that women have fewer teams and fewer participants than men, a much smaller percentage of women coaching women than before Title IX, and fewer women administering athletic programs. Why still are only approximately one third of school and college athletes women? This results from less societal approval for women athletes and fewer opportunities to compete in youth sport programs. Several factors have led to the increasing number of men coaching women. These include not enough women with expertise or interests in coaching, oversupply of men interested in coaching and undersupply male teams to coach, more equitable salaries for coaches of female teams than was the case and usually less pressure to win, unwillingness of many women to coach highly competitive teams, and hiring practices in which male athletic directors and school principals prefer to hire men. Also, in most instances, when female and male athletic programs have been combined, largely on the premise of equal opportunity, men have been placed in the top positions either because of seniority or the belief that they know athletics better. Thus the need for more qualified female coaches and administrators and the importance of achieving and maintaining quality programs for all women in schools and colleges remain.

EQUALITY FOR MINORITIES

Minorities have found themselves sports outcasts throughout most of this nation's history. Prior to 1950, sports were rarely integrated, with a few exceptions, such as Jack Johnson, Joe Louis, Paul Robeson, Satchel Paige, Jackie Robinson, and Jesse Owens. Following the Supreme Court's *Brown v. Board of Education* decision in 1954, school desegregation began to open more school and college sports programs to minorities.

Throughout the years, minorities have experienced blatant discrimination in the form of quota systems (only a small number allowed on a team), position stacking (certain positions were unavailable to them), social exclusion from clubs and parties, disparity in treatment by coaches, weak academic counseling, and little tutorial help. Minority athletes who were thrust into integrated schools were often ill-prepared for the academic work because of poorer opportunities in their earlier schooling or a lack of emphasis on education in their cultural backgrounds. Those with athletic prowess were often graduated from high school but were not educated in the process. Some enrolled in predominantly white colleges, where they were again ill-prepared for the academic demands. Many failed to earn degrees, thus eliminating themselves from possible coaching positions when their dreams of professional stardom failed to materialize. Many minorities oppose the National Collegiate Athletic Association's Rule 48, which requires first-year athletes at its Division I institutions, beginning in 1986, to have attained a minimum score on the Scholastic Aptitude Test (SAT) or the American College Test (ACT) or to have acheived a minimal standard based on their grade-point averages and test scores and to have maintained a C average in 11 designated high school courses. They state that the SAT and the ACT are culturally biased against minorities, and therefore that the test requirements prove that the predominately white institutions want to limit the domination by minorities on some of their sports teams. Another group of opponents of Rule 48 stresses that, rather than preventing the recruitment of minorities, the rule legitimizes the admission of poorly qualified students (often minorities) into colleges. (Rule 48 allows students who do not have the minimal scores to enroll in an institution and prove their ability to achieve at a C level on college work for 1 year and then to compete for the next 3 years.)

Whether the discrimination against minorities in sports is subtle or overt depends on the school or college, the team, and the leadership of both. Many interesting questions persist. Why are the starters on football and basketball teams predominately minorities when the student bodies are predominately white? Why are minorities seldom members of tennis, swimming, golf, and gymnastics teams? Why do fewer minority team members who are marginal athletes receive athletic scholarships than comparably-skilled whites? What is the status of the minority woman athlete?

Are minority athletes bigger, stronger, and generally more highly skilled than white athletes? Research does not substantiate this, yet their athletic opportunities in elite and expensive sports have traditionally been limited, resulting in their devoting greater amounts of time and energy into school-sponsored football, basketball, and baseball. These three sports also offer the potential for a professional career. In conjunction with this, coaches in predominately white institutions often experience pressure to win. For them, recruiting the best athletes becomes imperative, yet they also receive encouragement to have as many white players as possible. This may result in athletic scholarships being given disproportionately to marginal white athletes who play as substitutes, if they play at all.

The expense and the fewer opportunities for participation and competition have traditionally prevented many minorities from pursuing tennis, swimming, golf, and gymnastics. Private lessons, expensive equipment, club memberships, and travel requirements for quality competition discourage most minorities from entering these sports, while the virtual absence of role models only reinforces the status quo. The minority woman athlete must overcome both racial and sexual barriers against equality of sports opportunity.

Minority athletes, regardless of gender, sport, or level of competition, should be treated fairly and equally. They should be expected to complete their academic work in schools and colleges and to earn their degrees as preparation for later life. As with all athletes, minorities deserve to receive counseling to help them derive the most from their education and to learn marketable skills. Since prejudices change gradually, minorities must work to eliminate discrimination in athletics. Coaches must not allow mistreatment of minorities on their teams, and administrators must ensure equity for all.

Senior citizens and disabled persons have also had to face discriminatory biases to gain sporting opportunities. As the average age of the United States population increases, a greater awareness of the needs of seniors to exercise and to compete emerges. No longer are persons past 60 years old content to sit in their rocking chairs and let time pass them by. Rather, they are walking, cycling, jogging, swimming, lifting weights, and engaging in a large number of sporting activities with the blessing of their physicians, who favor such activities as preventive medicine. This enthusiasm for exercise and activity has rekindled in many a desire to compete. The Senior Olympics and Master's events in national, state, regional, and local competitions are providing opportunities for former and newly aspiring older athletes to achieve in sports in unprecedented ways. Whether competing for recognition or personal satisfaction, these older Americans are beneficiaries of enhanced strength, flexibility, endurance, and balance, factors that directly improve the quality of their lives. They also reduce the stress of lost spouses and friends and replace loneliness with new friends and social opportunities.

In recent years, disabled persons have increasingly desired equal opportunity to participate and compete in sports. Public Law 94-142 (discussed in Chapter 11) mandates that athletics be provided to disabled students. These two factors and an eagerness on the part of many to treat everyone equally have led to a proliferation of organizations and competitions in such sports as baseball, tennis, basketball, skiing, track and field, archery, bowling, and swimming. Through the International Games for the Disabled, individuals beginning on the local level compete for recognition as highly skilled athletes.

The Special Olympics, since 1968, has provided competitive opportunities for mentally retarded children. Although experts initially questioned this program, the overwhelming success of the state and national competitions has verified the importance of giving these special children the chance to achieve and to be recognized as winners. Minorities, regardless of sex, race, age, or disability, have proven that they both want and deserve equity in sporting opportunities.

YOUTH SPORTS

In the 1920s, the popularity of sports in the United States led many people to expect that schools would provide competitive sports for children. While junior and senior high schools assumed this responsibility (see the next section), physical educators stated that the negative outcomes outweighed the positive benefits for elementary-aged children. This refusal did not prevent the development of youth sports programs, however, as communities, private associations, and civic organizations, seeing these opportunities as deterrents to delinquency, tools for social control, promotional devices, and fun for the boys, got involved (Magill et al., 1982).

Along with the dramatic increase in sports teams for people of all ages and now for both genders have emerged several problems that physical educators sought to avoid. The major issues are an overemphasis on winning, poorly trained coaches, parental interference, and lost ethical values. When winning becomes the primary objective, individual skill development, participation for all, development of intrinsic motivation, learning and playing several sports and in varied positions, safety concerns, and even fun often lose importance. Coaches are usually the ones initially caught up in this win-at-all-costs attitude. To fulfill their own ego needs, coaches too often pressure their young players to play while injured, to violate the rules to their advantage, to quit if they are not good enough. Also, coaches' lack of preparation may result in poorly taught skills, improper treatment of injuries, and inability to understand and to deal with children's needs.

Parents, while usually well-intentioned, often impose their wishes on their children in youth sports as they force them to play a particular sport or several sports to fulfill their own needs to succeed in sports, rather than trying to fulfill the children's needs, because they either were or were not successful themselves. Children may experience considerable guilt because their parents invest large amounts of time and money in lessons and competitions, and

Soccer has become a popular competitive sport for children. (Courtesy of Winkie LaForce)

thus they want desperately to succeed. Parents too often reward results rather than effort and improvement. Interrelated with these problems are misplaced values. Coach and parental role models may reinforce cheating to win, abusing officials and opponents, circumventing the rules, and outcome (winning) over process (having fun and developing skills).

With such a long list of problems, why do youth sports continue to grow in popularity? First, children in America have a genuine interest in and enthusiasm for sports. Second, the positive outcomes in many programs exceed the negative aspects. There are leagues, organizations, coaches, and parents who emphasize fun and participation and who ensure the well-being of the children physiologically and psychologically. Through clinics, coaches learn how to teach skills correctly and progressively to children. Many programs require first-aid training for coaches and medical clearance for the participants. Through orientation programs, parents learn about program goals and how to help their children benefit most from their experiences. Program administrators are more aware that elimination of children from teams, overspecialization, extrinsic awards, and total adult control need replacing by a philosophy in which everyone plays in every event and in rotating positions, by certificates of participation and team outings instead of huge trophies and championship playoffs, and by asking children what they want from their sports experiences to ensure attainment of these aspirations. Coaches and parents should stress and reinforce cooperation, teamwork, and sportsmanship. Youth sports are here to stay, making it essential that those involved provide programs that incorporate these values. The philosophy of the physical education profession toward youth sports (Box 13—1) describes one approach to ensuring readiness for and appropriateness of these competitions.

BOX 13–1
GUIDELINES FOR SCHOOL-RELATED PROGRAMS

1. The physical activity needs of elementary school age children can best be served through a program of instruction in physical education supplemented by other opportunities for participation provided by school, home, and community;

2. Enrichment programs should provide opportunities for further development of knowledge and skills gained in the instructional physical education program during such periods as recess, noon hour, and extended school-day programs. The program should be varied in content and organization to provide for all levels of skill;

3. Intramural programs for continued participation in games, recreational sports, dance, gymnastics, and other activities should be offered to all children. This program should be varied in content and organization to provide for all levels of skill;

4. Competition at the elementary school level is a vital and forceful educational tool. It can stimulate a keen desire for self-improvement and create environments in which children, motivated by common purpose, unite in an effort to accomplish goals. However, to be beneficial, competition must be success-oriented for all children and relevant to the school program. Carefully structured competitive experiences within the school, involving individual and group opportunities and conducted to achieve specific instructional objectives, are usually more congruent with elementary education goals than are inter-school competitive programs. Consideration of inter-school competitive programs should follow only after a sound physical education program has been provided for all the children in the elementary school, including an intramural program for the upper elementary grades.

From AAHPERD.

Each year millions of girls and boys aged 8 to 18 years compete in the largest amateur sports program in the United States, the AAU/USA Junior Olympics. Organized by the Amateur Athletic Union, recognized by the United States Olympic Committee, and sponsored nationally by Sears, Roebuck and Co., competitions are held in 22 sports. These amateur athletes compete in more than 3,000 local meets, state championships, regional events, and the national finals. Benefits of being a part of the Junior Olympics are making friends, having opportunities to travel, gaining a sense of achievement, and enjoying the excitement of the competitions. Distractions from these outcomes include pressure to win and overspecialization in one sport. Youth also compete in state games, such as the Empire State Games (New York) and the Keystone (Pennsylvania) State Games, which provide a variety of sports opportunities for children of all ages. Most of the athletes in these state games have developed their skills through youth and school athletic programs.

INTERSCHOLASTIC ATHLETICS

Pressure to win is the major criticism lodged against high school sports today. In the United States, with its "we're number one" ethic, athletes in the schools have fallen victim to this compulsion, too. Year-round conditioning programs and practices, specializing in one sport, playing while hurt, and coaches' jobs resting on winning records are among the existing problems. Confusion between athletics and physical education in the schools adversely affects both programs. The teacher/coach must try to meet the demands of almost two full-time jobs. Coaching supplements are low when compared with the time expectations and pressures, although personal satisfaction and community and school recognition may compensate somewhat. Financial cutbacks for both programs have also hurt, since equipment and facilities are often shared.

The National Federation of State High School Associations promotes interscholastic athletics as an integral part of the educational experiences of high school students. Most physical educators have also traditionally favored and supported interscholastic athletics. They believe that adolescents are better able to compete developmentally and emotionally than are children. They stress the beneficial outcomes of fitness, sportsmanship, cooperation, self-discipline, and other values for the participants. In recent years, physical educators also have helped develop greater sport opportunities for girls in the schools. Box 13–2 summarizes the guidelines for interscholastic athletics that physical educators recommend if these objectives are to be met.

From a broader perspective, interscholastic athletics enhances school spirit

BOX 13–2
THE INTERSCHOLASTIC PROGRAM

The Interscholastic Sports Program is an outgrowth of the basic in-
structional program and provides additional physical education ex-
periences in a wide range of sports. The purposes of this program
should be to help participants to:
   Gain a better understanding of their physiological and psychological
      capabilities, and establish reasonable personal goals.
   View winning as a means to self-improvement and not as an end in
      itself.
   Assume leadership roles in planning and conducting intramural and
      interscholastic activities.
   Share in the decision-making process involved in those programs.
   Participate and/or compete fairly on the factors of age, ability, height,
      weight, physiological maturity and strength.
   Benefit from the expertise of coaches who are certified teachers pos-
      sessing either a major or a minor in physical education and/or state
      coaching certification.
   Receive appropriate medical attention before, during and after in-
      tramural/interscholastic sports programs.
   (1) Medical examinations should be required for all who participate
      in interscholastic activities.
   (2) A physician's statement indicating the student's fitness for re-
      suming participation should be required following a serious ill-
      ness or injury.
   (3) An athletic trainer or teacher/trainer should be present at all
      games and pratices.
From an administrative standpoint, all secondary school interscholastic
contests, including post-season games, should be conducted under the
jurisdiction of state high school athletic associations, and the programs
should be financed by local Boards of Education.

From AAHPERD.

and, in many locales, enlists strong community support for the school. In
spite of these benefits, many high schools are adopting a pay-for-play philosophy because of economic constraints. This concept means that no longer
will educational allocations finance athletic teams; instead, any student who
desires to participate on a team will have to pay for the experience. While
this excludes those unable to pay, this trend is a pervasive one nationally.

Basketball had become a popular school sport nationally by the early 1900s (Raylon School, Texas). (Courtesy of Thomas L. Ward)

Rather than this alternative, some schools have just eliminated athletic programs. Academic concerns, drug abuse, spectator violence, and required equal programming for girls and disabled persons, along with the increasing availability of community and club sports, contribute to the questioning of the future of interscholastic athletics. These same issues face the colleges, too.

INTERCOLLEGIATE ATHLETICS

Ever since the proliferation of college athletic programs for men in the late 1800s, college faculties and administrators have been concerned about the potentially detrimental effects of athletics on academic work. Associated problems then and now include missing classes, receiving unearned grades, being admitted although underqualified, and excessive training and traveling . The National Collegiate Athletic Association, the National Association of Intercollegiate Athletics, and the National Junior College Athletic Association each have attempted to base their administration of intercollegiate athletics on educational principles, although regulations concerning these issues largely rest with each institution. The problem that each college faces is how to deal effectively with regulations when winning is almost synonymous with survival, especially at the larger institutions (Underwood, 1985).

Winning teams appeal to spectators and lead to increased interest. More fans bring in larger gate receipts. More money contributes to hiring coaches with winning reputations and recruiting and awarding grants-in-aid to better athletes, who combine to win more games. This cycle (winning = fans = money = winning = fans = money) repeats itself and spirals upward. The resultant commercialism changes college athletics from an extension of the institution's educational activities to a business venture. When winning becomes the most important objective, rules frequently are skirted or blatantly violated, both during play and in the recruiting of athletes, while sportsmanship, character development, and other values may be lost or at least deemphasized in the process. Increasingly, college and university presidents are getting involved in examining the outcries concerning these problems and in seeking to resolve them. The NCAA, by enforcing its regulations more extensively, hopes to deter rule violators and to ensure the attainment of educational values.

Why do intercollegiate athletics continue to thrive? There are three major justifications. First, intercollegiate athletics reflect American attitudes, beliefs, and values. Many people advocate that colleges have the responsibility to

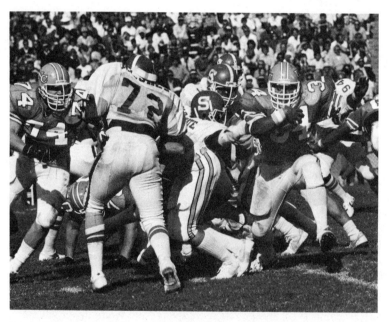

Intercollegiate football teams have become multimillion-dollar businesses in major institutions, thus challenging the accuracy of the concept of the student-athlete. (Courtesy of UNC Sports Information Office)

offer athletic teams for students to play on for the love of the game and defend the concept that athletics help prepare the participants for life by developing physical, intellectual, social, and moral skills. Second, the benefits already mentioned exceed the liabilities. Many people think that the problems listed above are sporadic rather than pervasive. They add that participants and spectators experience a cathartic release of tension and have fun while college spirit and allegiance are greatly enhanced. Third, athletics is a valuable public relations tool for the institution. College enrollments often increase due to successful athletic programs, especially in football and basketball. The provision of entertainment attracts large numbers of spectators to college athletic contests, with an accompanying surge in affiliation that positively affects legislative appropriations and private donations to academic departments, in addition to generous support for athletics.

Realistically, intercollegiate athletics, regardless of the extent of the negative features, will continue to thrive because of their entertainment value and because of their benefits. To accentuate the positive and to reduce the negative, Lumpkin (1982, pp. 14–19) recommends the following changes:

1. Censure violators (coaches and athletes) of intercollegiate athletic regulations, especially in the areas of recruiting and scholarships, for the first offense; place violators on a two-year probation from coaching and competing for the second offense; ban violators from college coaching and competing for life for the third offense;

2. Withhold from an institution one grant-in-aid for every athlete who does not graduate in five years;

3. Stipulate that coaches of non-revenue producing sports be employed full-time (either within athletics or some other aspect of the institution);

4. Base coaches' job security not on their won-lost records but on the fulfillment of their other job responsibilities and the provision of positive experiences for their athletes;

5. Restrict schedules of all sports to no more than three contests per week while classes are in session;

6. Eliminate freshman eligibility in all sports;

7. Restrict all athletes to no more than five days of absences from classes per academic year for athletics;

8. Limit grants-in-aid to athletes on non-revenue-producing teams to tuition and fees;

9. Allow athletes on revenue-producing teams to enroll in fewer hours of course work during their sport season;

10. Pay athletes on revenue-producing teams a salary (supplied from the same sources as grants-in-aid today) that would cover educational and living expenses for up to five years while they are athletes and students;

11. Require that all athletes meet academic standards of admission to the colleges they attend.

If some or all of these suggestions are implemented, intercollegiate athletics could become a more positive and educational experience for athletes.

Both high school and college athletes can take advantage of their state games and of the United States Olympic Festival as ways to develop further their sports prowess. This latter opportunity, through its qualifying events and annual competitions (except in Olympics years), gives developing athletes chances to demonstrate their skills against the other top athletes in their sports. Many Olympic sports use the United States Olympic Festival as qualifying events or training grounds for their team selections.

INTERNATIONAL SPORTS

Elite, nonprofessional athletes around the world have numerous opportunities to compete in championship events annually as well as in special events, such as the Pan-American Games, the Asian Games, the British Empire and Commonwealth Games, and the World University Games. These events, open to athletes from the countries implicit in the games' titles, are conducted every 4 years except for the World University Games, which are held every 2 years. All of these are important competitions, but the most prestigious internationally are the Olympic Games (patterned after the ancient Greek spectacle). Since 1896 (and 1924 for the Winter Games) athletes from around the world have competed every 4 years under the direction of the International Olympic Committee (IOC). The Olympic Games began with

Jesse Owens won four gold medals in the 1936 Berlin Olympic Games. (Courtesy of the University of Michigan)

nine events for men. Today they offer 14 summer and 3 winter sports for women and 21 summer and 6 winter sports for men.

The Olympic Games have been subjected to numerous detractions from their ideals, with politics being the chief detractor. From the inception of the Games through the attempt to prove Aryan supremacy in 1936 to the boycotts of 1976, 1980, and 1984, countries have attempted to use the Olympics to influence public opinion. The banning of some countries and the nonrecognition of others prove that the Olympic Games are political. Athletes competing as representatives of their nations, the playing of national anthems during the awards ceremonies, national medal counts, team sports, and national uniforms constantly reinforce nationalism. Governments, financially and ideologically, continue to increase their involvement because international prestige and promotion of their political ideology are at stake. Judging irregularities often result from political alliances, and increased use of drugs verifies the importance placed on winning.

Commercialism has grown exponentially. For example, the 1968 Mexico City Games cost $250 million to stage, while the 1980 Moscow Games reportedly cost $2¼ billion. CBS paid $660,000 to broadcast the 1960 events; NBC won the right to televise the 1988 Olympic Games with a bid of $300 million. The athletes are not immune to commercialism either. Although the Olympic Games were begun for amateur athletes competing for the love of sport, today the qualifying regulations use the word "amateur" and then proceed to describe what a potential competitor is allowed to accept monetarily. These regulations, which vary by sport, allow athletes to establish trust funds for their earnings and to maintain their eligibility as long as they do not use this money. Athletes can make commercials to benefit their national sport organizations and thereby profit indirectly. The list could continue, but the point is that few if any athletes are pure amateurs in the sense of never having profited from their athletic skill.

In spite of these problems, the Olympic Games thrive and continue to increase in popularity as people worldwide adopt the Olympic ideal. The development of friendships and the attainment of personal athletic goals are two of the many positive outcomes. Most disdain the boycotts, political maneuvering, unfair judging, and drug abuse, and these incidents only detract from but do not destroy the Olympic Games. Commercialization of their overall staging and of the athletes themselves seemingly is a nuisance to be tolerated rather than reasons to end the competitions. John Lucas (1980), a leading authority on and supporter of the Olympic Games, advocates either reducing the numbers of events and entries, or lengthening the Games and increasing the number of sites and sports. He supports a reduction in the excessive nationalism. Others suggest that one permanent site be chosen to help alleviate the tremendous cost of hosting the Games and that the Games be opened to all in an attempt to end the controversies concerning eligibility.

The United States is seeking to address several of the issues facing the Olympic Games as it restructures amateur sports. Following the passage of the Amateur Sport Act of 1978, the United States Olympic Committee (USOC) established the United States Olympic Training Center in Colorado Springs, Colorado. It offered to National Governing Bodies (NGBs) for each Olympic sport its resources and facilities as a training site for athletes. The USOC has received some federal funding but relies largely on corporate sponsorship and private donations to support its work.

One illustration of the progress made is the USOC's Sports Medicine Program. Located at the Olympic Complex in Colorado Springs, this group offers medical and clinical services, up-to-date physiological training assistance, bio-mechanical analyses, and educational services for athletes and coaches. In this one area alone, the USOC is greatly enhancing the support deserved by Olympic hopefuls as they train to compete against the athletes from the Eastern bloc nations, who are receiving similar training services.

The individual successes of many of the athletes from the United States in the 1984 Los Angeles Games were made possible by the services of the USOC as well as through the developmental programs of many of the NGBs. Because of increased funding from corporations and the monies from the surplus of the Los Angeles Olympic Games Organizing Committee, the USOC expects to continue to develop the best athletes possible.

SPORTS AND HUMAN VALUES

Sports participants seek to win. Human values emphasize people's self-worth. These two concepts may either contradict each other or peacefully coexist. From sports' perspective, "we're number one" seemingly has become the United States' motto as sports from Little Leagues to professional teams have become big businesses. To produce the best teams, athletes are often expected to specialize in one sport, to accept coaches' dictates without question, to practice and train with deferred gratification, to excel or face elimination, and to circumvent the rules when necessary. Ethical behavior often is disdained or negatively rewarded by coaches, teammates, and spectators, since winning surpasses it in importance.

Cooperation, discipline, emotional control, fair play, self-esteem, and teamwork are often outcomes of sports, if those in leadership roles seek their development in participants. Athletes can learn to respect their opponents both on and off the field and can be taught to accept officials' decisions without dispute. Even spectators are sometimes beneficiaries of these values by learning from the athletes. This is especially important for young people, who imitate the attitudes and behaviors of school, college, professional, and Olympic athletes.

Do sports contribute to or detract from human value development? If you ask athletes, invariably they will answer that sports are meaningful to them. Sports are fun. Sports provide a setting for people to develop their own identity by learning about their capabilities and their limitations. A genuine satisfaction results from maximal effort when the outcome is not overemphasized. A revitalization of body, mind, and spirit through sports can renew one's perspective of life. The potential for value development is present, while overly competitive and overcommercialized sports undermine this. Administrators, coaches, athletes, and fans must ensure that the positive side of sports is the right of everyone and must work to maintain value (Simon, 1985).

SUMMARY

Sports for minorities of gender, race, age, and those with disabilities, while often limited in the past, are today more equitable, although some barriers exist that only time will remove. Title IX's impact, while lingering, will no longer lead to greater opportunities for girls and women. Legislation helps bring change for minorities, but attitudes and behaviors change more gradually. Some youth sports overemphasize winning both in and out of the schools, yet most parents support their children's participation as valuable experiences. Weighing educational values against business concerns may be the dilemma facing major college sports today. Abuses abound, yet the public continues to expect colleges to offer athletic programs. Similarly, the Olympic ideals, whether real or imagined, seem to ensure people's support of the Games as politics, nationalism, and commercialism provide insufficient reasons to cancel the spectacle. The pervasiveness of sports in the United States means that people believe that sports contribute far more to society than they detract from it. It is the responsibility of those of us who work in any of these sports arenas to ensure that their values are realized by all.

MICHAEL DeLONG

Head Football Coach
Springfield College
Springfield, Massachusetts

EDUCATION

B.S., Physical Education, Springfield College (1974)
M.A., Physical Education, University of North Carolina at Chapel Hill (1978)

JOB RESPONSIBILITIES, HOURS, AND SALARY RANGE

The responsibilities of college and university coaches vary tremendously, depending on the emphasis placed on the institution's program and the sport. Mike organizes and administers an NCAA Division II football program, including directing a staff of 2 full-time assistant coaches and 12 graduate assistants, recruiting student athletes, working directly with admissions and financial aid officers, working with the alumni in fund raising, and carrying out on- and off-field coaching duties. He also teaches 4 semester hours in season and 15 semester hours out of season and advises physical education majors, a typical work load at a smaller institution. Like most coaches, Mike's weekly work hours, which vary from 84 in season to 64 off season to 30 during the summer, are demanding. Based on each coach's experience and won-lost record, the institution and its reputation, the sport, and the degree of pressure to win, salaries for this career range from $15,000 to more than $100,000.

SPECIALIZED COURSE WORK, DEGREES, AND WORK EXPERIENCES NEEDED FOR THIS CAREER

Although college or university coaching does not require a master's degree, teaching at smaller institutions may require attaining this degree. Physical education is the most common major for coaches at both the undergraduate and graduate levels, although many coaches have degrees in other disciplines. Opportunities to become head coaches usually follow years of coaching high school teams, serving as effective graduate assistants, or full-time assistant coaches, or completing successful college or professional playing careers. Volunteering to coach a youth, school, or club team may provide an entry into this career. Mike recommends that prospective coaches emphasize exercise physiology, oral and written communication skills, problem-solving techniques, organizational skills, and motivational strategies in their course work.

SATISFYING ASPECTS

People may choose this career because they love a particular sport, want to continue associating with it, enjoy teaching its skills and strategies, like to help athletes develop their talents to their optimal levels, or for a combination of reasons. Mike especially enjoys player-coach relationships, coach-coach interactions, and the feeling of accomplishment as the team improves. Coaching can be tremendously satisfying, not in terms of wins and losses, but in watching teams and players grow and mature. For Mike, helping individuals reach their goals is the most rewarding part of coaching.

JOB POTENTIAL

Mike states that to be secure in a college or university coaching position, winning is essential. If you perform, he says, you will be secure; if you do not perform, you can expect to be relieved of your duties. Promotion is also based on performance. Coaches who are proven workers have a good chance of "moving" in the profession. Politics also play a role, so it helps to know people. Since getting your foot in the door is difficult and highly competitive, a major part of the initial hiring process is knowing someone who can help you secure a full-time position. Once you have proven your abilities and made connections with people, things generally go a little easier.

ADVICE TO STUDENTS

Mike suggests deciding very early how much a coaching career means to you by asking yourself whether you are willing to work uncountable hours; whether you are willing to sacrifice most of your personal life; whether your family is totally supportive; and whether you can deal with setbacks. He states that many rewards from coaching are directly proportional to the commitment to the job and to the amount of work done.

REVIEW QUESTIONS

1. What are three ways in which societal factors inhibit girls' and women's involvement in sports?
2. What are the three areas of compliance in the Final Policy Interpretations (1979) of Title IX?
3. Is the concept of pay-for-play a viable alternative for funding interscholastic athletics?
4. What does the National Collegiate Athletic Association's Rule 48 require?
5. What are three ways in which youth sports coaches can be more properly trained?
6. What is the meaning of the winning = fans = money = winning = fans = money cycle?
7. What are three general justifications for the inclusion of athletics in colleges?
8. What are the three major issues facing the Olympic Games today?
9. What are two problems that pervade all levels of sports?
10. How can sports contribute to value development?

STUDENT ACTIVITIES

1. Interview students about their attitudes toward women in sports. Ask them what financial support women should receive, which teams they should have, who should coach them, as well as other related questions. What changes have they observed in society's acceptance of women in sport?

2. Interview minority athletes on your campus. Ask them whether they have experienced any discrimination during their sports careers and, if so, to describe it. Have they seen or experienced any changes in how they are treated today as opposed to how they were treated when they first began playing their sports on the college level?

3. Attend a youth sports event, and make a list of the positives and negatives that you observe.

4. Describe whether the intercollegiate athletic program at your institution is a business or a component of education. Can it be both? If so, how?

5. List 10 possible changes that could improve the Olympic Games by alleviating some of the problems. Which of these are realistic alternatives?

6. Interview individuals who have participated in the Senior Olympics or Senior Games or who are active sports participants. What are their reasons for competing and for being active? Has their involvement been lifelong or is it a recent life-style change?

REFERENCES

"In money, numbers—women athletes take leaps toward equity. *Journal of Physical Education, Recreation, and Dance, 55,* 3, October 1984.

Lucas, J. *The modern Olympic games.* New York: A. S. Barnes and Company, 1980.

Lumpkin, A. Intercollegiate athletics: bane or boon. *The North Carolina Journal, 18,* 14–19, Spring 1982.

Magill, R. A., Ask, M. J., and Small, F. L., (eds.). *Children in sport.* Champaign, Illinois: Human Kinetics Publishers, 1982.

Simon, R. L. *Sports and social values.* Englewood Cliffs, N.J.: Prentice–Hall, Inc., 1985.

Underwood, C. *The student athlete: eligibility and academic integrity.* East Lansing, Michigan: Michigan State University Press, 1985.

SUGGESTED READINGS

Coakley, J. J. *Sport in society* (3rd Ed.). St. Louis: Times Mirror/Mosby, 1986. The social phenomenon of sports provides a context for discussing social behaviors exhibited by children, women, blacks, and school, college, and professional athletes.

Edwards, H. The collegiate athletic arms race: origins and implications of the 'Rule 48' controversy. *Journal of Sport and Social Issues,* Spring 1984, *8,* 4–22. This article, which addresses the financial and academic consequences of the passage of Rule 48 for the Division I institutions of the National Collegiate Athletic Association, suggests that rather than being an alleged racist attempt to resegregate major college sports, Rule 48 is actually a weak attempt to address the crisis of academic quality and integrity.

Field, D. A. Opportunities for senior athletes. *Journal of Physical Education, Recreation and Dance,*

1982, *53*, 81–83. This article lists and describes competitions for older athletes offered by more than 20 sport organizations, including Senior Olympics in three states.

Frey, J. *The governance of intercollegiate athletics.* West Point, N.Y.: Leisure Press, 1982. This anthology critically describes college athletics from several vantage points—historically, administratively, academically, economically, legally, futuristically, and equitably for all participants.

Fraleigh, W. P. *Right actions in sport: ethics for contestants.* This book describes winning/losing and quality of play, rules and their functions, relationships of opponents, and values in the sports contest and provides guides for right actions.

Lucas, J. Future directions of athletic amateurism and the Olympic movement. *The Academy Papers,* December 1980, *14*, 15–19. Pierre de Coubertin founded the modern Olympic Games on the pure amateur spirit of Olympism and on the concepts of unity and fair play. The uniqueness and spirit of the Olympic ideal merit preservation, but the Games have a pressing need for reform and change.

The Miller Lite report on American attitudes toward sports. New York: Research and Forecasts, Inc., 1983. This comprehensive survey reveals that the majority of Americans have embraced sports as an essential component of their lives.

Oglesby, C. A. *Women and sport: from myth to reality.* Philadelphia: Lea and Febiger, 1978. These 13 essays describe women's emergence from a mythical involvement in sports to their active participation therein as societal attitudes slowly changed.

Seurin, P. The future of the Olympic Games, world championships and sport-for-all. *FIEP Bulletin,* July–September 1983, *53*, 29–34. The ideals of Olympism are defended because they contribute to the attainment of educational values in and through sport. One strategy to reemphasize these ideals is to try to change attitudes and ideas through sports for all. A second recommendation is to try to isolate the Olympic Games from the pressures of giantism, commercialism, and political interference.

Smith, R. E. Behavior assessment in youth sports: coaching behaviors and children's attitudes. *Medicine and Science in Sports and Exercise,* 1983, *15*(3), 208–214. This study found that coaching behaviors were highly related to players' attitudes toward their sports and players' enjoyment of sports participation.

Williams, J. M., and Miller, D. M. Intercollegiate athletic administration: preparation patterns. *Research Quarterly for Exercise and Sport,* 1983, *54*(4), 398–406. Differences in male and female athletic directors' coaching, competitive, and administrative background experiences did not warrant the almost total stereotyping of male athletic directors in head positions of combined programs.

Fourteen

Looking to the Year 2000

KEY CONCEPTS

- Physical educators should provide quality programs and publicize the importance of these programs.
- Schools and colleges should improve curricula, offer activity opportunities for all, and develop athletic programs to meet the needs of their students more effectively.
- Fitness can improve the quality of life for all people worldwide.

Physical educators have often followed, rather than led, in Americans' participation in sports and activities. As a result, physical education's importance and prestige have suffered and its survival as a school subject may also be in jeopardy. To take a leading role in the sports and fitness movement, physical education, in all its varied settings, needs to improve the quality of its programs and its publicity about the valuable outcomes of those programs. The future of physical education depends on its development of a viable rationale that will convince school administrators, legislators, and the public of its value and of how it can uniquely meet individual and societal needs. To add credibility to this advocacy, physical educators must become good role models of fitness and activity adherence.

Guaranteeing accountability in instructional quality by making curricula more humanizing to meet students' needs, keeping abreast of the knowledge explosion and applying this research-based information, providing equal opportunities for diverse populations, and refocusing athletics to ensure educational outcomes are imperatives for the future. Physical educators in non-traditional careers can lead the sports and fitness movement by responding to stresses in the work place and to the needs of senior citizens by providing them with skills and knowledge for self-direction and adherence to activity. The global nature of our technological and communications-based world will rely heavily on how physical educators convince people to respond to the challenges of living in the twenty-first century.

SETTING THE STAGE

A recent report of the Commission on the Future of North Carolina lists eight basic goals, three of which are especially applicable to physical education's perspective for the future. Briefly, the report recommends the following:

> *Education*: To offer every person access to high-quality, lifelong learning experiences. Education at all levels should be given the priority needed to help people realize their full potential to enjoy life and participate effectively in a free society. Educational opportunity is the major equalizer in a democracy.

312

Health: To maintain a high-quality medical-care system; ensure that it is accessible to everyone; and improve health education programs to reduce the need for care. This goal emphasizes preventive medicine but recognizes the necessity of backing and financing a modern and efficient care system that accommodates all people, including the underprivileged.

Recreation: To provide all persons the chance to engage in wholesome recreational and cultural activities during their leisure time, which is increasing because of the changing structure of the economy. People of all ages require programs and events that permit them to use their free time to renew and enhance their physical and spiritual well-being. Such social problems as juvenile deliquency and family breakups result in part from limited opportunities to use leisure time constructively. (*The Future of North Carolina*)

To ensure attainment of these goals, the Commission recommends equal educational opportunity for all school children, improvement of the quality of school instruction, preparation of students for the future, strengthening and expansion of the state's health education program, and expansion of programs and resources within the public and private sectors for recreational activities. Physical education faces numerous challenges as it seeks to attain these and similar goals.

IMPROVING PHYSICAL EDUCATION'S IMAGE

Before physical education can effectively meet the challenges of leading the sports and fitness movement, it must reestablish its identity, its jurisdiction, and even its ability to lead. Throughout this book, the term "physical education" has been applied to all of the various programs and careers that involve movement, play, sports, recreation, athletics, and leisure. Part of the image problem facing physical education as it seeks to lead into the next century is the accuracy of our name—does it describe what we do? Regardless of personal preference for terms, professionals in this field need to align themselves behind one label and pledge their full allegiance to it. Following this commitment, they all can more rightly claim jurisdiction in the areas mentioned above. Physical education, in every setting, must justify its existence on its own merits or contributions rather than on the basis of any traditional status or a fad.

While proclaiming the values and outcomes of activity programs, physical educators must also serve as positive role models—accept responsibility for living a healthy, fit life style so that others may be positively influenced to adopt similar habits. Physical educators now and in the future can greatly enhance their credibility by demonstrating their commitment to "practicing what they preach."

Accountability for program content is essential and will continue to grow in importance. Without quality and thus benefits accruing to those served, no program merits continuation. If children, club members, athletes, senior citizens, and corporate employees are not being taught the skills and knowledge that they deserve, in an activity or sports programs, then elimination of the activity is warranted, or at least replacement of the teacher or leader is mandated. Individuals who are hired to teach programs owe it to their participants and to the profession to educate. Abdication of this responsibility will lead to the places of physical educators being taken by others who, regardless of background, will do the job.

Linked closely with accountability is the importance of public relations. Traditionally, the perspective taken by physical education has been a willingness to serve but not a desire to publicize and, yes, even to market programs. Today, this is archaic. Physical educators, regardless of setting, must communicate the positive outcomes of their programs to enlist financial backing, participants, and general support. To make this a reality, the programs must be desirable and productive in meeting perceived needs. An additional benefit from this concerted effort to tell others what we can do for them is the drawing together, rather than the driving apart, of programs in the schools and colleges with those in nontraditional settings.

PHYSICAL EDUCATION IN SCHOOLS AND COLLEGES

One challenge facing schools and colleges today, as they look to the future, is to improve curricula at all levels. In general, physical education should focus on a humanizing curriculum to meet the individual needs of all students. First, we need to teach people, not things. At all levels, the nucleus of the curriculum needs to be individual fitness, but not to the exclusion of fundamental skills and lifetime sports. We also cannot emphasize fitness or sports to the point of excluding other worthwhile outcomes. For example, cooperation is often supplanted by competition, although the two are not mutually exclusive. Teachers need to structure classes so that students have opportunities to learn both.

Elementary school programs may hold the key to the future. Unfortunately, many children today do not benefit from physical education classes and thus often fail to learn basic motor skills during their developmental years. This is unjust and may be suicidal for our nation's vitality. Lifetime habits and skills are learned early in life. Without these, people may be paying substantial sums 20 to 30 years later to gain skills that they should have been enjoying during these years.

Most American children are physically unfit. Regardless of the data or study examined, school-aged children overall score poorly on cardiovascular, strength, and flexibility indices of fitness (Seefeldt, 1984; Franks, 1984). The National Children and Youth Fitness Study recommends remedying this situation by 1990 by achieving the following goals for 10- to 17-year-olds: 60% will attend physical education classes daily, 70% will periodically have their fitness levels tested, and 90% will participate in physical activities that help maintain an effective cardiorespiratory system (McGinnis, 1985). Yet this is not a final goal—only progress. Instead, curricula at all levels must include activities that attain and maintain at least minimal levels of fitness. If children learn in their younger years to enjoy exercise and physical fitness, there is a much greater likelihood that they will continue these in later years.

Faced with restricted budgets, many physical education programs in the secondary schools have been severely cut back and may be eliminated. Even though school physical education programs have not led in the instruction of lifetime sports, such as tennis and golf, and fitness activities, such as weight training and aerobics, they will have the opportunity to impact on the lives of adolescents. Traditional competitive, same gender team sports have greatly contributed to the lack of motivation of many students. Class calisthenics dictated by an uninterested teacher/coach who later rolls out a ball and sends students to line the football field is hardly viewed as a humanizing experience by students.

Instead, teachers need to offer classes that motivate students to become fit and to adopt healthy life styles through enjoyable activity. Teachers must upgrade their skills and knowledge and rekindle their commitment to teaching and their enthusiasm for helping students learn, welcoming student and parental input about new activities and instructional approaches. By sharing facilities and even some programs with communities, teachers can demonstrate their exciting and valuable programs to the public. This should convince taxpayers that school and community programs are not the same, nor are they adversarial.

In the midst of restricted budgets and in all school and college programs, equal opportunity for physical education is imperative. Girls and boys, although occasionally separated for competition in team sports in the secondary schools, should be taught together and should participate with and against each other. If any division of classes occurs, it should be based on skill, not on gender. Disabled students have rights, too. They can often be mainstreamed and can thereby profit physically and socially from interactions with nondisabled peers.

As undergraduate physical education curricula diversify to include preparation for nontraditional careers, faculty members must reeducate themselves to ensure that graduates are both qualified for and committed to their profession. This process will continue to intensity as new career directions develop. College faculty members also must assume a great deal of responsibility for closing the research-into-practice gap. As they discover new knowledge and techniques, they should not only report their findings but do so in such a way that physical educators in the schools and in nontraditional careers can understand and apply the information whenever appropriate. This process will become increasingly more difficult as faculty and graduate students become even more specialized. Too narrow a focus on a particular research interest may lead to an inability or an unwillingness to contribute to the

Tennis remains a popular leisure-time sport for players of all ages.

Karate is an example of a nontraditional activity enjoyed by people of all ages. (Courtesy of Delaine Marbry)

broader field of physical education. By the same token, school and nontraditional physical educators should seek out this available updated information.

Schools and colleges also have a responsibility to society to curtail the abuses in the athletic programs conducted under their auspices. While they cannot control those sports competitions outside their jurisdiction, they can exert a major influence. The primary aspect of interscholastic and intercollegiate athletic programs that is overemphasized is winning. Maintaining perspective is important in reinforcing the fact that, regardless of the opponent, the event, and even the outcome, a game is still only a game. The way to return these athletic programs to educational values foremost in the minds of players, coaches, administrators, and spectators is to structure the contests to reinforce and reward teamwork, sportsmanship, fair play, cooperation, and effort. Opponents become worthy challengers rather than hated foes. Fun and skill development far surpass outcome in importance. Striving to win is good, but winning at all costs is detrimental. Colleges, especially large ones, must consciously reduce the business mentality of athletics or risk losing control. Another real possibility is that college football and basketball teams may become semiprofessional farm teams for the professional teams or that all other college sports may become club sports instead of varsity teams. In the high schools the pay-to-play concept may become the norm for financing athletics. These last issues all result from the financial side of athletics, which is a major issue regardless of the level of the sport.

PHYSICAL EDUCATION IN NONTRADITIONAL SETTINGS

The Madison Avenue promotion of physical activity has contributed to its overwhelming surge in popularity, especially for the middle and upper classes. Because of their social needs and feelings of self-worth, people of all ages are motivated by the media to join exercise and sports programs. Sports clothing and equipment are essentials, and only the best will do. Club membership, attendance at sports camps, and making business contacts at sporting events or after exercise workouts are popular examples of this phenomenon.

By contrast, physical educators traditionally have not promoted fitness, nor have they led in getting people of all ages involved (Lupton, Ostrove, and Bozzo, 1984). The sports and fitness movement, recognized now as a part of the American way of life, rather than a fad, is initiating dramatic changes in physical education (Flynn and Berg, 1984). Consumer demand is readily evident for a healthy life style that seeks to improve the quality of one's life through physical activity. Physical educators must share their knowledge about physiology, nutrition, psychology, and fitness and skill development. We must conduct our programs at the work site as well as in public facilities and private clubs. While helping the corporate executive, we must not neglect lower-income individuals, whose level of productivity and life style can also be enhanced.

Probably the group whose needs will become paramount in the next century are individuals 65 years of age and older. Between 1982 and 2050, the percentage of people in this age category will almost double (11% to 21%). As Americans live longer, they need lifetime recreational activities not only to prevent disease and degeneration, but also as a way to enjoy happier, healthier lives.

Advances in medicine and technology not only help people live longer, but they greatly impact on our lives in other ways. Fewer and fewer household and mundane tasks demand our time and energy, as machines free us from routine jobs. While only some of our free time is currently spent developing fitness and enjoying sports and other leisure-time activities, free time will increase in the future. Technological advances directly impact on these pursuits, too. Better-designed running shoes, exercise cycles equipped to monitor fitness levels, biomechanical analyses of tennis strokes or other sport skills, and individualized training paradigms already exist. Undoubtedly, multiple advances in sporting equipment, clothing, and facilities will continue to enhance performance as well as pleasure.

Senior citizens have become enthusiastic participants in road races.

Yet already the age of technology is giving way to the communications age.
Personal computers and telecommunications of various types are only the
beginning. We will soon need skills to communicate with friends living in
space. Travel in space, currently for astronauts but in the future for possibly
everyone, requires at least minimal levels of fitness. Learning to live and
interact, to work, and to recreate in an environment in space will provide
interesting challenges for researchers in the upcoming years.

The realm of space travel and the establishment of space colonies broadens
one's perspective from this country to the importance of viewing how physical
education can influence the entire world. Our enthusiasm for sports and fitness is already altering attitudes in other countries. Many professionals share
their sports expertise with people in other countries. Successful businesses
worldwide implement our corporate fitness programs. All of these contribute
to greater international understanding through the sharing of activity.

SUMMARY

Physical educators must first improve their programs and then publicize
them to improve the image of the field. We must preach and demonstrate
through our lives the message that physical education is both fun and beneficial. You as the physical educators of the future really are the key to the
future acceptance and promotion of sports and fitness for all. Improved cur-

ricula that focus on meeting all students' fitness and lifetime skill needs are imperative for survival. Professionals in schools and colleges must apply practically the expanding research knowledge and seek to return athletics to their sound educational basis. The power and potential of physical education lie in a love for exercising, and our nation's health and maybe even its existence depend on this. We must give consumers the programs that will benefit them and, especially, meet the activity needs of senior citizens. Through technological advances and communications techniques, we must strive to improve the quality of life for ourselves and for others worldwide as we draw closer to the year 2000.

DONNA A. LOPIANO

Director, Intercollegiate Athletics for Women
University of Texas
Austin, Texas

EDUCATION

B.S., Physical Education, Southern Connecticut State College (1968)
M.A., Physical Education University of Southern California (1969)
Ph.D., Physical Education with a specialization in Athletic Administration, University of Southern California (1974)

JOB RESPONSIBILITIES, HOURS, AND SALARY RANGE

Donna formulates program objectives and utilizes resources directed toward achieving them, represents the university at appropriate athletic meetings, develops the budget and completes an annual report, recruits, supervises, and evaluates departmental personnel, assists in fund-raising, supervises the revenue-generating activities of income-producing sports, and coordinates public relations efforts. Her hours are normally 4:00 A.M. to 8:00 A.M. at home and 8:00 A.M. to 7:00 P.M. at the office Monday through Friday. Depending on the size of the program, salaries for this type of career range from $25,000 to $50,000.

SPECIALIZED COURSE WORK, DEGREES, AND WORK EXPERIENCES NEEDED FOR THIS CAREER

In preparing for an athletic administrator's position in higher education, students should take courses in organizational theory and behavior, philosophy of sports, higher education in the United States, accounting, history of sports, athletic governance systems, and management. Although a master's degree is minimal preparation, Donna states that a Ph.D. provides "instant" acceptance by and respect from college faculty, which is very important for a program. While in graduate school, Donna advocates that students take internships (with or without credit) in various athletic department areas and seek to get jobs working in the office of a vice-president for finance or in student services areas. She stresses learning excellent verbal and written communication skills, public relations skills with a realistic view of "politics," the ability to articulate achievable goals, and problem-solving skills, especially in the area of personnel. She adds that this career demands "doing your homework" with attention to detail and being willing to work long hours under stress.

SATISFYING ASPECTS OF THIS CAREER

It is imperative that an athletic administrator at a major university maintain a balance between the business aspects, such as funding and public relations, and the educational objectives of providing competitive opportunities for students while ensuring that they graduate. Interwoven with these two components is the essentiality of promoting and achieving values. Donna draws from these latter two in emphasizing that she enjoys seeing young people "grow up" and mature during their college athletic experiences.

JOB POTENTIAL

As athletic programs continue to expand, an increasing number of careers will become available in colleges, universities, and the professional leagues. These openings will include sports promotion, ticket sales, facility management, fund raising, business management, and actual athletic program administration. To gain experience and to progress in athletic administration, a willingness to relocate is helpful.

ADVICE TO STUDENTS

Donna advises willingly starting at the bottom and proving yourself so indispensable that a position is created for you. She suggests volunteering for every committee and every extra duty and then giving 150% so that everyone who has ever worked with you can proclaim that you are outstanding and incredibly competent. Furthermore, she recommends never saying "It's impossible" or "I can't."

REVIEW QUESTIONS

1. How can physical education change its image?
2. How is accountability associated with public relations?
3. What are three ways in which school physical educators can revise their curricula to ensure quality programs?

4. In what way can colleges and universities assist in the development of quality school programs?
5. Why are American children physically unfit?
6. Why are elementary physical education programs so important?
7. What has been the impact of financial cutbacks on school and college physical education programs?
8. How can the research-into-practice gap be closed?
9. Why are more exercise programs for senior citizens essential in the future?
10. Why is teaching fitness life style changes the most important outcome of physical education programs today?

STUDENT ACTIVITIES

1. Find 10 magazine advertisements that use physical activity or fitness in marketing their products. Are their claims valid?
2. Interview physical educators who teach in the schools or in nontraditional careers. Ask them what they think the problems and challenges are for people in their careers and the entire field of physical education today. What suggestions for improvement do they have?
3. Describe the curricula or program offerings of an elementary school, secondary school, college activity program, health club, YMCA, or recreation department that you think meets the needs of the individuals currently served. Will these needs differ in the year 2000?
4. Write a two-page analysis of what you think physical education should contribute to society after the year 2000.

REFERENCES

Flynn, R. B., and Berg, K. Community health promotion and wellness: a working model. *Journal of Physical Education, Recreation and Dance, 55,* 37–39, March 1984.

Franks, B. D. Physical fitness in secondary education. *Journal of Physical Education, Recreation and Dance, 55,* 41–43, November/December 1984.

The Future of North Carolina—Goals and Recommendations for the Year 2000. Report of the Commission on the Future of North Carolina, North Carolina Department of Administration, Raleigh, North Carolina.

Lupton, C. H., Ostrove, N. M., and Bozzo, R. M. Participation in leisure-time physical activity: a comparison of the existing data. *Journal of Physical Education, Recreation and Dance. 55,* 19–23, November/December 1984.

McGinnis, J. M. The national children and youth fitness study—introduction. *Journal of Physical Education, Recreation and Dance, 56,* 44, January 1985.

Seefeldt, V. Physical fitness in preschool and elementary school-aged children. *Journal of Physical Education, Recreation and Dance, 55,* 33–37, 40, November/December 1984.

SUGGESTED READINGS

Broekhoff, J. Prognosis: what can be predicted for the profession, *The Academy Papers, 15* 75–80, April 1981. Among the author's predictions are that elementary school physical education will not change, innovative programs will be developed in response to alternative career opportunities while teacher preparation will remain about the same, and graduate specialization in the academic subdisciplines will intensify.

Bryant, J. E. The year 2001 AD and future careers in physical education. *The Physical Educator, 36,* 197–200, December 1979. After estimating expected societal, technological, and life-style changes, the author states that it is essential that the profession plan for the potential of futuristic physical education careers.

Bucher, C. A. The future of physical education and sport. *Journal of Physical Education, Recreation and Dance, 53,* 12–14, October 1982. With today's conceptions of the physical changing rapidly, physical educators in all settings must effectively deliver the field's systematic knowledge base to consumers through effective instruction about the healthful impact of proper activity.

Dunn, D. R. Economics and equity: critical choices. *Journal of Physical Education, Recreation and Dance, 55,* 23–26, May/June 1984. Career opportunities in health, fitness, and recreation await the strategic choices of today's graduates who must analyze population demographics, technological trends, and economic factors while examining their personal goals and philosophies.

Lyon, R. M. Toward century 21: issues in aging. *Proceedings: National Association for Physical Education in Higher Education,* 125–132, 1979. The growing population of the aging requires that their unique needs be addressed, including health and leisure activity, for which physical educators can provide expertise and leadership.

Misner, J. E. Are we fit to educate about fitness? *Journal of Physical Education, Recreation and Dance, 55,* 26–28, 40, November/December 1984. The collective leadership of physical educators in all settings is the key to accomplishing the nation's physical fitness objectives.

Moore, C. A. Future trends and issues in physical education and athletics. *Journal of Physical Education and Recreation, 51,* 20–21, January 1980. This author predicts trends in athletics and describes major issues in physical education, including certification, accountability, budgetary constraints, staffing, unionization, and especially curriculum revision.

Powell, K. E., Christenson, G. M., and Kreuter, M. W. Objectives for the nation: assessing the role physical education must play. *Journal of Physical Education, Recreation and Dance, 55,* 18–20, August 1984. Exercise, as one of the 15 priority areas listed by *Healthy People: The Surgeon General's Report on Health Promotion and Disease Prevention* (1979), provides physical educators the opportunity to lead the health community in meeting our national goals in this area while *Promoting Health/Preventing Disease: Objectives for the Nation* (1980) advocates physical fitness and exercise as vital to our nation's health.

Razor, J. E. Meeting the challenge: physical education in the late 1980s. *Proceedings: National Association for Physical Education in Higher Education, 4,* 68–76, 1983. Financial realities will challenge mandated physical education in the public schools in the late 1980s, necessitating that the profession develop clearly stated rationale supported by applicable research to justify it as a viable ingredient in the educational process.

Sherrill, C. The future is ours to shape. *The Physical Educator, 40,* 44–50, March 1983. This futuristic essay looks at the diversity of American society for the year 2000 and its implications for school and university curriculum planning.

Glossary

Academic discipline—the conceptual knowledge of a particular field, discovered through scholarly procedures.

Accreditation—process of measuring institutions' attainment of established program standards to ensure quality.

Adapted physical education—program for exceptional students who are so different in mental, physical, emotional, or behavioral characteristics that, in the interest of quality educational opportunity for all students, special provisions must be made for their proper education.

Affective objective—educational outcome that focuses on the development of attitudes, appreciations, and values, including both social and emotional dimensions.

Agoge—educational system for Spartan boys.

Allied sciences—the areas of dance, health, and recreation that share some purposes, programs, and professionals with physical education.

Applied sciences—the areas of adapted physical education, exercise physiology, humanities, motor development, motor learning, sport biomechanics, sport history, sport management, sport pedagogy, sport philosophy, sport psychology, and sport sociology, which constitute the discipline of physical education.

Arete—all-around mental, moral, and physical excellence, valued by the Greeks.

Athletics—organized, competitive activities in which trained individuals participate.

Battle of the Systems—controversy raging in the 1800s over which system of gymnastics was most appropriate for Americans.

British Amateur Sport Ideal—belief in "playing the game for the game's sake".

Burnout—decreased performance quality and quantity due to stress, job repetitiveness, lack of support and reward, and overwork.

Calisthenics—Catharine Beecher's program of exercise designed to promote health, beauty, and strength.

Cognitive objective—educational outcome that emphasizes the acquisition, comprehension, analysis, synthesis, application, and evaluation of knowledge.

Competency-based teacher education—teacher certification based on the successful attainment of specified psychomotor skills and cognitive knowledge.

Complete education—development of educational objectives as advocated by the "new physical educators".

Dance—bodily movements of a rhythmic and patterned succession usually executed to the accompaniment of music.

Ethics—the branch of philosophy that deals with what is good and bad, moral duty and obligation, and principles of conduct.

Exercise—physically using and toning the body.

Exercise physiology—the study of bodily functions under the stress of muscular activity.

Existentialism—20th century philosophy that centers on individual existence and advocates that truth and values are arrived at by each person's experiences.

Games—activities ranging from amusement or diversions to competitions with significant outcomes governed by rules.

Greek Ideal—unity of the "man of action" with the "man of wisdom".

Gymnasiums—sites for intellectual and physical activities for Greek citizens.

Gymnastics—term used to describe Greek athletics, European systems of exercises with or without apparatus, and a modern international sport.

Health—soundness of body, mind, and soul or one's general well-being.

Hygiene—the science of preserving one's health.

Idealism—philosophical theory that advocates that reality depends on the mind for existence and that truth is universal and absolute.

Intramurals—recreational and competitive activities participated in by students within an institution.

Leisure—time free from work or responsibility that may be used for physical activity.

Light gymnastics—Dio Lewis' program based on executing Beecher's calisthenics along with hand-held apparatus.

Merit pay—rewarding quality performance financially.

Motor development—the maturation of the neuromuscular mechanism, permitting progressive performance in motor skills.

Motor learning—the conceptualization of cognitive processes underlying motor acts and performance associated with skill acquisition.

Movement education—both a methodology for learning movement patterns and sports skills and a portion of a comprehensive physical education curriculum.

Nationalism—pervasive theme stressing promotion and defense of one's country that was the desired outcome of several European systems of gymnastics in the 1800s.

Naturalism—a belief that the scientific laws of nature govern life and that individual goals are more important than societal goals.

Normal school—a teacher training institute.

Palaestra—Greek wrestling school where boys learned wrestling, boxing, jumping, dancing, and gymnastics.

Pancratium—an event in Panhellenic festivals that combined wrestling and boxing skills into an almost-anything-goes combat.

Pentathlon—a five-event competition that included the discus throw, javelin throw, long jump, stade race, and wrestling.

Philosophy—the pursuit of wisdom.

Physical education—process through which an individual obtains optimal physical, mental, and social skills and fitness through physical activity.

Physical fitness—combination of cardiovascular endurance, muscular strength and endurance, and flexibility.

Play—action of participants in various types of physical activity.

Pragmatism—American movement in philosophy emphasizing reality as the sum total of each individual's experiences through practical experimentation.

Profession—a career that requires an extensive period of training, has an intellectual component that must be mastered, offers opportunities for communication among its members, and provides an important service to society.

Psychomotor objective—an educational outcome based on the development of fundamental movement skills, sports skills, and physical fitness.

Realism—philosophical thought that stresses that the laws and order of the world as revealed by science are independent from human experience.

Recreation—refreshing or renewing one's strength and spirit after work and a diversion that occurs during leisure hours.

Renaissance—a rebirth of and eagerness for learning in the fifteenth to seventeenth centuries.

Sports—diversions and physical activities one does for pleasure or for success.

Sport biomechanics—the study of the effects of natural laws and forces on the body through the science and mechanics of movement.

Sport history—descriptive and analytical examination of the significance of sporting events within the broader societal context.

Sport management—the study of the management of personnel, programs, budgets, and facilities in various sports settings.

Sport pedagogy—the study of the most effective methods and techniques of teaching sports.

Sport psychology—the study of mental processes as they relate to human sports performance.

Sport sociology—the study of the origin, development, organization, and role of sports in human society.

Thermae—facilities in Rome for contrast baths and other leisure activities.

Wellness—term describing overall, quality mental and physical health and fitness.

Index

Credits

Chapter 1 Physical Education—A Dynamic Field
P. 11—Reprinted with permission of the American Alliance for Health, Physical Education, Recreation and Dance, 1900 Association Drive, Reston, VA 22091.

Chapter 3 Physical Education as an Academic Discipline
P. 42—This article is reprinted with permission from The JOURNAL of Physical Education, Recreation and Dance, September, 1964, p. 32. The JOURNAL is a publication of the American Alliance for Health, Physical Education, Recreation and Dance, 1900 Association Drive, Reston, VA 22091.

Chapter 4 The Profession of Physical Education
Pp. 63, top, 63–64—Reprinted with permission of the American Alliance for Health, Physical Education, Recreation and Dance, 1900 Association Drive, Reston, VA 22091. P. 66—FITNESSGRAM was developed by the Institute for Aerobics Research, 12200 Preston Road, Dallas, TX 75230. P. 75—Reprinted with permission of the American Alliance

for Health, Physical Education, Recreation and Dance, 1900 Association Drive, Reston, VA 22091.

Chapter 9 Early American Physical Education
P. 202, top—This article is reprinted with permission from the JOURNAL of Physical Education, Recreation and Dance, April, 1960, p. 27. The JOURNAL is a publication of the American Alliance for Health, Physical Education, Recreation and Dance, 1900 Association Drive, Reston, VA 22091. Pp. 202–203—D. B. Van Dalen/B. L. Bennett, A WORLD HISTORY OF PHYSICAL EDUCATION: Cultural, Philosophical, Comparative, 2nd ed., © 1971, pp. 415–416. Reprinted by permission of Prentice-Hall, Inc., Englewood Cliffs, N.J.

Chapter 11 The Changing Nature of Physical Education
Pp. 258, 259–260—Reprinted with permission of the American Alliance for Health, Physical Education, Recreation and Dance, 1900 Association Drive, Reston, VA 22091.

Chapter 12 Issues in Physical Education
P. 270—This article is reprinted with permission from The JOURNAL of Physical Education, Recreation and Dance, November–December, 1981, p. 35. The JOURNAL is a publication of the American Alliance for Health, Physical Education, Recreation and Dance, 1900 Association Drive, Reston, VA 22091. P. 276—This article is reprinted with permission from the JOURNAL of Physical Education, Recreation and Dance, March, 1984, p. 35. The JOURNAL is a publication of the American Alliance for Health, Physical Education, Recreation and Dance, 1900 Association Drive, Reston, VA 22091. Pp. 279–280—Reprinted with permission of the American Alliance for Health, Physical Education, Recreation and Dance, 1900 Association Drive, Reston, VA 22091.

Chapter 13 Issues in Sports
Pp. 296, 298—Reprinted with permission of the American Alliance for Health, Physical Education, Recreation and Dance, 1900 Association Drive, Reston, VA 22091.